night throbbed and quivered to the thunder of their motors; and back from
a sunny day long ago a phrase repeated itself in the General's mind: *I
guess I'll never have to be in a war.* The Commander-in-Chief paid off
memory with a grim smile. Then he knelt and prayed.

GENERAL IKE

A Biography of

DWIGHT D. EISENHOWER

ALDEN HATCH

Peoples Book Club Edition

Published by
CONSOLIDATED BOOK PUBLISHERS
Chicago, Illinois

ACKNOWLEDGMENTS

AN AMAZING NUMBER of people are willing to give with reckless generosity of their time and effort to assist in the research for a biography. They do it from no selfish motive, but either from affection for the subject or from a genuine desire to add to the sum of human knowledge. Never in my considerable experience have I received such unstinted co-operation as I did in preparing this book on General Eisenhower. The reason is that his friends love him so very much.

It is my invariable rule to seek out my subject's enemies as well as those who praise him. This usually is not difficult—in fact, his enemies come to me bursting with angry comments, all of which help to draw a balanced picture. But on this occasion I had no luck in that direction. As far as intensive investigation can show, General Ike hasn't got an enemy outside of the Axis.

To those who helped me to gather this material, I want to extend my heartfelt thanks. I am particularly grateful to Mamie Eisenhower and to Milton Eisenhower, both of whom read every word of the text, not in a spirit of censorship but simply in the interests of accuracy.

Others who rendered great assistance to me were: Mrs. Ida Stover Eisenhower, Arthur and Louise Eisenhower, Lieutenant John S. D. Eisenhower, U.S.A., Charles M. Harger, Orin Snyder, J. F. (Six) MacDonell, Amon G. Carter, Paul Royer, Commander E. E. (Swede) Hazlett, Jr., U.S.N. Ret., Mrs. Gladys Harding Brooks, Mrs. Cecile Curry Gans, B. L. (Joner) Callahan, J. W. Howe, William Kittrell, Fletcher Pratt, Major General Francis B. Wilby, U.S.A., Brigadier General George Honen, U.S.A., Major Sheridan Biays, A.U.S., Major General A. D. Surles, U.S.A., Assistant Secretary of War, John J. McCloy, Mrs. John Gunther, Mrs. Omar N. Bradley, Colonel Meade Wildrick, U.S.A., Weldon

Jones, Presidente Sergio Osmena of the Philippine Common-
wealth, Vice Admiral Raymond A. Fenard, Chief of the French
Naval Mission, Colonel Charles Gayley, U.S.A., Major James
Stack, U.S.A., Lt. Colonel W. J. Morton, U.S.A., Colonel Paul
Alfred Hodgson, U.S.A., Mr. and Mrs. John Doud, Mr. and Mrs.
Tim White, Colonel Francis M. Fitts, Colonel Robert Schow,
U.S.A., Mrs. Harry Butcher and General Dwight D. Eisenhower,
U.S.A.

ALDEN HATCH

CONTENTS

CHAPTER ONE

VIGIL AT MALTA

The Commander in Chief stood on the little point of white beach in front of the black mass of the rocky cliffs of Malta. The wind was so strong that he had to lean against it as he looked out at the tumbled waves and the whitecaps flashing in the light of a lopsided moon. He was quite alone, and since he was a man who liked to be surrounded by friends, he was very lonely. But tonight he had felt that for this little time he must be by himself. So he stood there on the beach, one hand in his pocket fingering the lucky coins he always carried, a silver dollar, a gold five-guinea piece and a French franc. He was waiting and listening.

The air was full of sound—the crash and hiss of the waves on the sand, the humming of the wind against the cliffs, and the rattle of the leaves on the tossing trees. But none of these was the sound for which he listened.

The orders had all been given, there was nothing now that he could do or undo. Off across the violent waters thousands of ships were plunging forward in obedience to his commands. Those ships were crammed with American and English boys, boys like his son John back at West Point, just as fine and honest and full of humor as John, just as dear to someone. Almost, in a peculiar way, as dear to him. Tomorrow they would land on the beaches of Sicily.

So much hinged on this throw: more than the conquest of Sicily; more even than the lives of those fine young men who in a little while would be climbing down the nettings into the landing craft. This was the first test of whether amphibious operations on a great scale were practicable against such a wily and resolute foe as Germany. It was the template for that grander design that next year would, God willing, strike at the heart of the Axis from the west.

Tomorrow! Deliberately he turned his mind away from tomorrow. For weeks now he had thought of nothing else. The whole plan was set and clear in his brain; worrying would only muddy the picture. He turned his mind away, and while he waited, in that tremendous pause, it raced backward down the years, and focused on a scene he had thought forgotten.

The little city stood almost in the center of a vast plain marked with the rich harmonious coloring of tillage and husbandry. The gold of wheat, the straight green rows of corn, soft fields of grass in which the cattle stood or slowly moved, blue-green patches of alfalfa and the varying shades of rye and barley made a tremendous, ordered pattern of agricultural abundance. Other cities, towns and villages were focal points in this grand design, but they were only incidental to its main purpose of raising and garnering the produce of the land. The inhabitants of this favored region enjoyed such peace, plenty and security as had never before been recorded in all the annals of the human race.

The tiny city in the midst of all this fertility was known as Abilene, Kansas, and the time was a hot summer day in the year of tranquillity, 1910.

Two very young men were sitting on the edge of the raised wooden sidewalk of Abilene's principal street in the shade thrown by the low brick building of the Citizens' Bank. One of them was tall and dark, and had the deceptive, lanky awkwardness of an athlete in repose. His face was thin and his gray eyes were keen and quick. He signed his name J. F. MacDonell, but he was always known as "Six." He was captain of the high school baseball team; he was the football captain too, but baseball was his game.

The other youth was not quite so tall and of a broader, stockier build. His hair was yellow, and his skin was ruddy and white. His round smiling eyes were a changeable shade of bluish green, that sometimes shifted to vivid blue. Ike Eisenhower was an athlete too, and played on MacDonell's teams. His favorite game was football.

The two young men were discussing a subject of paramount importance to them, though not, it seemed, of any great consequence to the rest of the world: the question of what to do with their future. Six was a senior in high school; Ike had been out a year, knocking around the little city, working at odd jobs from assisting his father in the engine room of the Belle Springs Creamery to exercising his mechanical talents by repairing the half dozen automobiles owned by the more prosperous inhabitants of Abilene. He knew that he was drifting aimlessly and the thought gave him some concern.

"Six," he said suddenly, "let's you and me get into one of the service schools."

"What's that?" asked Six lazily.

"You know, Annapolis or West Point."

"What are they like?"

"I don't know much about them," Ike admitted. "Only that the life sounds pretty good and the government pays you while you get an education and"—he grinned delightedly—"play football."

"Oh," said Six. "You've been talking to Everett Hazlett."

"That's so. He's all excited about going to Annapolis."

"Maybe he thinks he'd like his looks in a monkey suit with anchors on the collar. It wouldn't suit me."

"That's just a little part of it," Ike argued. "It needn't bother us. The main thing is that we'd get a chance to go to college which we couldn't otherwise afford."

"And play football for four more years," Six said, grinning.

"Right," laughed Ike. "Come on, let's do!"

"You do," said Six. "I'd rather play pro baseball."

"I'm not that good. Besides, there's no future in it."

"Future enough if you get into the Big Leagues. Imagine pitching a game for the Giants at the Polo Grounds in New York! What future is there in the Army?"

"I was thinking of the Navy, and I'm going to try for it," Ike said. "Anyhow, you don't have to stay in. Once you get an education you can go into other things. Engineering. I'd like to go to South America and help open up the country. Of course if there were ever another war it would be different."

"There ain't going to be another war," Six stated dogmatically.

"I hope you're right," Ike said, "but there always have been wars."

"You and your history books and your Clausewitz theories on war," Six gibed. "You read too much and don't look around. Can't you see the world's getting too civilized for war? Even Europe."

Ike looked around. He saw a farm cart piled high with garden truck moving slowly down the dusty length of Second Street. Beyond the railroad tracks were the huge brick walls of the creamery with black smoke drifting lazily from its high stack. A fussy switch engine was pushing a couple of freight cars up the siding. In the other direction he looked along a wide dirt road above which hung a dusty golden haze. At the corner of Fifth Street stood the ornate City Hall. His eyes followed the brickwork up to the elaborate bell tower with its beehive-shaped dome sharp against the deep blue of a cloudless sky.

He turned and grinned amiably at Six.

"You're probably right," he said. "And that makes it better. I guess I'll never have to be in a war."

The Commander in Chief lifted his head. There was a deeper vibration in the air, a humming that was not the wind. It grew in volume to a brazen diapason that drowned out the small sounds of wind and waves and trees. As the General looked up at the pale sky, the four stars on his overseas cap twinkled faintly.

Now he could see the black shapes against the pallor above, flying in vees like the wild geese crossing Kansas. Almost automatically his hand came up in a smart salute to the 82nd Airborne Division winging toward Sicily. The night throbbed and quivered to the thunder of their motors; and back from that sunny day long ago a phrase repeated itself in the General's mind: I guess I'll never have to be in a war.

The Commander in Chief paid memory off with a grim smile. Then he knelt on the sand and prayed.

CHAPTER TWO

HOME

David Dwight Eisenhower he was christened. Later he reversed
the first two names. He was born in Denison, Texas, and so that
breeding ground of heroes claims him as her own. But Denison
was only a whistle stop on the line of his life; for Kansas is home
to him and all his family.

The Eisenhowers left Germany to escape religious persecution,
and stopped off in Switzerland for a generation or two to accus-
tom themselves to the heady air of freedom before they finally
started westward. They came to the American colonies in 1732,
where they settled first in York, Pennsylvania, later moving to
Elizabethville in Dauphin County. The religion for which they
gave up their home in Germany was strong in them generations
later. Their name means iron ax or iron hitter. However it is
translated, there is iron in it, and there is iron in the men of
that name.

The Eisenhowers were Brethren in Christ, popularly called
River Brethren because they observed the custom of baptism
in rivers. The Brethren were a "plain" sect akin to the Quakers,
and their way of life was even more austere. Like the Friends,
they regarded war as a cardinal sin.

Jacob Eisenhower, who was a leader of the Brethren, built a
big brick house at Elizabethville in 1860. There Dwight's father,
David Jacob, was born, the youngest of four children.

In the decade after the Civil War, the River Brethren began
a mass migration to Kansas, for Pennsylvania was becoming too
worldly. Once again the Eisenhowers sacrificed comfort to conscience. Jacob, now a widower, sold his fine house, and with
his two younger sons, Ira and David, trekked west to help build
the town of Hope in the still sparsely settled prairies. David

was sent to study engineering at Lane College, recently founded by the Brethren at Lecompton, Kansas.

At Lane, David, who was a quiet young man with dark hair and intense brown eyes, fell in love with the most vivid girl he had ever known. Ida Stover was a plump girl with masses of yellow curls piled above a round fresh face. Her blue eyes were bright with the excitement of being alive, and her whole personality was vibrant.

The only girl in a family of boys, she had grown up in Mount Sidney, Virginia, where her family had lived since 1730. The Stovers, too, were River Brethren, though somewhat less strict than the Pennsylvania branch. As a child Ida had been a tomboy. Her great delight was to ride and hunt with her four brothers, who teased her unmercifully. When their parents died, three of the boys followed the westward urge of the times to Topeka, Kansas, and Ida went to live with her grandparents near Staunton, Virginia. But her one ambition was to rejoin her brothers. As soon as she was twenty-one, she collected her small heritage and started for Kansas alone.

Ida was happy in Topeka for a little while, but her ardent spirit was not content. Unlike most young females of that era, she wanted an education and was determined to get it. So she came to Lane College and her ultimate destiny.

Young David Eisenhower did not have the field to himself, however. There was, in particular, one dashing admirer who sported a black mustache with a sweep that rivaled a longhorn's spread. But quiet persistence and real devotion won. David and Ida were married at Lecompton on September 23, 1885.

Jacob did handsomely by the young couple. He set his son up in the grocery business in Hope and bought him a half interest in the local bank. But David had too gentle a nature to be a successful businessman. The bills ran high and the funds ran low, and he could not bear to dun his delinquent accounts. The bank, too, suffered from philanthropic mismanagement, and eventually the young Eisenhowers found themselves on the rocks. David then got a job on the Cotton Belt Railroad and moved his father, his young wife and their two small sons, Arthur and Edgar, to the junction town of Denison, Texas.

Ida had a job on her hands making a home for her family in that strange environment. Denison was rough, and anything but ready for the contemplative Christian, but it didn't faze

Ida. She rented a pleasant wooden house set on piles about a foot off the ground. It had a nice front porch that looked out over the cotton bales piled along the railroad tracks and across a wide stretch of barren country, which was usually enlivened by a herd of goats. Ida soon had the house fixed up almost as comfortably as the home they had left.

Dwight was born there on October 14, 1890. Both David and Ida were unprophetically disappointed that he wasn't a girl.

After two years, the Eisenhowers tired of Denison; they wanted desperately to be among people of their own faith. When Ira wrote from Abilene, Kansas, where he had settled, that there was a job open for an engineer at the Belle Springs Creamery, David applied for it and was accepted. With all their belongings in a freight car, the Eisenhowers started for Abilene.

They all felt a strong sense of excitement as the train pulled out of Chapman and rattled down the last straight stretch of the journey. Dressed in his good suit of dark broadcloth, old Jacob sat motionless, ignoring the heat and cinders, but his eyes were happy. Arthur and Edgar climbed over the red plush seats and craned their necks to see out the window. Little Dwight trotted up and down the aisle, making friends with everybody. Ida, too, stared out at the fields of Kansas, trying to see into the future.

A smooth green wave of land rolled up out of the prairie, and the trees on its crest were like green spray tossed against the sky. The engine whistled and the cars bucked as the brakes took hold. The low hills flashed past and there were the neat white wooden houses and the few brick buildings of Abilene.

Ira was at the station to meet them as they piled out of the cars. After the affectionate greetings, he said, "I'll take Father and the baggage in the spring wagon. You and the boys can walk—it's no more than a step."

The three men loaded the wagon with the hand baggage. It rattled off with Jacob sitting erect on the seat beside his son. David and Ida walked slowly across the tracks while Arthur and Edgar raced around like retrievers in an autumn field, and Dwight clutched his mother's hand. Ida was wondering what her new home would be like. Ira, who wanted to move to the far West, had suggested that they take over his house as soon as he left.

On the left they passed the big yellow frame building of the Union Pacific Hotel. Farther down the tracks they could see a weathered, barnlike structure with a tall brick stack, which faded lettering proclaimed to be the Belle Springs Creamery.

"That's where I'm going to work," David said. "I hope the machinery is more modern than the building."

"I hope so, too," said Ida. "Oh, David, I like this town. It looks so clean and quiet."

A little farther on they turned down a side street at the corner of the new wooden grade school. There, beyond a big vacant lot, they saw the spring wagon standing in front of a little two-storied white house. It was exactly square and had a front porch, a bow window and a steep roof like a small four-sided pyramid with the apex cut off. From the flat rooftop rose a chimney, informally off the center line. Like all the other Eisenhowers, Ira loved a garden. Flowering shrubs grew around the house and there were bright flower beds in the front yard. In the rear were a stable and the necessary outhouse, painted white, and beyond them a big green meadow.

When the family arrived, Jacob and Ira were unloading the luggage. The side door stood open and the late afternoon sun lit the interior of the little house with a red-gold light. From the meadow came the evening songs and chirpings of orioles, robins, meadow larks and dickcissels.

David grinned broadly as he walked slowly toward the house. "It's sort of pretty," he said. "Do you think you'll like it, Ida?"

"David," said Ida a little breathlessly, "I love it already."

Ira took plenty of time to wind up his veterinary business and start west. It was two years before the Eisenhowers moved into their permanent quarters. They were as happy there as Ida had hoped they would be. Even today, whenever one of her sons speaks of home, he is thinking of that small white house on South Fourth Street in Abilene.

By 1898 it was not quite so little as it once had been. The family was growing at such a rate that the house had to expand or burst. David built on two additions: a parlor-bedroom on the east side and a flat-roofed wing at the back that became a long bright kitchen in which the family life centered.

At seven Dwight was a bright, scrappy little devil. He had yellow hair, bright blue eyes, and a lopsided grin that got him out of lots of trouble. However much he changed as he grew older, that grin remained, and in an unimagined future even English reserve was not proof against it.

Dwight now had two younger brothers, Roy and baby Earl.

Another boy, Paul, had been born in 1894, but before his first year was out he died of scarlet fever. Arthur and Edgar at ten and twelve were capable of doing a man's work, and Ida saw to it that they all had plenty to do. It was the best way to keep them out of trouble.

The two and a half acres which surrounded their house were cultivated as intensely as any Chinese farm. Almost the entire pattern of Kansas agriculture was reproduced there in miniature. The Eisenhowers grew corn, alfalfa, most of the garden vegetables and nearly every possible kind of fruit tree. In addition they raised pigs and Belgian hares, and had a team of horses, a cow, and at least one dog.

The boys did all the chores, which kept them busy a good part of the day. Working in the earth seemed to give them an inner strength as well as physical vigor. Dwight could always remember the delicious feel of the cold, black dirt on his bare feet in the early summer mornings and the sense of well-being that seemed to flow through his body.

Each week in turn one of the boys had to get up at four-thirty to make the kitchen fire. That was a chore Dwight hated. But he liked to cook. On Sunday, after attending the River Brethren Sunday School, the boys got the noonday dinner so that their mother could have the day off. It was more like fun than work, particularly the way they made piecrust. After the dough had been mixed and kneaded, the boys would roll it into a ball and play a game of catch. Their system of washing dishes—when alone—was similar. The one at the sink would wash a dish and skim it across to the towel man, who, after drying it, would complete the play to the stacker by the shelves.

The three older boys went to the grade school beyond the vacant lot. Edgar and Dwight were known as Big Ike and Little Ike. Something about the name of Eisenhower seemed to the Abilene boys and girls to demand that nickname. Nearly all the boys were called by it while they were in school, but it stuck to Dwight.

The Eisenhowers did not have to go far afield in search of amusement. There was a baseball diamond on the vacant lot, and a workshop in the cellar for rainy days. Their friends came to their house because it was more fun. Of course, in summer they went swimming in aptly named Mud Creek or the clear cold waters of Smoky Hill River. In winter they played hockey on the river's frozen surface, using crooked branches for sticks and an old tin can for a puck.

Winter, too, was the time when they all enjoyed the great classic dish of the Eisenhower family—mush and puddin—for which Ike would still cheerfully travel half around the world. The mush was fried cornmeal, home-grown and home-ground. The puddin was a Pennsylvania Dutch concoction, slightly akin to scrapple, to which it bore about the same relationship as applejack to sweet cider. The otherwise inedible parts of a hog went into it: heart, liver and lights, marrow of bones and strips of debristled hide. It was chopped up fine and then rendered down in a great iron kettle until it became a glutinous composition of unparalleled flavor and richness. Poured over the mush it produced a dish to delight the palate of a gourmet and ruin the digestion of an ostrich.

1898 was the year of the Spanish-American War and the martial spirit was rampant. America seemed to regard the affair as a glorified picnic in fancy dress. Everyone was singing the old Civil War songs: "We'll Rally Round the Flag," "The Battle Hymn of the Republic," "Marching Through Georgia," which thereby happily lost its sting, and that crazy new pseudo spiritual in two-step time, "There'll be a Hot Time in the Old Town Tonight." The boys of Abilene marched and countermarched, shouldering wooden muskets and beating drums. There were splendid skirmishes between "armies" from the North Side of town and those from the South.

Ida Eisenhower hated it. She loathed war with a sense of spiritual outrage; it was to her the ultimate wickedness. The boys took many a thrashing from her that spring, and more than once she tried to explain herself to them. There was a passionate insistence in her voice as she talked to Ike one evening.

"You see, I remember that other war," she said, "though I was only five when it ended. We were Virginians, but Father held to the Union side. He believed that the North was right, and that slavery was all wrong. So all our neighbors suspected us.

"Once, toward the end, Confederate soldiers stormed through our house looking for my older brother. I still remember how frightened I was of those men, with their ragged uniforms and their harsh voices and their hard bitter eyes.

"When the Yankees finally came, they weren't any better. They treated us like enemies, as they thought we were, and their eyes were just as mean.

"That's the way war makes men, like cruel animals. They seem to forget our Lord and his teaching of love. Christ forbid that you boys should ever grow like that."

All his life Ike remembered the urgency of his mother's words. Especially did he recall them when it became his improbable destiny to lead an army of liberation through a war-weary land. In the eyes of the people, as they watched the tanks go by, there was a little hope, but a great deal of fear—*When the Yankees finally came they weren't any better.* . . . Because he remembered so well, Ike understood that look. It made him a considerate conqueror.

Milton, Ike's youngest and favorite brother, was born in the summer of 1899.

"If this one isn't a girl," David said to Ida, before the event, "I'm going to leave you."

He actually did leave for a long walk in the country to master his disappointment. Milton suffered ingloriously from his parents' frustrated desire for a female child. He was forced to wear his hair in long silky ringlets until he was four years old. In such a family it was worse penance than a hairshirt.

Meanwhile, Ike was having a series of gnat's-eyelash escapes, which miraculously preserved him for the service of his country. Once, when the Smoky Hill River went off the reservation with a whoop and flooded the whole town, he developed a misguided yearning for nautical adventure. Edgar and he borrowed a row-boat that was hitched to the front porch of a farsighted neighbor, and set sail without oars or other means of propulsion.

Wild-eyed townsfolk saw the boys float swiftly by, bound for the main stream and certain destruction. Some of the men mounted horses and splashed off in pursuit. They thought they heard the boys shouting for help and yelled encouragement. Then a keener ear discerned the words: "And so we sang the chorus from Atlanta to the sea . . ."

Fortunately the boat grounded on a rise of land, and before the doughty mariners could push off, they were forcibly rescued.

A year or two later, Ike again looked over the abyss, this time through no fault of his own. He fell in the stable yard and scratched his knee. That didn't bother him until his leg began to throb and fire burned in his knee and flowed through his body.

The doctor said, "Blood poisoning," and looked grim. The

miracle of the sulfas was far beyond the rim of the future; there was nothing to be done but pray or cut. Ike's leg grew as big as his body and began to turn black. The pain was almost past bearing. He asked for a fork and sat up in bed, chipping at his teeth with it, in some peculiar way finding relief in this distraction.

As the days passed very slowly, Ike often heard the word "amputation." "The only chance of saving your life," the doctor told him.

"No," said Ike. "I'd rather die."

It must have been on the fourth or fifth day that he became really frightened. Things seemed queer and far off; there were blanks in time when he couldn't remember. He realized that he was becoming delirious. What if the doctor came when he was unconscious?

"Edgar!" he called. "Edgar!"

His brother came into the room, looking very solemn and a little embarrassed.

"How's it going, Ike?" he asked, and the heartiness of his tone was so obviously forced that Ike smiled feebly.

"Look, Edgar, you've got to promise me something," he said earnestly.

"Whatever you want, I'll do it," Edgar replied.

"I'm going off my nut," Ike explained. "It sorta comes over me in waves and then I don't know what's going on. It'll probably get worse. You promise me you'll stay here on guard, so they won't cut off my leg. Promise you won't leave even for a second. Promise you won't let them!"

"I promise," Edgar said earnestly.

He sat down in a straight chair beside his brother's bed.

While Ike wandered off into the delirium he had foreseen, Edgar faithfully kept guard. He wouldn't even leave the room to go down to his meals, and his mother brought them up on a tray. At night he lay down on the floor in front of the door. The doctor came and wagged his head and argued, but Edgar only sat there scowling. He didn't know the sense of this thing; maybe the doctor was right and Ike would die. But he did know what he had promised.

The magnificent Eisenhower constitution, his mother's prayers, and his brother's steadfastness pulled the boy through. The fever dropped and the inflammation slowly passed away. Ike came out of his room whole and fit to pass an army physical.

CHAPTER THREE

A SOLDIER BY ACCIDENT

In 1904, when he was thirteen, young Eisenhower began to develop that interest in history which helped fit him for the task of making it himself. At first it was the discovery that history dwelt in those same prosaic streets which he walked daily.

Back in 1870, Abilene had been at the end of the Chisholm Trail along which longhorns from Texas were driven for a thousand miles to be shipped to the eastern markets on the Kansas Pacific Railway. Ike loved to picture the town as it had been then, with its stockyards crammed with cattle, and the waiting herds, a hundred thousand strong, spreading out over the prairies even thicker than the buffalo of Indian days. The old Drovers' Cottage Hotel used to be riotous with reckless Texan cowboys and buyers from the East with pockets bulging with money. Abilene ran wide open. There were thirteen saloons on First Street, and dance halls and gambling dens were going night and day. The legendary Wild Bill Hickok had been the second marshal of Abilene. Great were the tales they told of his lightning draw, his deadly aim and his deceptively elegant appearance.

From such lurid fare about his own peaceful town, Ike's interest carried him on to the wider spaces of history. It was, he discovered, a repetitive tale of slaughter, crime and bloodshed, as though the whole world were a frontier town in which gunplay flickered incessantly and law and order had not yet been made to stick.

Yet there was much enlightened thinking and there were many noble deeds in the long tragic story; the great majority of men were always trying to do the best they could according to their lights. Right triumphed surprisingly often. Now, in the first decade of the new century, it looked as though a pattern of peace were evolving, and the nobler aspirations of mankind seemed close to fulfillment. The world was at last becoming civilized, Ike thought.

He found the strategy of the historic battles intensely interesting, though only as a mental exercise, not as anything that could affect him personally. When he got older, he happened on a copy of *Clausewitz on War,* and while his mind delighted in the clear logic of the great strategist's thinking, he revolted against the ruthless assumption that military power was the main object of a nation's existence. Clausewitz seemed curiously out of date. . . .

Ike started his high school career in the City Hall, which was so used for lack of a suitable school building. It was an elaborate red-brick affair of bastions, Moorish arches and crenelations, topped by a bell tower shaped like a bandsman's busby. Its architectural pomposity was all the more striking because it was flanked by low sheet-iron sheds, containing a livery stable and a foundry.

The south portion of the City Hall was occupied by the primitive, man-powered equipment of the Volunteer Fire Department. On the north side was the big council chamber, with the rope from the iron bell in the tower hanging down through its ceiling. Here all the classes of the high school studied and recited.

This arrangement added enormously to the variety and excitement of academic life. Whenever there was a fire, a wild-eyed man would race through the makeshift schoolroom shouting at the top of his lungs. He'd swing on the bell rope and as a magnificent clamor burst out above, pupils and teachers would stampede for the firehouse and lay hold of the drag ropes of the hook-and-ladder and hose carts. Out of the doors they'd dash and up the dusty street, with the old machines careening wildly behind them, while men poured from stores and houses on the way, and dogs raced along beside them barking frantically.

Those were the good old days of the Abilene High School. When, in Ike's junior year, it moved to a handsome new brick building on the northern edge of town, scholastic life became far less spirited.

Small though Abilene was, many of Ike's new classmates were unknown to him, for the railroad that bisected the town formed a natural barrier between sections. There were two grade schools, and children from the North Side seldom encountered those from the South until they met in high school. Hence it was in that improvised classroom that Ike met many of the friends who have remained close to him throughout the years. Among them was Everett Hazlett—known as Swede because of his Nordic blondness —who inconspicuously carried the key to Ike's destiny in his pocket.

Six MacDonell, the lanky southpaw pitcher, who entered high school two years later than Ike, became his closest friend. Even at fourteen Six showed promise as an athlete and he soon became the best man on both football and baseball teams.

At the time Ike entered high school, he went seriously to work. Before that he had held many odd jobs such as helping at the bottling plant of the Abilene Water Company or sandpapering the horses in the merry-go-round factory. Now he and Edgar alternated as night fireman at the Belle Springs Creamery.

In 1903 the creamery had moved to a huge brick building on the former site of the Drovers' Cottage Hotel, and modern machinery had been installed. David Eisenhower was still the engineer and he got his sons their dual job.

Every other evening after supper, Ike reported for work at the front office of the creamery. Then he went to his own domain, the engine room. It was a great square room, perhaps forty feet high. Dominating it was the new stationary steam engine, with its supporting members painted fire-engine red. Two huge silvered boilers, reaching to the ceiling, shoved their business ends into the room, and opposite them was the great coal bunker.

Between the bunker and the boilers, Ike had an easy chair. Here he did his homework by the light of a naked electric light bulb hanging on a long cord, and here he dozed between hourly shifts of shoveling coal. It was snug and warm in the glow from the fire doors. Being so quiet, it was a fine place to study. If Ike hadn't had to tend the fires so often, it would have been a good place to sleep, too. As it was, he learned to snatch a few moments of sleep when opportunity permitted, like Napoleon and Jeb Stuart.

In the summers Ike had a full-time job at the creamery. Often he worked in the freezing room, the floor of which was a checkerboard of small trap doors. Under each door was a metal trough in which the ice was frozen into three-hundred-pound cakes. When the cakes had hardened sufficiently, Ike had to lift them

out with the iron hook of a hand-powered crane and drag them
to the storage room where they were stacked in pyramidal steps.

At other times he helped pack the ice cream by hand or took
charge of the loading platform. Milton and Earl often came down
to see him work. Their eyes opened wide with admiration as they
watched their big brother crack his sharp tongs into a gleaming
piece of ice and swing it expertly aboard the waiting wagon.

Despite all the hard work, Ike did not miss out on the social
side of life. He loved people and because of his friendliness was
well-liked by everyone. Often when he was on duty the other
boys dropped in at the engine room to sit around and "chew the
fat" or to exercise their voices in the old songs and the latest
popular hits. Ike loved to sing, but when he joyously gave forth
with "Casey would waltz with a strawberry blonde," those of his
friends who cared for music pleaded with tears of anguish, "For
Pete's sake, shut up!"

When the boys grew older there was often a poker game on
the floor between the boilers. "Joner" Callahan, who was six years
older than Ike and very much a man about Abilene, took a great
liking to the younger boy and often stopped in. It was he who
showed Ike that poker was not by any standard a game of chance.

"You got to know the percentages," Joner said, collecting a
handful of Ike's small change, "and then you have to calculate
the chances. Most of all you must study the other fellow and try
to figure out what he's thinking."

Ike boned up on percentages more assiduously than any other
branch of mathematics. He was naturally good at estimating
character and personal reaction, and his greatest delight in the
game was outguessing his opponents. Quite soon the pupil was
outmaneuvering his master. This aptitude for poker might have
been seen as a distant portent, if anyone had connected it—as
Ike certainly did not—with the dictum of old Karl von Clausewitz
that "War, of all branches of human activity, [is] most like a
game of cards."

With his earnings and his winnings, Ike was able to buy
a Winchester repeating shotgun. He loved to go out with a
friend or two after quail and rabbit and other small game that
still abounded on the prairies. In fact he liked hunting so much
that he got into considerable trouble at school by playing hooky.

Nor did Ike neglect the girls; he liked them in general, and
he always had a "best girl." The gayest clique of the Class of

1909 called themselves the "Bums of Lawsy Lou." Ike was a welcome, if perforce somewhat intermittent, member of the Bums.

As he reached his senior year of high school, Ike was doing well in his studies—well, though not brilliantly except in history. It was this year that he finally arrived as an athlete. Until then he had been small and weedy; quite suddenly he grew an inch or more, to his full height of five feet ten and a half inches, and his frame filled out to the solid build ideal for football. That was always Ike's favorite game, because it combined team play and tactical considerations with physical prowess.

Football prospects looked poor that fall at Abilene High. The school board had a bad attack of parsimony and decided they could not afford a coach; in fact, they were determined not to spend any money on football at all. There was black despair in the hearts of the team; but Ike was undismayed.

"Let's form an athletic association," he proposed, "and raise some money."

"Who, us?" asked Six MacDonell.

"Why not? We ain't hog-bound, chained or paralyzed."

The others promptly elected Ike president of the Abilene High School Athletic Association, which is still functioning today. Ike guided its first faltering footsteps with energy and intelligence. It didn't raise much money, but it saved football in Abilene.

The first real crisis the association had to meet was how to get the team to Chapman some twelve miles eastward on the Union Pacific for the traditional game with the high school team. Despite the best efforts of its members there was not enough money for carfare.

"You're president of the association," the boys told Ike. "Do something."

"All trains aren't passenger trains," Ike pointed out, "and all the people who ride on them aren't passengers."

When the eleven-thirty-three freight pulled out of Abilene that Saturday morning, the football team was distributed under the cars on the tie rods. Thus they rode to Chapman, nailed the hides of the Chapmen to their own goal posts and traveled triumphantly home again on No. 6 mixed freight. Ike had solved his first problem in logistics.

In June, 1909, Dwight D. Eisenhower was graduated from high school with thirty-one pupils of his class. He stood well in the upper third. Writing about him in *The Helianthus,*

Cecilia Curry expressed the opinion of his fellows when she prophesied: "Ike will wind up as a professor of history at Yale."

By the summer of 1910 Ike felt that his progress through life had become a series of unprofitable circles; there was no absolute motion, not even drift. He had been working hard for a year and had accomplished nothing. To his job at the creamery he had added other casual employments. When he wasn't working, he played around with Six MacDonell, who was still in school, and Joner Callahan. His poker game had become phenomenal, but that was about all he gained, except what he learned during the hours he spent in the office of his older friend, J. W. Howe, owner of the weekly Abilene *News*.

It was tremendously exciting to Ike to watch the news flashes come in—history hot off the griddle. Then, too, Mr. Howe had an excellent library and was generous about lending his books. Ida Eisenhower had bought more books for her boys than she could really afford; but she could not keep pace with Ike's needs. And she would not buy the military histories that he particularly enjoyed. When he was younger he had to read them surreptitiously, lying under the bed. Mr. Howe's library filled a big gap. Even so, Ike's activities during that year added up to about zero. Meanwhile, both his older brothers were on their way.

Arthur had been the first to leave home. He was determined to be a successful businessman, and so had set his course. Even as a schoolboy he had had the ability to handle money. One morning soon after he finished school, Arthur took the three-thirty train to Kansas City. He put up at a cheap boardinghouse and immediately set out to look for work. He knew that Tenth Street was the business district, and he started at Wyandotte Street, turning in at every door on Tenth to apply for a job. When he got to the National Bank of Commerce, Charley Moore, the vice-president, hired him as a messenger boy at twenty-five dollars a month.

Arthur started in the basement and doggedly began to climb. He is still doing business on the same corner, but he is now the dominant financial figure of Kansas City.

Edgar, too, was sure of his ambition: he wanted to be a lawyer. By 1910 he was making good progress, working his way through the Law School of the University of Michigan. The boys who were still at home contributed a little money to help Edgar out, and he in turn helped them when their day came.

Ike's other brothers were still in school. Roy, round and good-natured, was at the High, while Earl and Milton were now Big Ike and Little Ike in the grade school.

So Ike was the only one at loose ends. He didn't exactly lose sleep over his plight—not all the might of the Luftwaffe has been able to produce that effect—but it troubled him. The difficulty was that he didn't know what he wanted to do, beyond playing football a while longer. Sometimes when he was at the *News* he thought of being a reporter. He knew that he could write concisely and well. At other times he had a recurring dream of going to South America as an engineer, but it never had sufficient force to overcome his inertia. He had the uneasy feeling that he was Micawbering along waiting for something to turn up.

It was Swede Hazlett who turned up. He had been appointed to the United States Naval Academy that spring and had gone to a cramming school in Annapolis. But the time had been too short and he had failed in his entrance examination. Nevertheless, Swede's brief glimpse of the naval scene had applied a forced draft to the fires of his ambition. He bedeviled his congressman until the latter reappointed him for the following year.

Hazlett spent the summer of 1910 managing a small business in Abilene and studying furiously—he wasn't going to lose his second chance. He could talk of nothing but Annapolis, and his enthusiasm was contagious. Few boys in those long days of peace regarded a military career as offering much chance to get on in the world; but Ike caught some of Hazlett's enthusiasm. Swede liked Ike better than any other boy in town, and seeing that his friend was interested, he redoubled his arguments.

Ike turned the idea over in his mind; the more he scrutinized it the better he liked it. Then came his conversation with Six on the steps of the Citizens' Bank, during which he made up his mind.

Once settled on a course, Ike pursued it with energy. He went to see Charles M. Harger of the Abilene *Reflector,* Mr. Howe of the *News* and Postmaster Phil Heath, all of whom promised to use their influence with Senator Joseph L. Bristow of Salina to obtain permission for him to take the competitive examination for Annapolis.

Mr. Heath warned Ike that it would not be easy even if he got the opportunity.

"There'll be about a hundred other fellows out after that appointment," he said.

"Do you think I have a chance?" Ike asked.

Mr. Heath looked at the blond young man who stood before him, and noted the quality of his steady blue eyes.

"You impress me as the sort of guy who can do just about anything he wants to," he said, "if you hump yourself."

In September, Senator Bristow accorded the permission together with the information that the examination would be held at Topeka in November. That gave Ike only two months to prepare. It was not just a question of passing: he had to beat everyone else.

Swede Hazlett offered to help. Every afternoon Ike went to his little office, where the two boys studied together for three hours or more. What happened to the business was secondary to Swede, who unselfishly devoted all his energy to tutoring his protégé. When he saw the way that untrained but brilliant mind took hold, he felt that his labor was justified.

Ike was humping himself. Although he was now night superintendent at the creamery, he went back to high school in the mornings to brush up on chemistry and mathematics. According to the rudimentary athletic regulations of those days, this postgraduate work gave him the right to play on the football team once more.

At twenty Ike was bigger and stronger than ever, a blond giant among the schoolboys. He played tackle on the team, which was captained by Six MacDonell. The apotheosis of Ike's prevarsity career came in the game against Salina High, which being much larger than Abilene had a correspondingly better team. Eisenhower and MacDonell had to play through the whole game, for if either had taken time out all would have been over.

Salina had a trick play, which tore through the Abilene line like a rotary plow through a snowdrift, but after the first two times, Ike figured it out, and hurled his one hundred and seventy-five pounds of work-hardened muscle at exactly the right spot. Salina's play crumpled like a model T against a telephone pole.

From that time on the play was smashed every time and the Salina boys became decidedly irked. Nobody wanted to tangle with the big Swede, as they called Ike, but one bruiser deliberately knocked out Six MacDonell. Ike liked to play rough, but all his life he had loathed brutality with a violence that on occasion filled him with a tremendous rage. As he looked at Six lying limp on the grass, his brain burned with fury; he went berserk.

By the time the others succeeded in stopping Eisenhower,

MacDonell was already coming to, but four of Salina's linesmen were lying peacefully beside him, as limp as so many mackerel on a dock.

When Ike went up to Topeka to take the examination, he shared none of Hazlett's confidence. On the contrary, he was convinced that he didn't have a chance. Not that he hadn't sweated for it; he was conditioned to work hard for whatever goal he sought. But this was his first venture beyond the limits of Abilene. He knew that he had to meet competition from the whole state and he calculated that the odds were against his being able to outshine all the bright young men from the big cities. To give himself a better chance he took both the Annapolis and the West Point examinations on the theory that if he didn't win one he might make the other.

This pessimism regarding the outcome did not depress him, for in his temperament resolution was combined with a philosophical attitude toward events; he would do his best and not worry about the result. It was this quality which later enabled him to withstand the strain of awful responsibility and come through smiling. He had never been to a real city before, and he proposed to enjoy it. Between examinations he had a wonderful time.

When Ike got the news from the examining board, it was a shock of sheer delight. In the Annapolis test, he was top man with an average of 87.7 per cent, and in the West Point he ranked second.

Ida Eisenhower was one of those fabulous mothers who never try to interfere with their sons' lives. Having brought up her boys as God-fearing, hard-working citizens, she felt that she had given them the cornerstone of character. She well remembered that in her youth people had tried to sway her from her decisions. What a struggle she had had, first to go west and then to go to college. Since the way she had chosen had proved so right for her, she was resolute that her sons should make their own decisions.

Never had this determination been so hardily tried as when Dwight told her of his wish to enter Annapolis. Her abhorrence of war was so strong that it seemed almost like blasphemy that a child of hers should practice it as a profession. And yet her confidence in Dwight's character was such that if he chose this course she felt it must be right for some reason beyond her powers to perceive. It must, she thought, be a manifestation of God's inscrutable will.

But though she made no protest, she ardently wished that he would fail in the examination—without very much hope, for her belief in Dwight's ability was as strong as her confidence in his character.

When Ida looked out the kitchen window that wintry afternoon and saw her son come running across the vacant lot behind the school, leaping exuberantly over a fallen log, she knew the answer. For that one moment faith weakened and grief overthrew her spirit. She jumped from her chair in a flash and ran up the stairs to her own room.

She had perhaps thirty seconds in which to sorrow—thirty seconds for the tears she could not restrain—before Dwight's deep joyous voice boomed in the parlor below. "Mother, where are you? Mother, I made it!"

Ida Eisenhower came down the narrow staircase; her face was serene and she was smiling.

"It's splendid, Dwight," she said. "I knew you could do it."

Ike's appointment to the Naval Academy came through; but his jubilance was transmuted to despair when he discovered what nobody had thought to tell him, that the maximum age limit for entrance was twenty. By June Ike would be eight months too old. In his trouble he consulted his faithful older friends. One of them held out a ray of hope: the age limit at West Point was twenty-two; perhaps the appointment could be changed. They all wrote to Senator Bristow. That statesman had been considerably impressed by young Eisenhower's fine record in both examinations, and when the top West Point candidate failed in his physical examination, Ike was given the appointment.

So the train of his life was fortuitously directed past the maze of switches and sidetracks and probable routes onto the main line of his destiny. It almost seems as though some higher intelligence were in the dispatcher's tower, setting the signals and throwing the levers.

The afternoon Ike left for West Point there were only two members of the family at home—his mother and Milton, and of course, Flip, his fox terrier. They were waiting on the west porch when he came down the stairs carrying his heavy bag. Milton felt very solemn—he wasn't quite sure why. When the other boys had left it hadn't been like this; it hadn't seemed so final.

Ike came out on the porch in his familiar, casual way and set his bag down on the stoop.

"Are you sure you have everything you need?" asked Ida.

"Sure," said Ike. He smiled at her affectionately. "Don't look so unhappy, Mother," he said gently. "It won't be long till you see me. Only two years."

"Oh, Dwight!" she said. "You'll be so different."

She burst into tears. It was the first time her sons had ever seen her cry, and they were stunned. Milton looked up at his big brother. All Ike's casualness had vanished; his face was white and strained. He put a clumsy arm around his mother's shoulders and hugged her tightly. Then he turned to the younger boy.

"Milton," he said in a rough, commanding voice, "I'm depending on you to look after Mother."

It was too much for Milton. He uttered a grief-stricken howl. Flip joined in mournfully.

Ike gave the unhappy trio a look of agonized despair. Then, picking up his bag, he fled across the field.

CHAPTER FOUR

FORTRESS ON THE HUDSON

The United States Military Academy is designed for a single specific purpose: the education of the highest possible type of officers to command the Armies of the United States. It does not aim to give them a liberal education, and there is no time for frills; but nothing that can contribute to their efficiency is omitted. Since men with some understanding of the liberal arts and philosophical thinking are better fitted for their larger tasks than those whose minds are narrowly confined to the technicalities of their profession, the range of subjects includes many which seem remote from military education.

The plant at West Point is, in fact, like a munitions factory engaged in turning out the most complicated and delicate of all machines of modern war. It is concerned even more with the tempering of these weapons than with their shaping; the emphasis is on the building of character. The West Point code of honor is fantastically superior to even the highest civilian ideals; the standard of duty seems beyond any reasonable requirements, and love of country is an absolute.

The raw material which comes there for processing is the finest obtainable. The young men who enter are ascertained to possess a high degree of physical perfection and mental alertness. But conformation to these standards still leaves a wide human variation. Some of the appointees are already by temperament and environment rough-shaped for the mold. These are usually sons of officers or graduates of military preparatory schools. Others are very raw material.

Dwight Eisenhower, riding the wooden coaches of the West Point Special from Weehawken, was definitely in the latter class. It is true that he surpassed the minimum requirements for entrance. His muscles were toughened by hard work and hard play, and his mind, though sketchily trained, was an efficient precision instrument; but even to himself he seemed an unlikely prospect for military distinction. His whole training was opposed to the idea of war. His mother had succeeded in imbuing him with much of her idealistic pacifism. He was easygoing, tolerant and free from any great personal ambition. Furthermore, he was older than the average appointee, and for that reason less malleable. He had been knocking around for two years, and though he came from such a small town, he was in certain ways more sophisticated than the boys who were fresh from prep schools. In others he was as green as winter wheat.

The only indication of military aptitude was his fondness for reading history and the accounts of famous campaigns. But it had been a sort of intellectual game with him. Now he would play the game of soldiering for the sake of getting an education. He intended to conform to the rules as much as was necessary to keep from being ordered to the sidelines, but he proposed to take it easy.

The neat little station at West Point was a scene of unmilitary confusion as boys from all over the country boiled out of the West Point Special and milled around on the platform. The big, yellow-haired young Kansan was one of the last out of the cars— taking it easy. He shoved affably through the crowd and, setting his bag down in a clear space, looked around to get his bearings.

The broad Hudson River, which almost lapped the tracks, was the biggest, bluest body of water he had ever seen. The wooded hills on the other side of the river seemed to him enormous angry mountains that cut off half the sky, and the cliff behind him was like a rocky plain standing on end. This was an uncomfortable sort of scenery, he thought, as his mind turned back to the rolling prairie and gentle, friendly hills he had left in Kansas. Then he concentrated on his future classmates. They looked surprisingly young, he thought. They acted young, too, either grimly tense or nervously hilarious.

The crowd began to move up a steep road carved out on the face of the cliff. Ike picked up his bag and trudged up the hill through the intense heat. Crowning the heights above him was a gray stone fortress, which seemed rooted in the rock. From the high top of its square, battlemented tower floated a big

American flag. On the left, between the river and the cliff, a still larger fortress was in process of construction. Even in its half-finished state, it seemed an integral part of the granite on which it stood.

The climb up this natural rampart ended on a wide plateau commanding the full sweep of the Hudson. Beyond the level green of a parade ground were still more gray, fortresslike buildings; crenelated towers rose among the distant trees.

On the sidewalk in front of the great portcullis of the Administration Building stood a row of tables with an enlisted man at each, taking down the names of the new appointees. Ike fell into the waiting line. Suddenly he felt chilly in spite of the blazing sun. The immense weight of all that implacable masonry was bearing down upon his spirit; it enclosed him like a prison—stern, unbending and austere. He felt the impact of an inexorable tradition frozen in the timeless granite, the first strong pressure of the mold that was to shape him to the West Point pattern.

The others in line were solemn, too. Ike saw that his emotion was shared by virtually every man who looked upon that dedicated Plain for the first time. He shook himself, like a retrieve coming out of cold water; the menacing battlements became old-fashioned-looking buildings and the sun felt hot again. Almost carelessly he signed the form in which he promised to serve in the Army of the United States for eight years from the date of his acceptance.

After that, he had no further time for thinking. In rapid progression he was passed along the preliminary assembly line. He entrusted all his money to the safekeeping of the treasurer, for no cadet may carry cash. He received his final physical examination and was assigned to a company according to his height; Ike's five feet ten and a half inches rated F Company, the tallest on the left flank of the parade line. Next he was taken to check his baggage, where it would be stored for two full years until his second-class leave. From there he went to a stone barracks in a quadrangle, where he was assigned to a room and a temporary roommate.

Then the Third Classmen took over, having been given the task of whipping the new arrivals into shape. They were called the "Beast Detail," because they tamed the "Beasts." Compared to the sweating herd of appointees in their heterogeneous assortment of civilian clothes, the Yearlings were incredibly immaculate in razor-edged white ducks and poured-on gray jackets. **This was** the first opportunity of these plebes of yesterweek to exercise authority, and how they loved it!

At their advent the human conveyer belt speeded up. Ike and his classmates went on the run from the barbershop to the cadet store for their first issue of gray flannel trousers and shirts, and down to the basement for mattresses and bedding. Back to the barracks they trotted under their burdens, and out again for a quick drill by their new masters.

"Suck in your guts!" "Pull in your chins!" "You're the worst-looking lot that ever disgraced the Academy!" "Can't you even stand in line?" "Hey, you big Swede with the outsize tail, what's your name?"

"Ike Eisenhower."

"Say 'sir' to me, Mr. Eisenhower, and wipe off that smile!"

"Yes, sir!"

Ike didn't mind the orders and the gibes. In spite of the rush, he was mentally taking it easy. This was part of the game that he had expected to play. These military paragons who barked curt orders were for the most part younger than he, and, he began to suspect, less experienced in many ways. He knew he had to follow the rules of the game, but he didn't have to take it seriously. He wondered what Joner and Six would say if they could see him standing in this ill-spaced line of boys, with his guts sucked in, his chest bulging out and his chin down on his neck. He grinned again at the thought.

"WIPE OFF THAT SMILE!"

"Yes, sir!"

But Ike couldn't wipe the smile out of his eyes.

Later, however, near the close of the endless day, he was once more knocked off balance by the impact of tradition. At five o'clock the new cadets were lined up in some sort of order and marched for the first time onto the Parade Ground. As Ike stood there waiting in the ragged gray line of the class of '15, the enlisted men's band struck up a rousing march and the Corps of Cadets in their full-dress uniforms swung onto the field. Ike had never seen good marching before; had never thought much about the pictorial side of military display. The sight of those men moving with smooth precision, wave on wave of them flowing past in effortless rhythm and exact alignment, every movement synchronized, every gun at the same angle, and the fixed

bayonets catching the sunlight like little silver streaks of lightning, had the elemental appeal of any form of beauty. It lifted
Ike right out of the detachment with which he had regarded the
events of the day, and into the realm of pure emotion.

When the moment came for him to take the oath of allegiance
all his nonchalance was gone.

"I do solemnly swear that I will support the Constitution of the
United States and bear true allegiance to the National Government; that I will maintain and defend the sovereignty of the
United States paramount to any and all allegiance, sovereignty
or fealty I may owe to any State, county or country whatsoever,
and that I will at all times obey the legal orders of my superior
officers and the rules and articles governing the Armies of the
United States."

It was a dedication.

But little sense of that exaltation remained to Ike in the next
hectic weeks of Beast Barracks and intensive whipping into shape.
It seemed to him that he was on a dead run every minute of his
waking hours, and when he hit his bed he slept as if dead. Some
of his classmates began to crack under the strain, but Ike remained
secure behind the defense of his temperament, which enabled
him still to take it easy emotionally, though certainly not
physically.

In those first weeks personalities began to emerge from the
two hundred and sixty-five men of the largest class to enter the
Academy up to that time. Ike's temporary roommate was inevitably the first he knew well, but it was not from choice. Johnny
was one of those who began to crack. Though up to standard
on the surface, there were flaws in his metal which could not take
the tempering process. To Ike's utter amazement this uncon-
genial companion began to have fits of sobbing. Ike tried to help
him with his own philosophy, but the boy rejected it.

"It's different for you," he said, "but I was awfully popular
at home."

Ike was slightly irked.

"What's so different?" he demanded.

"Well, your not ever having had things the way I had. For
instance, I got seventy-nine presents when I graduated from high
school."

"How many invitations did you send out?"

"About five hundred."

"A very poor percentage," Ike remarked coldly.

His roommate laid his head on the bare tabletop and bawled. When Johnny took to fainting on parade, it was evident that his time was short, especially as it was remarked by the cadets that he invariably waited until he was in a conveniently shady spot before collapsing. He became an early reject.

Though Ike was unsympathetic toward his weak roommate, he extended a helping hand to another plebe who began to exhibit distressing symptoms.

"What's wrong with you?" Ike asked the boy, whom he really liked. "Don't you like it here?"

"I do," said the boy. "I like it too much. But I can't stay."

"Why not?"

"Because," said the other desperately, "I'm over twenty-two. I lied about my age to get in. I've got to tell."

The honor system had not as yet completely got Ike. In a decision between technicality and humanity he was always apt to weight the verdict. With magnificent disregard of ethics he told a whopping lie.

"Shucks! Don't you worry about a little thing like that," he said. "I lied about my age, too."

But such cases as these two young men were a small minority, far outnumbered by those who seemed to grow in stature under the strain. One of the first of his classmates to command Ike's admiration and unfaltering friendship was Omar Bradley. The plebe from Missouri first achieved distinction as the ugliest man in the class. He had a long, melancholy face with full lips, and in spite of regulation barbering his hair contrived to look long and dank. But in Bradley's case the bottle was no criterion of the wine, and it was not long before his inner qualities gave him another sort of prominence. He had tremendous enthusiasm and energy; though he looked slow, he was fast on his feet and in his thinking. His loyalty was exceptional even at West Point, and in addition to these attributes, he could make a baseball do everything but loop the loop.

Ike liked him from the first. The greatest rage he ever felt at the Academy was when a cadet called the Missourian "Darwin," because of his supposedly simian appearance. What Ike called the cadet didn't sound pretty and couldn't be printed at all.

When Ike wrote Bradley's portrait for the *Howitzer* four years later, the gift of prophecy descended upon him. "Brad's most important characteristic is 'getting there,'" he wrote, "and if he keeps up the clip he's started some of us will some day be bragging that, 'Sure, General Bradley was a classmate of mine.'"

Ike's finest friendship at the Point began by a curious current of mutual attraction. As he stood in the company ranks day after day, Ike found his glance frequently drawn toward a tall boy who seemed always to be looking his way. When their eyes met, Ike would grin amiably and the other, with a quick, shy smile, always looked away. By these exchanges they seemed to be friends before ever they spoke a word.

At the last parade before summer camp, the invariable announcement was made that the plebes might choose their tentmates. When the ranks broke Ike impetuously walked over to his unknown friend. He had a queer certainty of the outcome.

"I'm Ike Eisenhower," he said.

"Paul Alfred Hodgson. My friends call me P.A.," was the prompt reply.

"Your way of talking sounds mighty familiar, P.A.," said Ike. "Where are you from?"

"Wichita, Kansas."

Ike laughed in delight.

"I'm from Abilene. How about us living together in camp?"

P.A.'s face shone with pleasure.

"You bet!" he said.

Ike's instinct for choosing men was exemplified by this happy selection. He and Hodgson became inseparable friends, and shared the same quarters for their entire time at the Academy. In cadet slang P.A. was Ike's "wife," but often he acted more like a mother. He was a perfectionist, who regarded the rules as sacred and obeyed them meticulously, whereas Ike was constantly contriving ways of evading the regulations he did not like. As a result, P.A. worried through four years for fear that his roommate would get into really serious trouble and be dismissed. Ike's attitude, until his final year, was extremely casual toward this dire contingency.

"If I get fired," he often said, "I'll go to South America and help open up the country."

With respect to Ike's numerous transgressions it is important to record that never under any circumstances did he violate the West Point code of honor. This requires of every cadet a nicety

Arthur, Edgar, Roy, and Dwight (lower right) shortly after the Eisenhowers moved to this house in Abilene. *(Monkmeyer)*

The boys grow up, but Milton still wears curls. Dwight is at the extreme left. *(Monkmeyer)*

All the Eisenhowers have a reunion in Abilene in 1926. *(Monkmeyer)*

"The Huge Kansan." Eisenhower as a half-back on the Army football team in 1912. (*European*)

Lieutenant and Mrs. Dwight D. Eisenhower, San Antonio, 1916.
(Monkmeyer)

Lieutenant Colonel Eisenhower, Commandant, Tank Training Center, Camp Colt, October 1918. *(Monkmeyer)*

Eisenhower when he was promoted to the rank of Brigadier General at Fort Sam Houston. *(Signal Corps)*

Eisenhower and Giraud take the salute of the Spahis prior to Giraud's conferring the Grand Cross of the Legion of Honor on the American Commander-in-Chief. *(Signal Corps)*

Conference after the fall of Mussolini. Front row: Eisenhower, Tedder, Alexander, and Cunningham. *(European)*

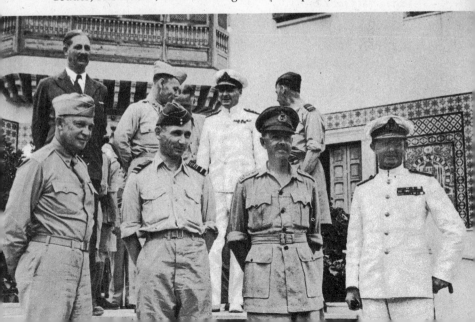

General Eisenhower, Field Marshall Gort, and Air Marshall Tedder chat after meeting of Allied Commanders on Malta, July 1944. *(Signal Corps)*

Eisenhower and Montgomery meet in Messina, Sicily, in August 1943. *(Signal Corps)*

The late Admiral Jean Darlan with General Clark and General Eisenhower after a meeting at Allied headquarters at Algiers. (*European*)

Eisenhower and Giraud start for the victory parade in Tunis. (*European*)

Eisenhower and Cunningham on the bridge of a British destroyer watch the surrender of the Italian fleet. *(Signal Corps)*

The Commander-in-Chief goes to see for himself. Ike starting a flight over the lines in Italy. *(Signal Corps)*

Winston Churchill and General Eisenhower reviewing airborne
troops in England. *(Signal Corps)*

The Supreme Command plans for D-Day. Air Marshall Tedder, General Eisenhower, General Montgomery at a conference before the invasion. *(European)*

They meet again in Normandy. *(European)*

The invasion armada crossing the Channel. *(Acme)*

General Eisenhower arrives on the beach at Isigny with
Admiral King (right) on D + 6. *(Signal Corps)*

General Eisenhower starts over the lines in Normandy with Major General Elwood Quesada, Chief of the 9th Air Force Fighter Command. *(European)*

Paratroopers receiving their orders from Ike before they start on their first invasion of the continent. *(Signal Corps)*

Ike in conversation with flight officer A. K. Asboe who, with others, escorted Ike to Normandy and back in their spitfires. *(Signal Corps)*

The General enjoys a hot meal somewhere in Germany. *(Signal Corps)*

The General chatting with two Norwegian airmen who are fighting with the Allies. *(Signal Corps)*

Ruth and Milton Eisenhower, Jr. take a walk with Telek II who was a gift from their uncle, General Eisenhower. (*Acme*)

Mrs. Eisenhower and John leaving their home at the Wardman Park Hotel. *(International)*

Eisenhower greets his cousin, Sgt. George Ethrington of Abilene, Kansas, who is attached to the Headquarters Company of an American Infantry Division. *(Signal Corps)*

Pearlie and Mickey with Colonel Ernest Lee.

Ike and Patton at the airport at Palermo. *(Signal Corps)*

Eisenhower with Lieutenant General Omar Bradley. *(Signal Corps)*

General Eisenhower and Major General Donald A. Strok. *(Signal Corps)*

Ike, with James V. Forrestal, Secretary of the Navy, after their conference with General Charles de Gaulle and Brigadier General Joseph-Pierre Koenig. *(Signal Corps)*

General Eisenhower wears his new five-star cluster, insignia of his new rank as General of the Army. *(Signal Corps)*

of conduct exceeding even the legends of the days of chivalry. Every statement a cadet makes must be the absolute truth, the whole truth, and no mental reservations. He must be rigidly honest in his work. If he is given a pass to go to a certain place, he must go there and not deviate from the straight line en route; if he is in charge of a barracks and sees a violation of the regulations, he must report it even though the offender be his best friend, even though it be himself. There are certain entries in the "skin sheets"—records of offenses and punishments—where Cadet Eisenhower was reported by Cadet Eisenhower.

But the code does not concern itself otherwise with the enforcement of regulations; that is entirely up to the Tactical Department. Therefore, except when a cadet is on his honor, it is perfectly all right to break every rule in the book—if he can get away with it. Of such evasive tactics Ike was a grand master, but his perilous maneuvers brought premature gray to the curly brown locks of the faithful P.A.

Poor Hodgson nearly went out of his mind one night in their first year when some upperclassmen ordered Ike and Cadet Larkin to appear after taps in their full-dress coats.

"It's an order," said Ike. "We'll obey it."

As the slow notes of the bugle call died away, Cadets Eisenhower and Larkin presented themselves as ordered. Brass buttons flashed in splendor, cross belts were as white as foam on their beautifully fitted tail coats. But military perfection ended abruptly at the waist.

"Nothing was said about trousers, sir," Cadet Eisenhower explained.

The association between the two men was amazingly free from the minor irritations usually incident to such close companionship. With good-natured resignation P.A. gave up eating onions for four years because Ike claimed that even the smell of them poisoned him. Long after graduation, Ike suddenly discovered that onions tasted better than they smelled and began eating great quantities of them. Then P.A. thought regretfully of those wasted four years.

Though it irked him, P.A. also forgave Ike his ability to toss off an English theme with no apparent effort. The compositions usually had to be in at two o'clock on Mondays. Hodgson would agonize over such a project for several days. At one o'clock on Monday, when they returned from lunch, Ike would say nonchalantly, "I need a nap. Call me at one-thirty."

P.A. would wake him at the appointed time and watch envi-ously as his friend sat down and scribbled rapidly. At one-fifty-five Ike would stop writing. His theme would be no more than two or three words longer than the required three-hundred-word minimum, and it invariably won a high mark.

When the football season came around, both men were in the Cullum Hall Squad, as the plebe team was called; and they both made brilliant records. Ike also went in for boxing, baseball and track.

At the end of his plebe year, Ike's academic record, though less brilliant than his athletic performance, was definitely creditable. He stood 57 among the 212 survivors of the entering class; his rank in English was 10, History 39, and Military Engineering 30.

But he had acquired a fine collection of demerits, and spent many an hour marching them off in the area, sweating under his dress coat and the apparently growing weight of his rifle. In the roster of his "skins," being late for breakfast formation is a frequent entry. He got two demerits for: "Asleep in chair at inspection, 8:30 P.M." It seemed as though he never would catch up with that lost sleep of boyhood.

Another demerit-catcher was his language, for Ike determinedly resisted any attempt to put a polish on him. He liked to affect the tough plainsmen. "Using profanity at supper—5" . . . "Im-proper expression about 2:33 P.M.—4."

In a later year he got a heavy slug for terpsichorean exuber-ance: "Violation of orders in reference to dancing, having previ-ously been admonished for same—8." It sounds like the Turkey Trot, the Bunny Hug, or perhaps the Grizzly Bear.

But in spite of his rugged resistance, Ike was shaping to the form. On June 30, 1912, he was promoted to corporal, though he was "busted" soon afterward. It was when the football season came around that he really began to be regarded as a credit to the Point. His game had come a long way since he rode the rods to Chapman to play for Abilene High. His work with the Cullum Hall Squad had brought him technical excellence which enhanced his basic ability. Playing now at halfback, he had developed into a "triple threat man," as dangerous in defense as in attack. Foot-ball was one game Ike didn't take easy.

P.A. also was an Army star, and the sports writers gave both friends a big play. They called Ike the "huge Kansan" and P.A. the "gigantic Kansan," and predicted All-American honors for Ike in particular.

Down at Annapolis the midshipmen shivered as news spread of a great new Army halfback who tore through the early games of the season like a Kansas tornado. Midshipman Everett Hazlett, surveying a two-column picture of his fellow townsman, felt immensely proud. It is safe to say that he was the only Navy man who enjoyed reading the accompanying article.

Ike was fairly proud himself. It wasn't just conceit, though of course a fellow's head was bound to expand a little when the plebes watched him go by with awe-struck eyes and even First Classmen looked respectful. It was a higher sort of pride—a joy in his strength and speed and quickness of mind, delight in the skill he had acquired, and satisfaction in a job well done. Most of all he was proud of being a worthy member of the Corps, the finest body of men in America. In the whole damn world! He exulted in bringing honor to them, and victory to their banners.

That's how he felt, standing on the athletic field on November 9, 1912, as the game with the Carlisle Indian School began. The cheering lifted his spirit—not the shouting of the civilians, but the disciplined, soul-stirring yell of those solid gray ranks in the wooden bleachers:

> "ssssSSSSS . . . . . BOOM! . . . . . Ahhh!
> U.S.M.A. Rah! Rah!
> Hoo-rah! Hoo-rah!
> Ar-MAY! Rah!
> Eisenhower! Eisenhower! Eisenhower!"

Ike's heart was almost at the bursting point.

That game was no victory; it was more in the nature of Custer's last stand without the glory; and, like that disaster, it was brought about by a redskin. The great Jim Thorpe of Carlisle slipped through the Army lines as swiftly and easily as his ancestors had sped through the clutching underbrush of their native forests. The cadets seemed to be just standing there watching him go by. Sunday morning papers stated that Eisenhower was the only Army man who even looked like a football player on that fatal field.

In the course of the game Ike sprained his knee. This caused even more consternation in the Army camp than the defeat. It was the Navy game that really counted, and they wanted Eisenhower for that. But Ike was destined never to play against Navy.

Doctors, coaches and trainers made feverish efforts to get the star back in condition. Marty Maher, the tough little Irishman who was custodian of the gym and took the honor of the team as seriously as any cadet, arranged for a special brace to steady the bad knee. Between them all they had Ike on the field again the following Saturday.

If the Carlisle game was a disaster, the one with Tufts College was a calamity. True, Army won, but it paid too dear a price, for Ike's knee was seriously injured.

It was a bitter blow, perhaps the heaviest of his life, though in retrospect it seems a trivial matter. It meant giving up the game he loved best of all—the end of a career scarcely begun. He could not play in the only contest that really counted—the Navy game. There would be no more cheers, no further chance to bring glory to the Corps—at least for that year, if not forever.

But as he lay in his bed in the hospital one thought comforted him. He had just received a slug of "six demerits and twenty-two punishment tours in the area during the next thirty days." Owing to that official wording, which has since been changed, Ike was able to walk off his punishment metaphorically, for the thirty days passed while he lay comfortably on his back.

Dr. Charles Keller, the chief surgeon, was hopeful.

"If you are careful," he said, "and obey my orders absolutely, there's a good chance that you will play again someday."

Keller was beloved by the whole Corps and loved them all. They sang about him affectionately:

> "We will send you down to Doctor Keller,
> He will make you very sick or weller.
> He will part you from your inmost thoughts."

That last line was the key to their regard for him. Knowing that he would always stand by them and weight the scales in their favor, the cadets trusted the kindly doctor with their most secret fears and hopes.

Not that Keller was soft. No one could put anything over on the doctor; and he had a robust humor. Once a malingering cadet reported on sick call. He was loath to describe his trouble, but under Keller's questioning he mumbled various complaints. When he had done, the doctor pondered a while and then announced in carrying tones, "Mr. Ducrot, I have checked your symptoms carefully and I find that you are pregnant."

In his profession Dr. Keller stood very near the top. He had a special gift for patching up broken football players which saved many a good officer for his country's service. He nursed Ike's knee as though it were the most precious object belonging to the United States Army, as perhaps it was. Within a month he had his patient walking again, but his final advice, as Ike left the hospital, still stiff in his movements, was: "Favor that knee! Don't do anything to strain it. You may take part in light drills, but in riding drill stay on your horse. I don't want you constantly mounting and dismounting."

"Yes, sir," said Ike, and added hesitantly, "Thank you, sir, for all you've done."

"Don't thank me," said Keller, "I did it for the good of the service. We can't afford to lose a halfback like you."

It was Ike's firm intention to follow the doctor's advice to the letter. Unhappily he broke the resolution. It happened in the huge new Riding Hall by the river, that same fortress which had been under construction when Ike first climbed the hill. The drillmaster was a martinet, who grumbled ferociously when Ike told him of the doctor's orders. During several drills he watched discontentedly, muttering gibes as Ike sat his mount while the others leaped off and on their horses at the word of command. One afternoon his patience snapped.

"Mr. Eisenhower," he shouted. "I believe you are malingering. Hereafter you will complete all the movements of the drill."

Ike's eyes were black with anger as he answered, "Yes, sir."

P.A. managed to get near enough to him for a word. He was ablaze with such rage as Ike had never thought could possess him. "Don't you do it, Ike," he whispered fiercely. "You'll wreck yourself. Tell the bastard where to head in."

"I've got to do it," said Ike. "He as good as called me a liar."

"You fool!" P.A. growled.

All through that long afternoon, Ike dismounted and re-mounted with exact precision. His knee complained from the first, then muscle and sinew gave warning with sharp stabs of pain; finally the nerves screamed in agony. Nevertheless, with his face set like the granite of the cliffs and his eyes as bleak as the plains in winter, Ike continued to perform the evolutions of the drill.

When Ike finally left the Riding Hall, he was half helped, half carried to the hospital by P.A., cursing him at every breath. Dr.

Keller examined the knee, and looked as though he wanted to cry.

"The bloody beast," he muttered. "I'd like to tear him apart with his own damned horses. And you, you poor little fool, I ought to throw up your case."

"Is it so bad?" asked Ike between clenched teeth.

"So bad," answered Dr. Keller, "that you'll never play football again, so bad that you may not even be good enough to graduate."

That was no more than the truth. Though Dr. Keller gave him devoted care, Ike's knee took so long to heal that even two and a half years later the doctor had to shade the truth in order to get him through his final physical. It was something less than a strict interpretation of Keller's duty as a medical officer thus to foist upon the Army a half-cracked second lieutenant, but perhaps it won't be held against his memory.

CHAPTER FIVE

DUTY, HONOR, COUNTRY

The locomotive whistled, its undulating wail streaming out across the plains. By the very sound, which was not thrown back from mountains or muffled by trees, Ike knew he was coming home to the wide prairies. Beyond the blackness outside the window he could almost feel the familiar contour of the country as the train rattled and roared down the last straight stretch from Chapman to Abilene. He looked very correct and military in his perfectly fitting gray uniform, sitting erect in the red plush seat with his shoulders set square by long habit. But his grin was almost cherubic.

It was two years since he had gone away from these plains, this home he loved. Now, on his second-class leave, he was coming back. Two years was a long time; he hoped that nothing would be different, or that he himself would not be so altered that things would *look* different. He didn't feel changed, though he supposed those years must have had some effect on him. He passionately wanted to find everything just as he remembered it.

The train got in a little after ten in the evening. There were no other passengers and since Ike had not sent word when he would arrive, no one was down to meet him. The station looked familiar, but suddenly a faint chill fell upon his exuberance. He felt a little lonely and uncertain. Things couldn't be the same.

He picked up his bag and started walking, looking eagerly for reassurance. The creamery was comfortingly bulky against the stars; Cedar Street looked all right, too. Boys and girls were coming out of the drugstore on the corner, but they didn't know him from Adam's off ox. He went on to Buckeye and turned south across the tracks. The Union Pacific Hotel seemed to be in its familiar state of disrepair. He thought how, long ago, he used to meet his brothers there, so they would not have to walk down the last dark stretch alone. As he entered that final phase of his journey, he felt a faint, reminiscent tingling of nerves, and laughed inwardly at himself. "Some soldier!"

The little white house was dark. They were all in bed, Ike surmised, and felt unreasonably disappointed. The sweet summer smells seemed somehow very sad.

Then he heard a sharp, cocky bark, and answered with a low whistle. A white streak shot out of the shadows and flashed across the field. Ike dropped his bag and braced himself. Flip took off five feet away and landed in his arms.

A moment later Ike was in the familiar kitchen, shouting. Lights came on; his father appeared in his dressing gown, looking very sleepy; his mother came running downstairs with her little white cap over one ear.

"Mother!"

"Dwight."

She hugged him hard.

"My buttons may hurt you, mother."

"Bother the buttons. Dwight, you're back again!"

"Mother, I've missed you so."

Milton and Earl came down, rubbing their eyes. In their pajamas they didn't look very much older.

Suddenly Ike left them standing there in the kitchen and dashed into the sitting room. It was all right: the piano on which his mother had taught Arthur and Milton to play still had the old songs on its rack. He looked into the parlor; the chairs were in their familiar places, and the fancy marriage certificate hung on the wall above the table where the great family Bible lay. Ike remembered its brightly colored maps, which he had loved to study, and the engravings of exciting Biblical scenes. He ran on up the stairs, in and out of the different rooms.

"What are you doing, Dwight?" his mother called up to him.

He came back downstairs to the homely kitchen.

"Just making sure you hadn't changed anything, mother."

"As if I would . . ."

The town thought that Ike had changed a great deal; for the better, they said. All the older people found his manners charming, for the daily polishing he had received was bound to leave a shine on the roughest texture. Ciel Curry looked at him with adoring eyes and begged him to dress up in his best uniform, which he did to please her.

Another of the local girls, Gladys Harding, was more sophisticated. She was an unusually pretty girl, as bright as a flag; her eyes were vivid blue, her skin was very white, and her hair was the color of a new ten-dollar gold piece. Having taken up "expression" at college, she had been offered a position with a concert company doing pianologues and singing, and was going on tour in the fall. In spite of her worldliness, however, she was tremendously attracted by the warmth and vigor of Ike's personality, and his boisterous spirits. You couldn't exactly call him handsome, not with that round face, split by a wide laughing mouth. But his eyes were exciting; you never knew whether they'd be bluish green or vivid blue, whether they'd be laughing or serious. There was nobody with whom she had so much fun.

They went out a lot together, to the airdrome to see the movies, to parties; and to the new natatorium, as Abilenians called the pool which had replaced the old swimming hole. Ike certainly was keen on West Point, Gladys thought. His enthusiasm kept bursting out; he talked about it all the time.

"What is so remarkable about West Point?" she asked him one day.

Ike looked very serious as he tried to tell her.

"It's pretty hard to explain," he said. "But it isn't what most people think—just a place where they teach you about war. There's a lot more to it than that. You learn so many things that aren't in the book. It gives you standards to go by. Duty, honor, country —those words have a tremendous meaning to us. Then there are the fellows themselves, the Corps. They're the finest bunch you can imagine, the sort of guys you can trust absolutely, the kind that would stand by you in any pinch. Because they live by those standards. In one way they're like one of those ancient orders of chivalry you read about, but they're better than that, because they're really just hell-raisin', common fellows like me."

"I think I understand how you feel about it, Ike," Gladys said. "It must be something very special."

"That's a good word to describe it," said Ike.

He thought that Gladys was the most understanding girl he had ever known, as well as one of the prettiest.

But he didn't spend all his time with her; he enjoyed being with his old friends too much for that. Joner and Six, Harry

Makin and Paul Royer—all the boys were glad to see him, though they acted a little defensive at first. He soon reassured them that he was the same old Ike. His poker was as good as ever. Of course, he did have new prestige. It was pleasant and perhaps he swaggered a little, but it had its disadvantages. Bill Sterl brought that to his attention.

"Look, Ike," he said one day, "you're quite a boxer at West Point, aren't you?"

"Sure," Ike said brashly, "I box some."

"Well, there's a little match some of the fellers would like to make for you."

"What is it?"

"We want you to challenge Dirk Tyler to a bout."

"Who's Dirk Tyler?"

"You know, the colored boy who works down at the barbershop. He's been doing some pro boxing lately, and says he can lick anybody in town. He's anxious to take you on."

It didn't sound good to Ike, but he felt his responsibilities. The prestige of the Point seemed vaguely at stake.

"If that's how it is, let's go over there right now."

"That's talking," said Bill admiringly.

When Ike saw the big Negro porter in the barbershop, he liked the look of things even less. It occurred to him that for once he might have done too much talking. Tyler was clearly built for fighting.

"When will it be?" Dirk asked.

"What's the matter with right now?" Ike suggested, carrying the bluff.

"You can come over to Pop's gym," Bill put in excitedly.

The whole crowd, including a citizen with his face half shaved, moved across the street to the "Champ's Gym" in the basement of Sterl's Department Store. Only the barber remained disconsolately behind. Ike would have liked to keep him company.

There was a ring set up in the basement gym, with funeral chairs arranged around it. A board closet made a dressing room at the back. As Dirk began to strip, Ike liked the look of things still less. Muscles were bunched like baseballs under that black satin skin. Ike felt very pink and white and naked as he walked out in his shorts. His bad knee, under an elastic stocking, moved stiffly and gave a warning throb. He was quite literally scared stiff.

Mr. Sterl himself came down to officiate, followed by all his clerks and the customers. Word spread by the human wireless through the town, bringing in more spectators. It was a full house. The owner of the store saw to the gloves and gave instructions.

"No monkey business," he warned. "Markess o' Queensbury rules, and keep your punches high."

He pulled out a silver turnip watch. "I'll keep time. Are you ready? Go!"

Ike saw Dirk assume an awkward cross-arm stance and almost laughed in relief. He jigged around, and dodged a couple of haymakers. In a few moments the expected opening came. Ike walked in and straightened up Dirk with a left. Then he swung hard with his right . . .

The barber, looking gloomily across the street, was surprised to see his porter being returned to him, feet first.

Poor Dirk's life wasn't worth living for a while after that. Everybody who had cowered before him now wanted to have a crack at him. He took to dodging into alleyways. Ike didn't like that either and said so publicly.

"Lay off Dirk, fellows," he ordered. "He's all right now. If you keep picking on him, I might have to have a couple more fights."

They laid off.

Ike's thirty days seemed to pass like thirty minutes. It was a wrench to tear himself away from home, from his mother. It would be two more years before he saw her again because Christmas leaves were too short to allow a trip to Kansas. But when he got back to West Point it was like coming home in another way. The gray austere buildings, the bugle calls and parades, the discipline and order seemed to enclose him in a clean familiar world.

Of course he grumbled a lot to P.A. "Back in the old Hell Hole!" But in his heart he didn't mean it.

It was about this time that he decided he was a woman hater, in spite of his flirtations in Abilene. Cadets Louis Merrilett and Charley Benedict were of like mind, and they formed a sort of misogynists' club. One of its features was a pool to which each was obliged to pledge ten dollars, the entire sum to be won by the last one wedded. All three were married the year after graduation.

The Misogynists did not go to hops, unless they were boodle hops—that is, dances where food was served. In that case, they would rush in, glut themselves and rush out again.

Any evening when a hop was in progress was a fine time to play poker, because there was little chance of discovery. Gambling was, of course, strictly against regulations, and for his first two years Ike had had little opportunity to exercise his special talent. But in his later period there were many clandestine games; the women haters were frequently joined by other young gentlemen with exaggerated opinions of their ability to draw to an inside straight. Since nobody had any cash, all bets were on the cuff, to be paid after graduation. For some years after that event checks kept coming in to Ike from every Army post in the world.

Not all Ike's good friends of this time were ascetic devotees of the Royal Flush. There was, for instance, that "brilliant spoonoid," "Snookums" Mendenhall, whose admiration for the feminine gender extended from girls to boats. Snookums had passed his long leave making a cruise on the Sound in his sailboat *Cascarina*. Ike delighted in his nautical yarns, which despite their briny flavor needed to be taken with more than a grain of salt.

Ike could no longer play football, but he still loved the game. Since he was congenitally unable to be a sideline athlete, he became a cheer leader, in which capacity his powerful lungs and bounding enthusiasm served the Army well. He even displayed a solitary burst of artistic talent when he designed the colored cheesecloth capes and hoods which certain designated cadets put on at a given signal to form the letters ARMY in black and gold against the solid gray of the Corps massed in the stand.

The forward pass was legalized at this time, and Ike was leading the cheering on that famous day in November, 1914, when Army defeated a far more powerful Navy team by a surprise aerial offensive.

In his First Class year, Ike helped Lieutenant Shelleck coach the Cullum Hall Squad, with the gratifying result that the plebes beat the best freshman teams in the East. Their big contest of the season was against their ancient and doughty foe, New York Military Academy. This was the plebes' "Navy Game," played on the big field with the whole Corps present. It was a perfect day, brilliant and cold and still. Because the boys on the team had worked so loyally for him, Ike cared more about winning that game than any in which he had played himself. As the long afternoon passed with never a score for either team, he was, in his favorite phrase, "fit to be tied." It looked like a scoreless tie until the last quarter. In the uncertain light of the early winter dusk a last-minute substitute kicked an impossible field goal from the forty-five yard line, and the plebes won the game.

By the beginning of his First Class year, Ike was taking his military career seriously. He knew now that this was what he wanted to do, that he would stay in the Army. But he had little hope of ever gaining high rank.

"I'm a lot older than most of the fellows," he explained to P.A. "By the time I get enough seniority it will be time to retire. I'll be lucky if I make colonel."

"You can't tell about that," P.A. objected. "Supposing there is a war."

"I hope there won't be," Ike answered seriously. "If all the progress we've made in these last few years means anything at all, it ought to mean that men are getting too civilized—too sensible to go out and massacre each other. And that's what war would be now, with all these new weapons. Just think of what machine guns can do, compared with the stuff we had in Cuba."

"It's horrible to think about," P.A. agreed, "but it could happen. They are spending an awful lot of money on armaments in Europe. Those fellows seem to think it's quite likely."

"Perhaps it will happen there," said Ike. "They're pretty backward in politics, with their Kings and Kaisers."

"Don't you think we ought to have a good Army and Navy?"

"Of course, but we don't get itchy to use it, and feeling that way, we probably won't have to."

So, though Ike was taking it seriously now, soldiering was still a kind of game to him. He played it with all his heart, yet he could not bring himself to believe that he would ever have to play for keeps.

That was in the early summer of 1914.

West Point is a cloistered place. It is true that the papers come every day and the cadets are encouraged to read them. But there is a feeling of inviolableness inside those walls; nothing that happens beyond them can affect the men inside. So when the papers carried black headlines about a duke of some sort who got himself shot at a barbarous place in the Balkans, it didn't mean a thing, and even the gathering tension of that fateful July stirred no more than casual interest among the cadets. Ultimatums, flying back and forth between the capitals of Europe, were after all a commonplace of diplomatic usage; they probably didn't really mean what they seemed to.

But when declarations of war followed the ultimatums, and the huge armies, swollen by a tremendous influx of reservists, spilled across the borders like rivers in flood, the embryo officers began to take notice. Even so, their attention was at first purely professional. They thought they were about to see the theories of modern warfare demonstrated practically; it was very interesting. They had no sense of reality, no premonition that the secure world they knew was about to blow up in their faces.

This attitude did not indicate any particular obtuseness on their part; virtually everyone in America was complacent. Even in Europe, the people most nearly involved—the statesmen and the generals, and the soldiers marching down the long white roads and deploying through the fields in which the crops stood ready for the harvest that never came—had no notion where they were going. The peoples of Europe went into that war gaily, with songs on their lips, and bright flags waving and pretty girls throwing flowers. The troops acted as though they were off on a holiday, laughing and cheering as the trains pulled out, bound eventually for the Marne and Tannenberg, Verdun and Vimy Ridge.

Ike had that same sense of unreality at first. The little flags that moved across the maps as the Germans flowed over Belgium and France seemed only symbols, like pieces on a chessboard. He followed the moves with the same intellectual excitement with which he had read about battles long ago. As the German line, pivoting on Metz, swung up through France, driving the French and English before it, he recognized the strategy of the opening gambit, and wondered if they could get away with it. Then General Alexander von Kluck, ignoring the "contemptible little British Army," turned left in front of Paris in a great gamble to crumple the whole French line back on Verdun. But the right wing, it seemed, wasn't quite strong enough; the British and the garrison of Paris flung themselves at his exposed flank, and it collapsed. The whole German plan was abandoned, and the little flags marched backward again until they froze in a vast entrenched line, which stretched from the Channel to Switzerland.

So far it had all been according to Hoyle—war in the grand old manner, charge and countercharge, cavalry on the flanks and the horse artillery galloping up to unlimber the guns. The only new note was the fragile little airplanes scouting the lines, French and German sometimes flying side by side with their pilots glaring impotently or, perhaps, taking pot shots at each other with revolvers.

But as the troops dug interminable trenches in the viscous mud made by the autumn rains, the color and dash were drowned in the gray drizzle. Poilus changed their red pants for less conspicuous attire and the stench of death hung like a miasma over the grim battle lines.

As the appalling details of that bloody struggle began to drift back in the newspaper dispatches, Ike lost his sense of detachment. Owing to his early training, his attitude toward human relations never fell into the military mold. In spite of his professional attitude, he always kept the civilian point of view; hence the misery of war struck him more forcibly than it did many of his fellow cadets. Like the great majority of his fellow countrymen, he reacted with pity and horror; and, as in their case also, it took a peculiarly barbarous action really to awaken him.

To understand the terrific emotional impact of the sinking of the *Lusitania,* with a loss of eleven hundred and ninety-eight civilians, of whom sixty-three were children, it is important to remember that the American people had not yet become accustomed to brutality. The world they had known was far gentler and more civilized than the one we have lived in since. Sensibility had not yet been dulled by the mass slaughter of women and children; not for several hundred years had a city been put to fire and sword. It was erroneously supposed that humanity had become too humane for that sort of thing. The torpedo from *U-20* did more than sink an ocean liner; it blew up a whole concept of civilization.

Ike's first reaction was a terrible rage against this barbarity. Then he realized that he must re-evaluate all his previous conceptions of the world in which he was destined to live.

On a Saturday afternoon in May, 1915, he sat on a slope beyond the Battle Monument trying to think it out. From his position he could see long vistas up and down the river, which was constrained between the steep granite walls of the mountains. It was easy to understand why West Point had been the key to the Hudson in Revolutionary times. Against a plunging fire from this bluff no ship would have a chance; it would not even be able to elevate its guns sufficiently to fire back.

The jutting point narrowed the fairway to a few hundred yards. During the Revolution a chain was stretched across the river to prevent the British ships from sneaking past at night. Some of the great cast-iron links were still lying around the Battle Monument. By this means West Point had cut the armies of the enemy in two and prevented supplies or reinforcements from making use of the one practicable route from the sea to the northern lakes. Otherwise, the British General John Burgoyne would never have been defeated at Saratoga and the Revolution would have been lost.

That was the beginning of national existence. Except for the secondary disturbance of the War of 1812, the United States had never since been seriously threatened by a foreign power. They had remained secure and apparently impregnable—free to grow into greatness and nourish the happiest civilization mankind had ever known.

But Ike could see that the end of this era of security was at hand. He had thought it unlikely that he would have to exercise his chosen profession in any great war. His whole mental outlook had rejected such a prospect. Now things looked very different. A large part of the country was calling for war against Germany; and in spite of his pacifist training, it seemed to him that such a war would be righteous.

Ike knew that an era in his own life was ending, too. In a few weeks he would be graduated and leave this clean, hard, uncomplicated existence to take his place among the infinite complexities which had descended upon the world. He compared the callow boy who had climbed the hill to the Plain four years ago with the person he now was; he felt grateful to West Point, for it seemed to him that those years had worked an enormous change for the better. He knew that he was a different and finer sort of man.

Half turning, he let his eyes sweep over those gray towers and battlements which once had oppressed him and now seemed so dear and full of memories. The bright flag flying from the square stone tower of the Administration Building stirred him now, as it could not have done then. The Chapel, rising in beautiful perpendicular lines of stone from its high hill above the Plain, brought to him a feeling of religious fervor, a sense of high purpose under God. The technical knowledge he had acquired was, he realized, the least of the things he had learned here.

America had been singularly protected while she grew strong and built a civilization and a faith. Now her great age of insulation was ending and that strength and courage and faith were to be tried by forces of a world whose aspect had suddenly grown strange and terrible. Similarly, he had been secured against the trials of life, while the great traditions of the Academy—its code of honor and its love of country—had made him strong and given him a standard to live by and a faith to hold. Secure in them, he felt that he was now fit to go out to serve America in the time of her need.

It is recorded that Dwight D. Eisenhower was graduated from the United States Military Academy on June 12, 1915. His record was satisfactory but by no means brilliant. He stood 61 in a class of 168. His conduct order was only 125, but he stood high in Engineering, Ordnance, Gunnery and Drill Regulations. His general rating was 2083.96 out of a possible 2525. The highest rank he held in the Corps was color sergeant.

Moving in the normal course of events he was commissioned as a second lieutenant in the 19th Infantry.

CHAPTER SIX

MAMIE

Marie Geneva Doud was a very pretty girl. Of this she was aware, not in a conceited way, but simply in recognition of an agreeable fact, like the other pleasant circumstances of her life. She had dark-brown hair and eyes of so deep a blue that at some times they seemed violet and at others a cloudy sapphire. She was small and very slim, and so full of animation that she almost seemed to ripple like the surface of a lake in a stiff breeze. She loved people and gaiety, and everybody called her by her nickname, "Mamie." Her father and mother doted on her, so did her small tomboy sister, "Mike."

Mamie's father, John Sheldon Doud, was as American as Uncle Sam. His family had come over from Guilford, England, to found the town of Guilford, Connecticut, in 1648. Holding to English custom, the eldest son inherited the farm while the younger boys moved on to make their own way. John Doud was born in Rome, New York. Shortly afterward his father, Royal H. Doud, removed his family to Chicago, where he became one of the original meat packers.

Young John Doud was full of restless energy and that adventurous spirit which ran so high in the 1880's. It was a family trait, too; some years later, at the age of sixty-odd, his father had a sudden acute attack of venturesomeness and left his prosperous but boring business to join the Alaska Gold Rush. By that time, however, the flesh was weaker than the spirit, and he came back to Chicago to die in 1899.

The younger Doud did not wait so long to go off in search of adventure. When he reached his teens he ran away three times within two years. The first time, he started off with his great school friend, a Jewish boy. They got as far as South Bend, Indiana, before they got discouraged and turned back.

His next adventure was more successful. He hoboed to Memphis, Tennessee, where he enlisted in a levee building squad. The work was rather hard, but since John Doud was ambitious, he got promoted until he was third cook. It meant getting up at 3:30 A.M. to make coffee for the crew with water dipped from the Mississippi in a bucket, but it was a lot easier than toting bags of cement. He held the job for three months. Meanwhile, his family wondered where he had gone, but knowing how self-reliant he was, they did not worry overmuch.

John Doud made one more excursion—this time to Council Bluffs, Iowa—before he settled down to a college course at the University of Chicago. After completing his education, he went into the stockyards at Omaha, Nebraska, with his uncle, Jim Doud, who was hog buyer for the T. J. Lipton Company, which at that time was venturing into meat packing. When Sir Thomas decided to give up meat and stick to tea, Uncle Jim Doud and John raised some capital and built a packing house of their own at Boone, Iowa.

At Boone, John Doud met and married Elvira Mathilda Carlson, and there Mamie and an older sister were born. The Douds had four daughters in all, but two of them died tragically in their teens.

John Doud was extremely successful in business, as was to be expected. He eventually settled in Denver, Colorado, and purchased a winter home in San Antonio, Texas. Every fall the family trekked down south in the big Winton Six, while the servants and Mrs. Doud's electric coupé were shipped on by train.

It was still hot in San Antonio when the Douds returned there in October, 1915. Mamie was immediately besieged by numerous beaux, who had been waiting all summer for her return. On the first Sunday after their arrival, Mrs. Doud told her daughter, "The Ingrams are coming to take us for an automobile ride this afternoon. I think it would be nice if you went with us."

"I'd love to," Mamie said, "if you'll promise to be back by seven. I have a date."

They drove slowly in the heavy Sunday traffic through the city, where the steel beams of modern skyscrapers were rising among the low frame buildings of the passing era, and the stone Spanish structures of historic memory. The narrow streets and wide green squares were crowded with ebullient Mexican families in their gala Sunday clothes, and soldiers from Fort Sam Houston strolling with fair, deceptively fragile-looking Texas girls.

"Let's go by Fort Sam," suggested Mr. Ingram, "and call on the Harrises."

"I've got to be back at seven," Mamie warned him.

Her host looked at the clock on the dashboard.

"It's only a little after four," he said. "We've plenty of time."

They found the Harrises sitting in lazy chairs on the putting-green lawn in front of the Bachelor Officers' Quarters. They were delighted to welcome their old friends. A group of young officers who were with them snapped out of their Sunday languor at the sight of Mamie in her starched white dress and big floppy hat.

"Why don't you stay on the post for supper?" Miss Anabelle Harris suggested. "You know what fun it is at the mess Sunday night."

"That sounds delightful," said Mr. Doud. "Think you could break your date, Mamie?"

"It's awfully important, Daddy," Mamie answered. "You know I'd love to, but it's the first date I've had with this man since we've been back."

"We've a most attractive new officer here, who will make you forget all about him," Miss Lulu Harris urged. "He's a football star!"

"Do we have to let Eisenhower in on this?" asked a captain, who had been on the Post the year before.

"I have Mamie's interests at heart," said Miss Lulu.

She cupped her hands and called across to the long low building of the Bachelor Officers' Quarters, "Hey, Ike, come over here!"

A cheerful bellow answered, "I'll be right there."

Mamie began to feel a bit frantic about her date; she didn't care a hoot about meeting this paragon of shavetails. But she adjusted that impression when she saw him walking across the lawn. He was a big fellow, but dapper, with the shine of West Point still on him. The brass of his buttons and insignia was like new gold and his field boots fairly flashed in the late afternoon sunshine. The service revolver that swung from his belt indicated that he was Officer of the Guard. Mamie admired the fit of his khaki tunic over his hard broad shoulders, and liked his round, pleasant face, which was so friendly that it somehow made everyone feel warm. In fact, she thought he was one of the handsomest men she had ever seen.

In a moment he had joined the group and was laughing with Miss Lulu and Miss Anabelle and being introduced all around.

With his cap off, Mamie saw that in the sunshine his hair was as bright as his buttons. When he bowed over her hand in the best West Point manner and she looked into his eyes, she discovered that they were a lovely shade of bluish green, and full of laughter; but as he looked at her the laughter went away and they seemed to change to an intense blue.

"How about staying for supper, Mamie?" Miss Lulu asked softly.

Mamie felt herself blush slightly.

"Perhaps it would be all right," she answered, "if I could telephone my date to meet me here."

Ike had supper with them at the officers' mess. He was in such tearing high spirits that he carried the whole crowd with him to peaks of gaiety. When they finished the meal he turned to Mamie.

"I've got to inspect the guard, darn it!" he said. "Would you care to walk post with me?"

If there was one thing Mamie hated it was walking, but now the prospect seemed delightful.

They had a long and leisurely stroll through the wide straight streets in the first cool air of early evening. Lieutenant Eisenhower inspected post number 5, and they walked still farther to the hospital post. After the guard had turned out and had been duly examined, they sat down on the broad wooden steps of Brooke Hospital and talked. They had, it seemed, a number of tastes in common.

When Mamie got back to the club, her young man had been waiting for quite a while.

Ike happened to be in San Antonio by one of those series of chances which seemed to shape his life. He had originally expected to be ordered to the Philippines; had in fact acquired an outfit of tropical uniforms. But, though President Wilson's diplomatic dexterity in persuading Germany to modify her submarine tactics had temporarily postponed America's date with Destiny, the Mexican pot was boiling furiously and it was considered advisable to keep the young hopefuls of the Army near home.

Ike was ordered to report to the 19th Infantry at Galveston. He got there to find that his regiment had been floated out of their barracks by one of that city's famous floods, and removed to Fort Sam Houston. He had only just reported there when he met Mamie.

From the first he had that same sense of certainty about her, that hunch by which he chose his closest friends—only this was so much stronger that it had the force of a revelation. He had been "sweet" on other girls, had almost thought himself in love with Gladys Harding; but the surging emotion he felt for Mamie was entirely different. He knew absolutely that he had found his girl—the One and Only, as West Point slang had it—and that he would marry her. With characteristic energy he didn't waste a minute.

Mamie came home from a day's fishing expedition on Medina Lake the following evening to find the Douds' Negro houseman looking harassed.

"Miss Mamie, they's been a Mr. Eisenhart calling you, an' ef he's phoned once he's phoned fifteen times."

"You must mean Mr. Eisenhower," she laughed.

"Yes, ma'am, Mr. Eisenhart. Oh, Lordy! They he is again!"

It was Ike, very formal but confident.

"Miss Doud, I wondered if you would like to go dancing with me this evening?"

Mamie almost giggled.

"That's very kind of you, Mr. Eisenhower, but I'm afraid I have an engagement."

"Tomorrow, then?"

"No, I'm having supper out."

"Well, when can you come?"

"I'm afraid I'm dated up all this week. Perhaps next Monday."

"Do you mean I'm not going to see you for a week?"

Mamie relented.

"Well, I'm usually home about five in the afternoons. You could call on me sometime."

"Fine. I'll be there tomorrow. Don't forget about next Monday."

Ike spent many tomorrows on the broad, columned veranda of the Douds' big white house on McCullough Street. He pursued his courtship with the same intense drive with which he went after anything he wanted badly. Nothing was going to stand in his way.

The Douds, who were very particular about Mamie's beaux, approved of him from the first. Certainly he had no material advantages, but they liked him immensely; everybody did. And they recognized absolute integrity when they saw it.

The routine duties at an Army post in peacetime, even when complicated by the intensive courtship of a girl who lived on the other side of town, didn't begin to absorb Ike's energy. He was used to working harder than that. In spite of his bad knee, which still required an elastic stocking, he retained his love of football. His West Point reputation had preceded him to San Antonio. Almost as soon as he arrived he was asked if he would coach the Peacock Military Academy Football Team. He delightedly accepted the job.

Though a small school, Peacock had high standards and lots of spirit. Ike took charge of the team with as much enthusiasm as he had felt toward the Cullum Hall Squad, and the boys responded with the touching devotion which a leader who really cares can inspire. They worked harder and played harder for him than ever before in their lives.

At that time competition was keen in San Antonio and Peacock had a tough schedule. Most of the teams they met came from larger institutions with far more material to draw upon. But Ike succeeded in giving them that imponderable of sport—and war—which occasionally proves that God isn't always on the side with the biggest artillery: the will to win. And win they did.

Ike was so full of enthusiasm for "his team" that he even inspired the Douds with a passionate loyalty for Peacock, which, when they thought about, it, surprised them considerably. When Saturday came around Mr. and Mrs. Doud, Mamie and the younger sister, Mike, would almost invariably be on hand, rooting frenziedly for a school of which they had hardly even heard before that season.

It soon became evident to Mamie's other suitors that she was showing marked partiality for her big blond lieutenant. They pointedly reminded her that San Antonio was called the "Mother-in-law of the Army" because so many of the girls married officers.

"All the women fall for brass buttons," one beau said reproachfully, "but I didn't think it of you, Mamie."

"It isn't the brass buttons," said Mamie.

She held out until midwinter. On St. Valentine's Day, 1916, she accepted Ike's class ring.

Ten days isn't much time in which to get married and have a honeymoon, but in view of the tension along the Mexican border in the summer of 1916, Ike was lucky to get that long a leave. He and Mamie were married in Denver on July 1—the same day Ike got his first promotion—and as soon as the ceremony was over they headed straight for Abilene.

Ike looked forward to that visit with the highest hopes. It would, he believed, be the culmination of his happiness to bring together the two women who shared his devotion, to introduce his lovely bride to his fellow townsfolk, whose opinion he always valued beyond anyone else's, and to show Mamie the town and the home he loved so deeply.

The visit might be extremely trying. What if his mother and Mamie disliked each other? Such a thing happens more often than not. What if Mamie found Abilene provincial, or Abilene thought her uppish? The circumstances pointed to one or all of those dismal possibilities, but they never occurred to Ike's direct mind. Those he loved would love each other, because they were fine people. It seemed to him as simple as that. And his instinct was confirmed by the outcome.

At their first meeting, at the unpropitious hour of four on the morning after the wedding, a deep affection sprang up between Ike's two women; they had much in common, sharing his love and their devotion to him. David Eisenhower was shyly admiring of his new daughter-in-law. Mamie already liked him, because of a letter she had received from him before the wedding, written in his beautiful Spencerian script. The classic formality of his language had not concealed the sincerity with which he welcomed her into the family and invited her to his home.

Milton and Earl came downstairs at about seven that morning and were immediately captivated by Mamie, whose first words to them were, "Now I've got some brothers, like I always wanted."

At nine o'clock there was a formal wedding breakfast with the neighbors invited and small corsages provided for Mamie and Ida. Oh, they were very formal—for at least ten minutes. Then that wedding breakfast must have been a joy to watch, with Ike beaming like a birthday boy and Mamie darting about among the guests like a happy dragonfly.

Those few days in Abilene were probably the highest peak of happiness Ike ever reached. Mamie was, he thought, enchanting, but it is likely that he did not realize at the time how much he owed to her tact and social grace. Their visit was just as he hoped it would be, only better. It all looked as easy as breathing; Mamie made it seem that way.

There was, however, one first-class row. Shortly after noon dinner one day, Ike started for town with the nonchalant remark, "I think I'll look up the gang."

When he had not come home by suppertime Mamie turned into a small frenetic fury.

"Where is that no-account son of yours?" she demanded of her mother-in-law.

"I figure he's down to Joner Callahan's, playing a little poker," said Ida calmly.

"Jonah's, eh!" Mamie snapped. "He'll wish he was in the whale when I get through with him."

She telephoned Joner's and got her husband.

"I'm sorry I'm so late," Ike said amiably, "but I got a little behind and have to make it back."

"You come home this minute," stormed Mamie.

"Honey, I can't do that," Ike explained patiently. "I told you I was loser."

"Come now or don't bother to come at all!" Mamie said, and slammed down the receiver.

"That ought to fetch him," she told Ida.

"Don't get too upset if it doesn't," Ike's mother advised.

It didn't, and Mamie got very upset indeed. Ike ambled in at two in the morning, feeling well-satisfied with his evening's work, and sure that he could soothe Mamie with the logical explanation that he had to get his money back. He found that it would have been easier to soothe a Kansas tornado, and probably would not have taken so long.

The days passed rapidly. When they returned to San Antonio, they moved into quarters at Fort Sam, where they had a miniature living room, bedroom and bath. For Mamie it was quite a change from the spaciousness to which she was accustomed. But since Mr. Doud had old-time American ideas about young people's standing on their own pins, there was no financial aid from that quarter, nor did the young Eisenhowers want it. They subscribed to the same idea.

Mamie took hold and made a home out of their cramped quarters. She worked some minor miracles in her miscroscopic kitchenette, though Ike was always a better cook. The tiny apartment fitted her as though it were custom-built, but when Ike came home the walls seemed fairly to bulge. He was so big and clumsy and gentle that Mamie's heart bulged, too, with happiness and love.

The hard part was the nights he was on duty. He had charge of the Military Police detail, with the thankless job of rounding up Uncle Sam's strayed lambs and settling occasional acrimonious differences between the military and the citizenry. Knowing that he was patrolling the toughest quarters of the town, Mamie worried about him a good deal while she waited alone for long hours, and not without reason.

There was, for instance, the night Ike was leading a patrol up Matamoros Street, the Mexican red-light district. He swung along easily, looking sharply at the dim fronts of the buildings in which cracks of light slipped through drawn blinds, noting without really noticing dark-haired girls walking slowly with the characteristic twitch of well-rounded buttocks.

Suddenly he was jerked backward by the strong arm of his sergeant. There was a flash and crack from a somber doorway and a bullet zipped unpleasantly past his nose.

Ike turned fast and sprinted toward the place, followed by his patrol, boots echoing noisily. A heavy wooden door banged in their faces and a bolt squeaked home. Behind them the street was suddenly as deserted as a church on Monday morning; the girls had vanished like cockroaches into a crack.

By the time the patrol had gained entrance to the building their quarry was probably over the border. Ike never knew whether the shot was an expression of personal dislike or a matter of public sentiment.

It might well have been the latter. Our relations with our nearest neighbor were in an unusually distressing state, that summer. Back in March, 1916, a troop of fifteen hundred Mexican horsemen, reputedly led by Pancho Villa, a bandit who was also a prominent politician, made a sortie across the border into the town of Columbus, New Mexico. It has never been proved that Villa was one of the party, nor has the purpose of the raid ever been clarified. But it certainly made complications for President Wilson, who was about to campaign for re-election with the slogan: "He Kept Us Out of War."

Even the most peace-loving administration could scarcely ignore American dead lying in the streets of an American town, and the President acted with dispatch and energy. Brigadier General John J. Pershing was given six thousand men and ordered to pursue Villa through the arid mountains of Chihuahua. When President Venustiano Carranza of Mexico objected, Woodrow Wilson called out the National Guard and stationed the troops on the Mexican border.

These border disputes were, as it proved, of far-reaching importance to the United States. They provided a testing ground for our military leaders, who were hamstrung by pacifist sentiment. Few of our general officers had ever seen together in one place any body of soldiers larger than a regiment. It was extremely fortunate that they got a chance to maneuver a few divisions before they were sent overseas to take part in World War I.

After this show of strength, the Mexican government cooperated energetically in the attempt to subdue Villa. That the Imperial German government was somewhat less impressed may be explained by the fact that there were more casualties before Verdun every month than there were men in all the Armies of the United States.

Many of the younger officers of the Regular Army were detached to help train the Guardsmen. Ike's turn for this duty came in August, 1916, when he was ordered as inspector instructor to the Illinois National Guard at Camp Travis. The camp was sufficiently near San Antonio so that by rising before dawn he could commute to work.

The same qualities which made Ike an inspired football coach made him an excellent instructor. He did his new job well and earned the approval of his seniors. But he did it too well for his own good.

CHAPTER SEVEN

WORLD WAR I

In January, 1917, the Imperial German General Staff did some intricate calculating. From a lifelong study of war and two and a half years of practical experience, they knew that Germany was at the peak of her power; from where they stood the road led downward. Some way had to be found to break the deadlock on the Western Front. The obvious method was to stop American supplies from getting to England. The U-boats could do it, Admiral Alfred von Tirpitz believed, if all pretense of humanity were cast aside and they were given orders to sink on sight. But that might bring America into the war. How much would that mean?

The General Staff examined long columns of figures and read thousands of secret reports from agents scattered throughout the United States. After weighing all the factors with the minute thoroughness for which the Germans are so famous, they decided that American power could not possibly be effective for at least two years—if ever. Basing their action on this conclusion, they proceeded to commit the most colossal blunder in recorded history.

On January 31, Ambassador Johann Heinrich von Bernstorff handed the State Department a note announcing that on February 1, Germany would begin absolutely unrestricted submarine warfare. The note went on to state that Germany would forcibly prevent any American vessel from reaching England.

The German démarche came like the detonation of a sixteen-inch shell fired from beyond the horizon. In a flash the American people saw clearly, at last, the ghastly lineaments of their enemy. The arrogance of the note was not to be borne by a nation with any vestige of spirit. But deeper than that went the realization that, if Germany should win and so accrete to herself the entire control of European manufacture and manpower, America would ever after be in deadly peril, facing across a narrowing ocean a mighty empire whose cynical disregard of honor was matched only by its barbaric indifference to human suffering.

The German note made war inevitable, but it did not come immediately. Rather it moved slowly upon us like the charted approach of a hurricane; the American people, watching it creep forward, seemed hypnotized into inaction. They were apparently unable to make the primary preparations to defend themselves. President Wilson could not even get a bill through the Senate to arm our merchant ships.

To Army officers that period of waiting for the inevitable was particularly nerve-racking because they knew what a tremendous task we faced and how unprepared we were. Even after the small increases achieved by Wilson's preparedness program, the total strength of the Regular Army was less than 140,000 officers and men, more than half of whom were needed to garrison our defenses. The National Guard added a few hundred thousand more, but these were by no means ready for combat. And we needed an army of at least 2,000,000 highly trained men if Germany were to be defeated.

These were facts that every intelligent officer knew, yet, knowing them, had to wait almost in idleness while the precious months went past.

Release came in April, when the national paralysis was broken by the declaration of war. Not that these officers went into it gaily or with any false notions of glory—the horrid view of Europe's battlefields had knocked that sort of nonsense out of everyone, civilian and soldier alike—but at last their energies were released to do the things that had to be done, and quickly. For the Allied missions made it clear that Germany was actually winning the war. Russia was knocked out; England and France could last but a few months more . . .

Ike, like virtually every West Pointer in the Army, wanted active service. This was the job for which they had trained so long, and however clearly they realized the grimness of modern war, they were impelled by every instinct to take an active part. No matter how important a noncombatant duty might be, they could not feel at peace with themselves unless they justified their existence by actual combat.

In Ike's case, this universal feeling was intensified by the football player's desire to be in the thick of things. For years his injured knee had forced him to sit on the sidelines; now he was intent on getting into the fray.

But it was evident that with 2,000,000 men to be trained and less than 4,000 experts available, many of the West Pointers must be left behind for the arduous task of creating an army. Fervently each one hoped that it would not be he.

On April 1, 1917, a few days before the declaration of war, Ike was assigned to the 57th Infantry at Leon Springs, Texas, as regimental supply officer. Mamie, who was expecting a child in September, stayed in San Antonio since there were no possible accommodations at Leon Springs. Ike was so busy that he was seldom able to come home even on Sunday, and Mamie was very lonely. One Saturday when he had telephoned to say that, as usual, he was unable to get leave, she felt she could not bear the separation any longer. Leon Springs was not far away and in the garage behind her house stood the Douds' perfectly good automobile; only Mamie had never learned to drive. Well, she decided, now was the time. She called the man next door. Sitting in the garaged car, he showed her how to start it and what to do about shifting gears.

Sunday morning at five o'clock Mamie slipped out of the house and opened the garage doors. She climbed into the car and carried out the previous day's instructions. The engine caught. She pushed the gearshift into what she remembered as reverse. Surprisingly, it was and the car shot backward; it careened to the street, where happily the engine stalled. Mamie yanked the gear to neutral and started the motor again. When she shifted gears this time, the car moved forward and she was off.

Thirty miles to Leon Springs, thirty miles over empty morning roads, wobbling erratically, spurting forward and then slowing to a crawl, Mamie fought her way. In a deserted village street, an early riser gaped and shouted as the car caromed from curb to curb, straightened itself out and dashed on. Perhaps he thought the glazed expression of the pretty girl at the wheel was alcoholic and decided to vote for Prohibition. But in a trance of terror and determination Mamie drove on.

Outside the gates of the camp, Ike, forewarned, stood gazing anxiously up the road. There she came at last; the familiar car, undamaged, moved slowly and eccentrically toward him. Ike grinned and waved.

"Hi, Mamie!"

"Ike!" shouted Mamie. "Jump on the running board quick. I don't know how to stop!"

Things looked good for Ike in September, 1917. He had been promoted to captain on June 1. The 57th Infantry was fast shaping up for foreign service, and the baby was due to appear any minute. Ike hoped he would remain in Texas just long enough to see his child and then be off on the long trail that they sang about.

But on September 20 he was sent as instructor to the Officers' Training Camp at Fort Oglethorpe, Georgia. The order hit him like the kick of a mule. There went both his hope of getting to France soon, and his chance of being with Mamie when her baby was born. In San Antonio four days later she gave birth to a son, who was christened Doud Dwight Eisenhower.

Ike hoped that his next move would be something constructive toward achieving his ambition. Instead, on December 1, he was sent to Fort Leavenworth as instructor of provisional officers. He was altogether too good at training men.

He worked through the winter, teaching luckier men than himself the knowledge he had hoped to employ at first hand. Always there was that deep uneasiness, the unhappy feeling that he was not doing his part, that somehow, in spite of himself, he was shirking the hardships and dangers which his classmates were facing on the bitter fields of France.

On March 1, 1918, new orders came. Ike read them with a mixture of acute disappointment and satisfaction in having done his work well. The post to which he was assigned was one of extraordinary responsibility for a mere captain of infantry, and indicated the confidence which his superiors had in him; but the fields of France faded still further into the mists of an improbable future. He was to command the Tank Training Center at Camp Colt, Gettysburg, Pennsylvania.

With Icky, as they called little Doud Dwight, Mamie joined him there, taking a tiny house in Gettysburg. It was the first of a bewildering series of moves over a period of twenty-five years, in the course of which she was to provide beauty of living and a gay gathering place for their friends under every conceivable circumstance and in places geographically and spiritually as far apart as Paris, the jungles of Panama, and Manila, Philippine Islands.

Camp Colt was under canvas. There were no barracks or facilities for comfort, but it was an inspiring place to train men for war. It was on the very battlefield of Gettysburg. The straight rows of khaki-colored tents marched in orderly ranks along the Emmetsburg road, across which Pickett had led the immortal charge in which the hopes of the Confederacy had fallen with the elite of Lee's army. To the west the ground sloped up to Seminary Ridge, which once had flamed so fiercely with the fire of massed Confederate cannon, and to the east it rose more steeply to the rocky Round Tops and the heights of Cemetery Ridge, where the Army of the Potomac made the desperate stand that saved the Union.

The landmarks of heroic deeds were all around. Tents were pitched by the orchard where General Sickle's Union troops were shattered by Longstreet's tremendous attack, and at the head of one company street was the monument to Pennsylvania's lost regiments. When they dug trenches the men were always finding bullets and other debris of war, and when they went on practice marches they followed routes over which Union and Confederate armies had moved in desperate haste to add their weight to the tilting scales of battle.

Ike, traversing the field in the course of his duties, was constantly reminded of this or that episode of the engagement, for he knew where every brigade had been stationed and the tactics of every shift of attack and defense.

But, though the scene was inspiring, the conditions of training were not, for a very good reason. When he took over, Ike found a very knotty situation on his hands. Under his command were thousands of men, especially selected and eager to be trained in tank warfare. But there was not a single tank!

Later they got one—a two-man French Renault of the type they called whippets. This absurd little contraption, with its long woodpecker's tail, running playfully through the green meadows and raising a cloud of dust on the battle-scarred road, was the only evidence of mechanization which met the eyes of all those men who had come to learn the ultimate technique of modern war.

Tank procurement was in a deplorable mess between Washington, where orders were given and countermanded, and Dayton, where engineers were trying to build the whippet tanks. This snarl was not unraveled until after the Armistice, and almost the only members of the Tank Corps who saw an American tank during World War I were those who went to Dayton.

Under such circumstances it was not only necessary to improvise a method of training troops in tank warfare without any means of practical demonstration, but also to maintain the morale of the disappointed officers and men. It was like trying to coach a football team, consisting of thousands of men, without any footballs.

It is a matter of record that young Captain Eisenhower succeeded brilliantly in this baffling task. His system of theoretical instruction enable American crews to handle French and British tanks in battle after only a few weeks of practical training abroad. And, by the character of his administration and the force of his enthusiasm, he made the Tank Training Center a model of soldierly smartness. It has been said that an experienced officer can always judge the state of morale by the way the men salute. Those who visited Camp Colt were everywhere accorded a snappy salute which reminded them of West Point.

The fact that the camp was as smart as a military academy did not indicate that its young commander was a martinet. In fact, some of his subordinates thought that Captain Eisenhower was a peculiar sort of commanding officer. He didn't like people around who always agreed with him. They still tell the tale of a downy lieutenant who thought that everything at Camp Colt was wonderful. It was Ike's first experience with a yes-man and, on the spur of his irritation, he developed one phase of his theory of command.

"Get out and find something wrong with this camp!" he snapped at his astonished junior officer. "It's not that good. Either you're not being frank, or you're as big a fool as you make me feel."

It must have been nearly that good, though, for eleven years later, in 1929, Ike was belatedly awarded the Distinguished Service Medal: "For exceptionally distinguished services. While Commanding Officer of the Tank Corps Training Center from March 23, 1918, to November 18, 1918, at Camp Colt, Gettysburg, Pa., he displayed unusual zeal, foresight and marked administrative ability in the organization and preparation for overseas service of technical troops of the Tank Corps."

In June, 1918, Ike was promoted to major (temporary) of infantry. And in October, 1918, the oak leaves on his shoulders were transmuted by the reverse alchemy of the War Department from gold to silver. But Lieutenant Colonel (temporary) Eisenhower never gave up striving to get to France. Men he had trained in the early spring were now driving French tanks through the shell-swept forest of the Argonne. He felt that he had earned his right to take his place among them, and he figured that there was yet time, for the confidential reports of American losses in the October battles were staggering. The German Army was still a tough and war-tempered foe. The best official opinion was that they would not crack until the great offensive which was planned for the spring of 1919.

Early in November, Ike came to Mamie, grinning and waving a piece of paper, shouting as he had shouted to his mother on a day long ago, "I've made it! My orders for France have come!"

Mamie felt the sick upsurge of her stomach that every woman must experience when the blow falls, and the man she adores is tapped on the shoulder by Mars. But she loved her big smiling Ike so truly that after those first few seconds she could really feel glad—glad because she knew how much this meant to him, glad because, despite the dreadful danger, it was right for him to go.

Her eyes shone as she said gaily, "It's grand, Ike! I'm truly happy. When do you go?"

"Very soon," he said delightedly. "Here, read it."

He handed the flimsy sheet of paper to her and she read aloud: "You will proceed to Camp Dix for embarkation on *November 18, 1918.*"

CHAPTER EIGHT

ARMORED CAVALRY

There were many tanks at Camp Meade, Maryland, in 1919:
great, clumsy Britishers, captured Germans with their steel sides
ripped by death wounds, and little French Renaults with bullet
burns on their turrets. And now that the Armistice was signed
there were plenty of whippets from Dayton.

Camp Meade had been made the Army Tank School. Lieutenant Colonel Eisenhower was ordered there in March, 1919.
In the interim he had been at Camp Dix, New Jersey, and Camp
Benning, Georgia. It had been a period of torpidity. No matter
how eagerly peace may be awaited, the aftermath of war is
inevitably a period of letdown. Morale goes to pieces, for the
temporary soldiers naturally want only to get home, and the
regulars ponder lost opportunities and the inevitable reduction
of activity. They are all marking time.

Ike found it good to be in a place where something constructive
was going on. The Army, conscious of its lack of experience in
tank warfare, was taking this precious opportunity, while the
means were at hand, to study the lessons of experience and work
out plans for the future. Ike, in command of the Heavy Tank
Brigade, threw himself into the work with all his abounding
energy.

Perhaps the most interesting man at Camp Meade, and the
one from whom Ike learned the most, was Lieutenant Colonel
George S. Patton. He had organized and commanded the American Tank Center at Langres in France, where Ike's pupils from
Camp Colt had gone to finishing school. Before that, he had been
with the British at the Battle of Cambrai, where the first great
tank attack of history took place, after a previous tentative experiment at Ypres. At Saint-Mihiel and the Meuse-Argonne, Patton

had commanded the 304th Tank Brigade with terrific fire and dash. In fact, he had been all the places where Ike had wanted to go.

They became good friends, though never were two personalities more divergent. Patton was six feet tall with broad shoulders, narrow hips and powerful limbs. His face was like a chip of flint with steel-blue eyes peering from beneath a balding dome, thinly thatched with lightish hair. He was rough and tough and gave no quarter to his men any more than to himself, and his language made the mules in the picket lines bashfully cast down their eyes.

But underneath Patton was wildly romantic. He was as great an advocate of "death and glory" as any knight-errant who ever cried, "Avaunt, varlet! Unhand yon maiden on peril of thy life!" This was obvious from the flamboyance which he succeeded in attaining even within the rigid confines of uniform. Contrary to regulations, a pair of pearl-handled forty-fives, legacy of the California ranch where he was born, swung from his hips, and he wore the khaki like a caballero. In leisure moments he wrote poems about the bitterness and glory of battle, and his romanticism appeared also in his philosophy of war.

"Soldiers fight primarily for two reasons," he often proclaimed: "hero worship for a commanding officer, and the desire for glory."

Ike thought that more often they forgot about glory, but fought for more impersonal ideas.

Nothing could cure Patton of his zest for battle. In the Argonne he had been wounded and left for dead, but he had come out of the encounter in fine fettle and ready for another fight at the drop of a helmet.

In 1919 nobody had ever heard of an inferiority complex, but sometime when Georgie Patton was a boy, there may have been some uncertainty in his soul, a vulnerable spot which caused him to grow that protective shell which clothed his romantic spirit in chrome nickel steel. Once in a burst of unaccustomed confidence he told a friend, "I talk of blood and guts because I'm scared half the time."

His joy in battle lay in mastering this fear.

The sharp contrast of personalities did not interfere with the growth of friendship. There were points of common interest between Patton and Eisenhower. The former was a fine athlete and Olympic champion target shot in 1912. He liked poker, though his own game was craps. And both Mamie and Ike grew fond of gentle Beatrice Patton, who understood so well how to handle her obstreperous husband.

Despite the light-years which separated their personal philosophies, the two men were in close agreement on military strategy. Ike knew that George Patton was a splendid soldier. He was as profound a student of military history as Ike himself. And he delivered the goods. There had been that time in Mexico, when Pershing sent Patton with a small force after one of Villa's bandit chieftains who had holed up in some inaccessible mountains with his cutthroat followers. Patton brought the bandit back trussed to the hood of an old Dodge car. "The first mechanized action of the American Army," he called it. And his handling of the tanks in France had covered his chest with a satisfactory rainbow of ribbons.

Both men agreed that there was much to be learned about tank combat. Patton described the action at Cambrai to the younger man. Three hundred and seventy-eight tanks were employed, and they had broken the German Army in its moment of pride. That was a weird and awful spectacle: the ungainly black monsters creeping through the dawn fog, clanking and groaning forward at three miles an hour, flattening the thickets of barbed wire with relentless unconcern. They plunged and bucked across the narrow trenches, spitting fire from their ports at the frightened white faces below them. On they plowed, while the British infantry, following behind, had only to gather in the paralyzed prisoners. Ten thousand Germans surrendered in ten hours.

"It was a complete break-through," Patton said. "The road to Berlin was as clear as a damned parkway. But nobody knew how to use it. The British were just as surprised as the bloody Jerrys. They fumbled the chance and it was lost."

Ike and Patton spent hours discussing the strategy of this new weapon. They agreed that its possibilities had not even been indicated. The squadrons of tanks should be handled by radio. They were already experimenting with that infant invention at Meade. Whippet tanks were equipped with sending and receiving sets. Fishpoles were stuck up through the turrets to carry the aerials. But the radio apparatus was so bulky that all armament had to be removed; the only weapons of a radio tank were revolvers fired through the ports.

"Wait till we get good radios and fast tanks," said Patton, his eyes shining. "We'll handle 'em like cavalry—the armored, impregnable cavalry of medieval days with the mobility of motorcycles. Smash right through their bloody front, sweep around cutting their lines of supply. Hit 'em from the rear. Grab 'em by the nose and kick 'em in the tail!"

Ike's research into the habits and temperament of tanks was temporarily interrupted when he was ordered to be an observer on the first transcontinental trip of a motor truck train. This experiment in mechanized logistics was fruitful of much valuable information of the negative, or what-not-to-do, sort. It definitely proved that at that time the way to get across the country was on a train. The trip was made in summer, and its opening phases held some of the enjoyment of a mass picnic. However, crossing the American desert in August was definitely seamy. Over the buffalo trails and the tracks of the covered wagons, the last word in motor transport, model 1919, made pretty heavy weather of it. Thermometers were popping like firecrackers in the heat; the motometers on radiator caps of the trucks were permanently red. The last word spoken by the personnel was profane.

But they had fun too. Comic relief was provided by a young lieutenant who was nicknamed Greeney because he believed everything that anyone told him. Ike thought of plenty of things to tell.

When the caravan reached the arid plains of West Texas, Greeney consulted Ike as an expert.

"Are there many snakes around here?" he asked.

"Snakes," mused Ike. "Yeah, there's quite a few."

"Poisonous?"

"You know rattlesnakes. One little scratch and you die in awful agony."

"I know," said Greeney. "But they do give you warning, don't they?"

"The rattle doesn't do you much good when they slip into your tent and get into bed with you."

"In bed with you?" quavered Greeney.

"Sure. Rattlesnakes love good beds. But there's one good thing," Ike said seriously, "they won't cross rubber."

"I never heard that," said Greeney.

"We all know it out here. Been proved a thousand times. Something to do with electricity, I guess. Snakes are full of it. You're safe as long as you're in a car or a truck."

That night and every night thereafter, Greeney gave up his comfortable tent and slept on the hard floor of a motor truck.

Then there was the day when Captain Serino Brett was taken with a mysterious form of hydrophobia. Greeney caught a horrifying glimpse of the Captain's face, peering from the back of a staff car. Eyes rolled wildly, and Greeney thought he saw blood and foam. At the next halt Captain Brett was clearly in bad shape. He raced around like a demented squirrel. Colonel Eisenhower was making courageous efforts to control him.

"What's wrong with Serino?" Greeney shakily demanded of a fellow officer.

"Gone mad, poor devil," was the answer. "The heat, you know. Ike's the only one who can handle him. Better keep clear—he's bad medicine, and whatever you do, don't let him *bite* you."

At that moment Serino let out a war whoop that would have made a sissy of Sitting Bull, and charged straight at Greeney, with bloody foam spurting from his lips. Greeney's yell of terror streamed out behind him as he made the length of the convoy in 0.44 flat and dove into the last truck.

Throughout the rest of that day Greeney ardently sought inconspicuousness. Whenever his duties forced him to appear, the mere sight of him seemed to drive the demented officer to frenzy, and only Ike's strength and persuasion saved his life again and again. But before the game was ended, Serino was awfully tired of the taste of shaving soap and ketchup.

With the exception of that trucking jaunt across the continent, Ike did not leave Camp Meade for nearly two years. In July, 1920, he was reduced to the rank of major (temporary) of infantry, and given the status of student officer at the Tank School. Such regressions in rank were necessitated by the rapidly shrinking army; otherwise there would have been an opéra bouffe collection of field officers with not enough privates to go around. No matter how necessary, these reductions are inevitably depressing. But Ike continued to study with enthusiasm. He squeezed the last ounce of knowledge of tank tactics out of the master minds and made a number of original contributions to Army thought on the subject.

Ike would have liked to go on to the Infantry School. This was officially his branch of the service and it was the general, though not invariable, rule that officers should attend their own service schools before being eligible for the General Staff School at Fort Leavenworth, which was a prerequisite of high command. When Ike's application was capriciously refused by his commanding officer it looked as though his career was approaching a dead end.

But there were other compensations. No matter how worried he was or how hard he worked, Ike could always find time for fun. Mamie's hospitality and his geniality made their quarters at Meade a rendezvous for all ranks from generals down to shavetails and, more often than not, half the droppers-in stayed on for potluck and a little game of poker.

A greater source of delight to Ike was the companionship of his small son, who was now three years old. They played violent games together, and never a night passed that the Major did not tiptoe heavily down the hall for a peep at the sleeping child. But this period of happiness came to a bitter end.

Little Icky fell ill of scarlet fever and was taken to the post hospital. Mamie was sick also, too ill to go with him, and Ike spent all his time at the hospital. There, on January 2, 1921, Icky died in his father's arms. Never has Ike been able to forget the horror of that day, the desperate love which was powerless to help. His grief was equaled only by his solicitude for Mamie, whose eyes were so shadowed that he wondered if they would ever sparkle again. His strength supported her during the terrible trip to Denver, where they took the little boy for burial; it encompassed and sustained her throughout the lonely days. And never since, wherever he may be, has Ike forgotten to send Mamie flowers on Icky's birthday.

CHAPTER NINE

"THERE WILL BE ANOTHER WAR"

On January 8, 1921, six days after the death of his son, Major (temporary) Dwight D. Eisenhower graduated from the Tank School in command of the 301st Tank Battalion. He had orders to report to General Conner, commanding the 20th Infantry Battalion at Camp Gaillard in the Canal Zone.

These orders were inspired by General Conner himself, who had met Ike through George Patton the previous year. Friendship had flourished fast, and Conner had been impressed with the younger man's technical knowledge and enthusiasm. When the time came for him to select a chief of staff for his new command, Conner thought of the brilliant and genial young Major. Those were the very qualities he needed: brilliance, because completely new plans must be drawn up for the defense of the canal, based on the drastic lessons of the war and the new shifts of military and naval power since the Armistice; geniality, because friction was one of the risks of close association in a primitive tropical community. He wrote to Ike asking him if he would like the job, and was enormously pleased by a quick affirmative reply.

The house at Gaillard had been built by the French in the days when Viscount Ferdinand de Lesseps was trying to cut a canal through the mountains of Panama by the handicraft methods which had worked in the sands of Suez. It stood on stilts on a hillside near Culebra Cut. There were galleries all around it, and lattices for windows, since the warm breath of the jungle need never be excluded by panes of glass. Mamie and Ike liked it in spite of its drawbacks, the first and greatest of which was the bats. The French had tried to control the malarial mosquitoes, which decimated their ranks, by importing these alleged friends of man in large numbers. When George Washington Goethals took over at Gaillard, he had retained their services as auxiliaries in his campaign of insect extermination. It was still against the law to kill them.

The bats lived in great towers especially built for their convenience. By day they hung in pulsating tiers, and, as the dusk came down, they streamed out to fill the night with the flutter of furry wings. They seemed dissatisfied with their own apartment houses, and exercised a malevolent intelligence in securing entrance to the human habitations.

One night soon after she arrived, Mamie was awakened by an unpleasant whirring sound. She snapped on the light. Her eyes confirmed the horrid implication of what she had heard: a bat was performing acrobatics above the bed.

"Ike!"

Her husband woke instantly. "What is it, Mamie?"

"Ike, please kill that bat."

"It's against the law," he argued.

"Law or no law," Mamie shrieked, "kill that bloody bat!"

Ike knew when it was safer to disobey the law than Mamie. He jumped out of bed and dashed into the hall. When Mamie heard him come back, she stuck her head out from under the bedclothes and saw her husband standing in the middle of the room in his pajamas. His eyes gleamed wildly and the naked blade of a saber flashed in his hand. He cut and thrust as though he were fighting a duel with the Invisible Man. Whoosh went the blade, whiz-z-z went the bat. Mamie covered her head with the sheet and peered from beneath it. The bat came over low and zoomed up to the molding. Ike leaped on the bed brandishing his sword. Swish! Crash! Squeak!

"Got him!" shouted Ike triumphantly. "Now help me dispose of the corpus delicti."

There were other drawbacks to Camp Gaillard besides the bats. It was on the other side of the canal from the railroad, and all supplies had to come in by a tortuous dirt road cut through the jungle. Every so often the houses would tremble to an earthshaking roar as a large section of landscape went down the slope into the canal, carrying the artery of commerce with it. The whole camp might be cut off from fresh food for as long as a week until a new section of road could be hacked out.

They were not entirely isolated by these mishaps. In fact, the normal way of going to the outside was to walk across the lock gates and take a train. Ike tried driving a Model T Ford over and found that it could be done if, at the critical point where the gates met at an angle, everybody piled out and helped to lift the rear wheels around.

There was no post hospital at Camp Gaillard. The 20th was a Puerto Rican regiment officered by Americans, and was about ninety per cent married. The small dark soldiers and their luxuriant wives seemed to be fountainheads of fecundity. Babies were born all over the place, and because of the lack of facilities, the officers' wives were kept busy helping out.

In a climate where the effort of lifting a glass from the table to the lips causes a man to break into perspiration, a certain degree of tropical languor might be excused, but Ike set himself a strenuous schedule. There would be no slovenliness around any camp with which he was connected. He began by making his own small grounds a model of neatness. Then he did the same for the Headquarters Building. Soon all over the camp white-painted rocks began to line the drives and walks, flowers were planted and the lawns trimmed like putting greens.

Ike's close association with General Conner was in itself sufficient stimulus to overcome any climatic lethargy. The General was a man who could inspire others by the force of his mind and character. Ike soon became utterly devoted to him. Conner valued the loyalty of his young subordinate most highly, the more so since it was unaccompanied by any false humility toward his rank. Knowing that Ike would not hesitate to poke fun at anybody if he got a chance, the general was anxious not to lay himself open, as he revealed in a ridiculous incident soon after Eisenhower's arrival.

Being very fond of horses, General Conner was personally seeing to the shoeing of an old crock which he feared would not be given proper attention by the men. Just as the first shoe was being put on, the horse heaved forward and jabbed her nose into the General's stomach. Conner toppled backward out a low window of the blacksmith shop, beneath which stood a large tub of water.

A young aide who was with him dashed frantically out the

door to his commander's rescue. As he rounded the corner of the building, General Conner, who was sitting in the tub of water, roared out a command, "By gawd, don't you tell Eisenhower about this!"

General Conner and his chief of staff had on their hands the very important job of reorganizing and modernizing the defense of the Culebra area.

The whole naval strategy of the United States was based on the assumption that the canal could be kept open so that the fleet could be shifted to whichever coast was threatened. The old plans had further assumed that the Navy would be able to protect the canal against anything but a sudden naval raid or an arduous military expedition through the jungles. But the tremendous advances in aviation during the war had created a new and terrible danger. As things stood, the vital locks were virtually defenseless against aerial bombing.

The new plans not only had to take into consideration the lessons of that war and the present potentialities of aircraft, but they also needed to be sufficiently flexible to provide against a future that could not be clearly foreseen. And they had to make the best possible use of limited means, for this was the Age of Disarmament.

To the assistance of his chief in this vital undertaking, Ike brought his own considerable knowledge of strategy, his enthusiasm, and his tremendous capacity for hard work. In addition to his regular office hours he fitted up the second-story porch of his house as a workroom with maps, drawing boards and technical books. Here he often sat up late at night, either working on the plans or, for relaxation, refighting the campaigns of the old masters.

But it wasn't all hard work. The Eisenhowers' house was, as always, a center of sociability. There were good poker games, none of your deuces-wild stuff, but scientific play—either straight draw or five-card stud. Early every morning Ike went for a ride along the narrow jungle trails, where the jade-green light, filtering through the fantastic foliation, splintered prismatically on the brilliant plumage of tropical birds, and the damp heat of the earthy air made it seem as though the whole forest were enclosed in a vast greenhouse.

In the summer of 1922 Mamie went home to have her second child. Ike missed her unreasonably, for he was always miserable unless someone dear to him was close at hand. One day that fall, he stood on the dock looking up at the towering plated wall of a transport. Mamie came stepping carefully down the steep gangplank, carrying a small pink and white bundle, which was impressively known as John Sheldon Doud Eisenhower. When Ike looked into her eyes, he saw that the last shadows were gone. He made Mamie let him carry the baby across to the train, while she walked beside him, talking very fast about the extraordinary brilliance of the three-months-old child.

Everything seemed perfect to Ike after that. Even his reduction to his regular rank of captain failed to dampen his spirits. It just didn't seem to matter, what with all the work there was to do and all the joy he found at home.

Another pleasant and, as it proved, exciting incident of the winter was the unexpected reappearance of Swede Hazlett. Though they had maintained a regular correspondence, the two friends had seen each other only three times since entering their respective service schools—twice at Army and Navy games and once when Swede had used part of his graduation leave to pay Ike a visit at West Point. Now Hazlett surprised him by telephoning from the Submarine Base at Coco Solo.

"I've got a submarine here with a burned-out motor," he explained. "We'll be laid up at the base for several weeks."

"Come up, come up, wherever you are!" Ike chanted joyously.

"I'll make it this weekend," Swede promised.

Mamie and Ike drove the Ford across the lock gates to the railroad to meet Hazlett. On the way back they had so much to talk about that Ike forgot to stop and switch the wheels around. He nearly took his friend and Mamie for an unpremeditated dive. During that weekend and those following they hardly got any sleep at all. Ike had to explain all his wonderful plans to his old friend. He dragged Hazlett out of bed at dawn and got him on a horse for the first time since he'd become a sailor, in order to show him the exotic trails. In the evenings they played poker and, when the game ended, they went up to the study to talk a while longer.

On the last day, Swede made what Ike considered a brilliant suggestion.

"The motor's fixed and we're making a trial run tomorrow," he said. "Would you like to come along and take a dive?"

"Wouldn't I!" Ike exclaimed.

The next day Ike stood beside Hazlett on the little railed bridge atop the conning tower of the *S-32*, as it cut across the brilliant blue water of Panama Bay.

"This is the life!" he exclaimed, feeling the wonderful coolness of the wind on his face. "It almost makes me wish I'd got into the Navy."

"You seem to be doing pretty well where you are," laughed Swede.

"Oh, I wouldn't change," said Ike, "but you certainly have a lot of fun playing with your intricate little toys. When do we dive?"

Hazlett studied the chart.

"We've got plenty of depth now," he decided.

He gave the necessary orders; the submarine slowed and settled until the deck was awash and the brisk waves were slapping at the foot of the conning tower, flinging rainbow spray over it.

"Get below," he ordered Ike, and followed him down the ladder.

Ike watched the men bolt the hatch home. The beat of the Diesels died away and the electric motors whined in crescendo. Hazlett issued further orders, and Ike nearly fell on his face as the deck tilted sharply.

Once a submarine is underwater a dive can be somewhat dull, but Ike was as excited as a boy on his first flight. He ranged from one end of the submarine to the other, squeezing through narrow spaces, looking and questioning. It was more interesting to him to watch the working of this complicated piece of mechanism than to be able to see what was going on outside; the sight of the depth gauge registering sixty feet was more thrilling than a sunset.

Hazlett brought her back up to fifteen feet.

"Up periscope!"

After studying the scene he turned to Ike.

"Want to take a peek?"

"Sure."

Ike put his eyes to the instrument and saw the blue circle of the sea cupped in the reflector like water in a finger bowl. A destroyer, curiously distorted by the lens, slid along the slope of blue, and he swung the periscope until the cross hairs met on the target.

"This is the life!" he repeated.

After Hazlett left and the plans for the defense of the Panama Canal were finished, there was a lull; Ike felt the letdown. The strenuous life in that debilitating climate had begun to tell on him. He was thinner, and sometimes he had a pain in his right side, which the doctors said could be chronic appendicitis. "Nothing to worry about, though it might kick up sometime." Ike didn't bother much about it; he never was the worrying kind. And with the interesting part of his work completed, nothing seemed especially worth bothering about. The career that stretched before him was apparently cut and dried and full of routine. The whole world was at peace and heartily sick of war. In February, 1923, with America leading the way by scrapping a large portion of her mighty navy, the five principal powers had signed a disarmament treaty which reduced and limited their fleets. The Four-Power Treaty, signed by England, France, America and Japan, in which they agreed to respect one another's island possessions, seemed to assure stability in the Pacific. It was considered likely that a treaty of military disarmament might follow. Baron Tomosaburo Kato of Japan remarked fervently, "We realize that a new spirit of moral consciousness has come over the world."

Ike thought the world might have progressed at that. It was time. After four years of such terrible suffering, such hideously senseless destruction, the men of all nations must wish only for peace. And surely mankind, who had conquered the earth, the sea, and now the sky, who had developed the art of government so highly, could devise a technique for preserving the peace that everyone desired.

So Ike thought, until he talked one evening with his commanding officer.

General Conner was a man of unusual vision; he saw, not what he wanted to see, but what was really there. His mind cut through the gaudy wrapping of verbiage and emotional thinking to the bitter core of truth. He had been taking a hard, clear look at the future and what he saw there was not good.

One night General Conner and his chief of staff were sitting late in Eisenhower's veranda workroom, which seemed to float like the cabin of an anchored dirigible at the level of the treetops. In the course of their talk Ike casually referred to the "Great War."

"Call it the 'Great War,'" said General Conner, harshly. "Why, as far as we're concerned, that was only large-scale maneuvers."

"Do you mean you think that there will be another soon?" asked Ike.

"There will be another war," Conner said, "sooner than anyone thinks. It's implicit in every phase of the European scene, and obvious in the Pacific situation."

"In spite of the Four-Power Pact and the Disarmament Treaty?"

"They have hastened it by a good ten years," the General replied. "Look, you, at what they mean. We have secured the so-called 5-5-3 ratio of naval tonnage. That seems to give us a comfortable margin of superiority, but with two coasts to guard, you can cut that by a third or more. Then add the fact that the theater of war in the Pacific will be thousands of miles from our nearest base. I don't count Manila—it will be captured or made useless at the start. You know your logistics. What does that mean?"

"The distance will cut down our comparative strength at least by half," answered Ike. "According to your reasoning we are really at a 1-to-2 disadvantage."

"Right. Now we have agreed not to fortify our islands and so have the Japanese. Which of us will keep to that agreement?"

"We will, of course. But what about Kato's 'new spirit of moral consciousness'?"

"The only moral in the consciousness of a Jap," Conner said, "is the greater glory of Nippon. That is their creed and any other is wicked nonsense to them. That is why they will trick us as long as they can, and strike like a snake when the moment comes.

"In Europe," he went on, "things are far worse than in 1914. France is a formidable façade shored up by rotten timbers, like the front of a movie set. England is weary of greatness, and Russia lies chaotic in the hands of fanatics, who may succeed in making her strong to serve their purpose. God knows what that will be. Only Germany is strong in defeat, for she is essentially untouched and her people concentrate on one burning thought—revenge."

"You believe," said Ike thoughtfully, "that England and France will be unable to stop the revival of German military power?"

"The old men are in the saddle, as they were after the Napoleonic Wars," said General Conner, "and the reins of power will slip through their stiffened fingers. In Germany, the old ones are discredited and the young officers of the German General

Staff are working feverishly on new and daring plans, which this time must not fail."

Fox Conner sat silent for a moment, staring at the scattered lights of the sleeping camp. He looked tired in repose, but as he began to talk again a sort of exaltation filled him and seemed to enlarge him.

"America is in deadly peril," he said. "In the last war we fought for an ideal and the right to live in peace. This time we shall be fighting for our very lives. For I believe that Germany and Japan will combine against us, and Russia may be with them, too, while for allies we shall have an ebbing empire and a republic in the last stages of a mortal illness."

As Fox Conner talked Ike felt his own conviction growing. The General's ideas were exactly contrary to those which he, like the vast majority of his fellow countrymen, had held. But now it seemed to him, enclosed in that balcony above the world, that the older man was touched by the spirit of prophecy. The words had more than the power of logic; they were the utterances of a seer who saw the truth.

In his next question Ike tacitly accepted the revelation.

"When do you think it will begin?" he asked.

General Conner moved his hands indecisively.

"Fifteen, twenty, at most thirty years," he answered. "You see, that puts it right up to you. I may be too old. The men of your time at the Academy will be the generals. You must get ready! Make yourselves strong and cunning. Don't waste a moment or overlook a single bet. The sentiment of the country is so strongly pacifistic and we are so damned gullible that you will have little to work with when the time comes. The survival of America and all that it means to humanity will depend on your skill and fortitude alone, you and your classmates and the others of your time, from West Point and Annapolis."

Suddenly he pointed at Ike and shouted, "I mean you in particular. I've worked with you for two years now. I know that fine brain of yours, its skill and foresight, and the drive of your energy. Men will always follow you because they like you and put their trust in you. Those qualities will be wanted sometime, desperately. The moment you leave here, get to Leavenworth. You must qualify at the General Staff School."

"God knows I want to," said Ike, "but not having been to my service school . . ."

"That can be fixed," said the General. "I'll make them send you!"

He was silent again. Ike noticed that the night was fading, and as he watched, the sky gathered light and its color changed to the brilliant green of a macaw's wing. Bugles sounding reveille pierced the brittle moment.

Fox Conner got stiffly to his feet.

"I've talked too much and too long as usual," he said. "Mamie'll kill me."

"It has been a great experience to hear you," said Ike.

"Damned tiresome, I expect," said the General, taking Ike's hand. "Probably I'm all wrong."

Then just for a moment more the spirit was on him.

"But I know I'm right," he said. "Remember what I have told you. For years yet America will go on unheeding, then she will cry for help in panic and distress. Make yourself ready to answer when she calls!"

As Ike went downstairs he phrased his new conviction in the homely manner of his thought, "I guess I'm elected." It indicated a sense of consecration.

When Ike went into the house, Mamie came up the stairs carrying the baby's six o'clock bottle. She looked sleepy and disheveled and very pretty.

"You must be a wreck," she said, "talking all night. What did you find to say to each other?"

"Oh, international politics," Ike answered vaguely.

"Come watch John have his bottle."

Ike followed her into the room, noticing the sweet-sour baby smell that was somehow touching. John had pulled himself up by the side of his crib.

"He's a big guy," Ike said admiringly.

"Like his dad," Mamie answered. "In no time he'll be starting for West Point."

Ike figured mentally.

"About 1941," he said somberly. "That may be just about it."

"What's it?" asked Mamie absently.

"Nothing. Say, Mamie, I think when we go to Denver on leave I'll go to Fitzsimmons Hospital and get them to whip my appendix out. It might kick up sometime when I'm really busy."

CHAPTER TEN

MONTAGE

In September, 1924, Eisenhower, restored to the rank of major (permanent) of infantry, was ordered home. He returned, filled with the zeal of an acolyte. That talk with Fox Conner had made an abiding impression which had been strengthened by many another serious conversation, until his sense of impending necessity transcended conviction and became a personal article of faith. He was determined to fit himself for whatever service might be required of him. But authority had just the spot for such a man. Ike was ordered to Camp Meade to coach the Third Area Football Team!

1925. Although Fox Conner was pulling the strings for the General Staff School at Leavenworth, the obstacle of Ike's missing his own service school bulked big with the "brass hats." Major Eisenhower was ordered as recruiting officer to Fort Logan, Colorado. "A good place to mark time. Nice for Mamie to be with her folks. Meanwhile, *nil desperandum*, Fox Conner."

Ike didn't despair, nor did he mark time. Wherever he was, that feeling of urgency drove him hard. Recruiting for a diminishing army was not exacting work; there was plenty of time for study.

It *was* nice for Mamie and her folks. The Douds were enthralled by their grandchild. They found Ike so affectionate and considerate that they came to regard him as their own son. They did their best to spoil both son-in-law and grandson. Ike was happy, but restless.

Then a telegram: "BE READY MAKE NO MOVE DON'T EVEN BREATHE FOX CONNER."

Orders came for Leavenworth!

1926. The General Staff School was tough. Competition for

first place was so keen that many a fine officer broke down under the strain. But Ike was fortified by his intense interest and years of study. Seeking knowledge rather than honors, he gained both. He was graduated first in his class, and was placed on the General Staff Eligible List. He was now marked for advancement.

There followed a routine tour of duty as post executive, Fort Benning, Georgia, in command of "2nd Bat. 24th Infantry." Then exciting new orders.

1927. "Major Dwight D. Eisenhower: You will report to headquarters Battle Monuments Commission, Paris, France, for special duty preparing book, 'A Guide to American Battlefields in Europe.' "

So Ike saw them at last, the bitter fields of France—to write a tourist's guide. But the irony had no sting. There were things to study besides past glory, since now he knew that the last battle had not been fought. Even before he and Mamie sailed, he had made himself so familiar with the theater of war that when they drove through France he would describe exactly the scene which they were approaching, never having seen it except in imagination.

Ike visited every American battlefield as well as many on which no Americans had fought. He also made a careful inspection of certain areas which were potential battlefields. What he saw was recorded in his minute notes and more indelibly in his brain. The fields of crosses made him wonder: *Must it be again?* Still the civilian point of view.

In August, Major Eisenhower returned to become a student officer at the War College in Washington. It was his first tour of duty in the capital. Mamie loved it—so many old friends and delightful new ones. Milton was now in the Department of Agriculture. With him was his pretty young wife, Helen Eakin, whom he had met while studying at Kansas State College at Manhattan, Kansas. In spite of the difference in their ages, Milton had always been Ike's favorite brother; it was grand being near him after all these years.

Milton's close friends, Harry and Ruth Butcher, became almost part of the family circle. They were good at bridge and poker. Butch had just opened Columbia Broadcasting's new Washington station, WJSV. Ike, with his old interest in news and communications and his new trade of writing, found him congenial and stimulating. Butcher was much younger than Eisenhower—he looked like a movie star, tall and broad-shouldered with chiseled features and wavy light-brown hair. But he had ideas and was not afraid to talk back. Ike loved to test his mind against high-calibered opposition.

Meanwhile, young John was growing up: six years old. One night he came in when his father's army friends were gathered— L. T. Gerow, a close friend since the days in San Antonio; Hughes, Stone, Dr. Beach. Shy though he was, John blurted out his question, "Will you be my blood brothers?"

They gravely agreed, and John fetched a darning needle and his iodine kit. After due sterilization the ceremony began. John worked on his thumb for what seemed like hours. Finally he achieved a beautiful, big red drop. The others, following suit, seriously mingled their blood with his. Ike may have had the civilian point of view, but John was a soldier's son.

1929. Major Eisenhower was ordered back to the Battle Monuments Commission, for his guidebook and reports were minor masterpieces. Ike and Mamie found themselves in Paris again in June. Their pretty apartment on the Quai d'Auteuil near the Pont Mirabeau was a gathering place for the officers of the commission and other Army men who found themselves in Paris that gay summer. The Americans rechristened the bridge "Pont Mamie" and the nearby square "Place Eisenhower." John began his schooling at MacJannette's near the Trocadéro.

The Eisenhowers planned to take a trip to North Africa when the cooler weather came, but in September they were ordered home. Ike was terribly disappointed.

"I've always wanted to go to Africa. It sort of fascinates me."

"You'll get there someday," Mamie prophesied.

1930-1933. The years of "normalcy" had run, and the tone of life deepened as the tide of prosperity ebbed. There were repercussions offstage as America carried with her over the economic precipice the nations of Europe which had fattened on her financing. Ike was in Washington as assistant to the Assistant Secretary of War. He hated staff duty, but he was in for a long dry spell. At first his job was planning industrial mobilization— the arrangements for M-day, which didn't seem quite so distant now. He familiarized himself with the potentialities of automobile factories for the manufacture of airplanes and tanks, of locomotive plants for armored matériél, and typewriter plants for small arms ammunition. He took an important part in founding the Army Industrial College, and endeavored to interest the authorities in the production of guayule as a source of crude rubber in case Japan should sometime cut our communications with Malaya—a fantastic idea, people thought.

General Douglas MacArthur, so brilliant and dashing that he might have been written by Richard Harding Davis, was chief of staff. Here was one soldier who not only knew his business, but understood public relations. He was inevitably brought into close contact with Eisenhower and appreciated the quality of the man—his technical knowledge and, especially, his ability to write concise literate reports.

Those were trying times for a chief of staff. The mounting deficit drove President Herbert Hoover to frantic retrenchment. His policy toward Army appropriations shifted from the economical to the penurious. Maintaining a military establishment on the dole was a headache to MacArthur, who didn't like the look of the skies over Europe and the Far East. But worse trouble was marching toward him over the new concrete highways of the Middle West.

There was a movement to raise the country out of the economic muddle by paying the veterans of World War I a huge bonus. A majority of the veterans thought it a wonderful idea, but the President preferred more orthodox economics. While Congress was debating the issue, the bonus lobby organized a march on Washington by out-of-work veterans. The Bonus Marchers arrived by the thousands and pitched their camp near the Washington Monument. Nothing persuaded them to move out, and as the months passed, their encampment became a stench in the nostrils of authority. Since something had to be done, the Commander in Chief sent the order down to the Chief of Staff, "Clean 'em out, but for God's sake don't kill anybody."

MacArthur loved personal publicity, but not this kind. He knew only too well that a victory over the veterans would bring more odium than defeat at the hands of an enemy. However, he was too fair to hang it on a subordinate. Under his personal command, the troops went in with tear gas, and the veterans decamped with howls and imprecations. It was a nice neat job, but the public reaction was what might have been expected.

Now more than ever MacArthur needed a good staff. The conduct of his administration must be above criticism. He wanted a proven assistant, and one whose ability to write would help in public relations. Eisenhower was the man. MacArthur requested him, and put him in the office next his own.

1933-1935. For two years MacArthur and Eisenhower worked in close harmony. The Chief of Staff's reports took on new luster and clarity. There were erudite references to the campaigns of Genghis Khan but the prose was clear and trenchant. Taken as a series, the reports elucidated a sensible theory of military preparation based on a small regular army and an adequate reserve of trained citizens; they even persuaded a little money out of Congress.

This was a vital necessity. Peacetime attrition had reduced the Army to the ridiculous figure of 118,000 men, far below the barest minimum of safety. The sentiment of the country was fanatically pacifist. Its motto seemed to be: "Millions for tribute, but practically nothing for defense." However, the General Staff did manage to get an authorization to recruit the Army up to 165,000 men and a small appropriation for tanks. The 1935 report mentions that: "We have initiated a procurement program in modern tanks and combat cars, of which 78 are now in production and 69 are provided in the current bill. A total of 3,340 of the new semi-automatic rifle has been authorized." Hitler had been in power for over two years and the Krupps works were running day and night.

1935. There was to be a New Deal in the Philippines too. No longer would an American governor general rule; the Islands were to have their own government under the guidance of a high commissioner for a probationary period of ten years, after which they would be granted full independence. It was a revolutionary step in colonial history—a big country actually turning a little one loose. The new Presidente, Manuel Quezon, was distinctly nervous. He cast an anxious eye toward the menacing cone of Fujiyama and consulted MacArthur, whom he trusted. In ten years, MacArthur told him, it would be possible to build a system of defense for the Islands. Quezon accepted independence on condition that MacArthur take charge of creating a Philippine army.

MacArthur decided to take his key men with him. He invited Major James Ort and Major Eisenhower to accompany him. Ike liked the prospect; he had always wanted to go to the Philippines, and this was a magnificent opportunity. Besides, the need was great. The disarmament and naval limitation treaties were shot full of holes. Japan had grabbed Manchuria in 1931, and was flicking her paw at China. Eisenhower figured he could serve his country best by doing what he could to strengthen its farthest bastion. Delightedly he accepted the new post.

CHAPTER ELEVEN

"THE DANGER FROM THE NORTH"

In October, 1935, Major Eisenhower started for the Philippines. Mamie stayed behind in Washington to give John a chance to finish junior high school; they were to join her husband the following spring. As usual when Ike was separated from his family, he was lonely. Philippine service was an adventure to which he had long looked forward; before he graduated he had bought tropical uniforms in anticipation of being sent there. But it wasn't much fun without Mamie and John.

The boy had become very companionable in the last few years. Ike missed their morning talks a great deal. These conversations had been going on ever since John was old enough to bathe himself. While John washed and the Major shaved, everything from military strategy to morals came up for discussion. Ike never talked down to his son, but "laid it on the line" the way he felt. His code was so simple and straightforward that it made sense to a boy.

One thing Ike was always talking about was the value of athletics. No matter how hard up he might be at times, he was determined that John should never lack the best equipment and instruction that could be obtained. In his large offhand way —he never thought about money at all—he gave John the run of Santa Claus's sports factory. "Anything you need in the way of athletic equipment, just tell me and I'll get it for you."

Years later, when they came back to America, he made an equally spacious gesture.

"You're just about the age when a fellow wants to begin smoking and drinking," he said to John. "I won't ask you not to, but it will ruin your wind, and you'll want that if you're going to make the tennis team."

"I sure will," said John. "Still—"

"Tell you what I'll do," Ike said. "If you stay off cigarettes while you're at the Academy I'll give you what they'd cost over four years. That'd be about three hundred dollars."

Then he had a sober second thought and turned to his Keeper of the Purse.

"Say, Mamie, have we got three hundred dollars?"

There was plenty of work in the Philippines to keep Ike occupied. The situation was that MacArthur was commander in chief of the Philippine Army, and so in the service of the new government. Ike was assistant military adviser to the commonwealth government, but still in the service of the United States. Except at formal reviews, none of the American Military Mission wore uniform.

They all had to start from scratch, for there was no Philippine Army whatever. The Philippine Scouts, a fine body of men who showed what good soldiers Filipinos could become, were an integral part of the United States Army. The Philippine Constabulary was just what its name implied—a police force. In fact, MacArthur and his advisers were really starting behind scratch, for the Philippine Assembly had first to pass an act authorizing an army and providing appropriations. That was Ike's first business when he arrived, and a delicate business it was.

MacArthur figured that in order to provide any sort of defense it would be necessary for the commonwealth government to spend $8,000,000 a year. That seems a moderate sum for a country within the orbit of Japan, but the proposal raised an awful howl. There were plenty of pacifists who didn't want any military establishment at all, and owing to the new government's obligation to provide schools and sadly needed public improvements, and a thousand and one new responsibilities, they had some powerful arguments. Frank Murphy, who was the last governor general and the first high commissioner, was one of those who were against it. He was responsible for seeing that the Islands met their bonded indebtedness, and as an advanced liberal, he didn't like armies at best.

But Presidente Quezon, Vice-President Sergio Osmena and General Valdez were determined that their country should be able to defend itself, and many patriotic Filipinos followed their lead. Quezon publicly admitted that, had MacArthur not promised to provide them with an adequate defense against "the danger from the north," he would not have accepted independence at all.

In collaboration with Philippine officials, Ike went to work drawing up a National Defense Act which embodied MacArthur's theories of a citizen army and was based on the Swiss system of compulsory military training. Meanwhile, MacArthur took on the task of publicizing it, by means of speeches and broadsides and conversations. He stuck his official neck way out, but he carried conviction. Quezon and the government backed him, and in spite of all opposition, the National Defense Act was the first bill passed by the new Philippine Assembly.

Now they were even with scratch, and could get to work. The Philippine Constabulary could serve as a sort of training cadre. The United States Army lent officers for training purposes, and the conscripted men of the first class began to pour in.

They were an odd lot: Filipinos from the big cities, who had had considerable education; Moros from the outer islands and Igorotes from the north, who arrived wearing breechclouts and long knives. But they were first-class fighting men. It was amazing what could be done with them. Within two weeks the naked savages were smartly clothed in khaki and drilling in ordered ranks. They already looked like soldiers, and soon they would be—damned fine soldiers. It was unfortunate that they had to carry wooden guns, but real ones would come in time.

Ike put his pet project into effect—a Philippine West Point. He selected a site for the Academy at Baguio, up in the hills where it was cool and dry. Many of the instructors were Filipinos who had been graduated from the real West Point.

The Americans began to feel that they were really getting somewhere; it was rewarding work. Eisenhower, who had been promoted to lieutenant colonel, acted as MacArthur's chief of staff. His tremendous enthusiasm inspired the Filipinos just as it had the boys on his football teams and the men at the Tank Training Center so long ago. He went from one cadre to another, constantly organizing, and enjoying his work enormously.

Frank Murphy had retired and the acting high commissioner, Weldon Jones, was more sympathetic to the plans for defense and was personally very fond of Ike. Eisenhower got along wonderfully with the Filipinos. His talent for diplomacy, which was always based on his straightforwardness and his genuine liking for people, no matter how much they differed from himself, first became evident in Manila. Quezon, Osmena and Valdez relied on him more and more—especially Quezon, who became a devoted friend.

It wasn't all work. There were weekend cruises on the Presidente's splendid yacht, *Casiana*. The company were always men, except for the Presidente's own family, and while the *Casiana* sailed over the brilliant, peaceful waters of the China Sea and the grateful coolness off the ocean replaced the mugginess of land, the men gathered for terrific games of bridge and poker. The Presidente was a master of these arts and liked keen competition. Ike had a standing invitation on the *Casiana*.

The American group were saddened during the first year by the death of Jimmy Ort. He flew up to Camp John Hay at Baguio with a Filipino pilot in a light sport plane to spend the weekend with the Fairchilds, who had a lovely place on the edge of the golf links. Baguio was at the 5,000-foot level, a place of high mountains and deep valleys, where the winds played strange tricks in the rarefied air.

As they came to the camp, Ort told his pilot to jazz the motor over the Fairchilds' house, and leaned out of the cabin to wave as the little plane swooped down below the tall pines on the ridge. He was still leaning out and waving when the plane staggered in a sharp downdraft and crashed among the trees.

It wasn't a bad smash; the pilot was only slightly hurt, but Jimmy's ribs were crushed against the frame of the cabin window.

In the fall of 1936, Mamie and John finally arrived in Manila. Ike, beaming from ear to ear, met them at the dock. Mamie thought he looked very well and extremely handsome in his immaculate white sharkskins. But when he took off his panama hat she got a nasty shock; his head looked like a pink cannon ball.

"Ike! What have you done with your hair?"

Ike grinned apologetically. "It's so hot out here that I shave my head whenever I shave my face. Can't be bothered with hair."

"You haven't had much to bother with for some time," Mamie said.

The Eisenhowers took rooms at the Manila Hotel because Ike thought it would be the most comfortable place for Mamie. Even that had its drawbacks, for there were no screens on the windows and if they wanted to read at night they had to pop into bed and pull the mosquito netting tight. There were lizards everywhere, especially on the ceiling. A minor hazard of life in Manila was the lack of discrimination which these reptiles showed in their habits. At any moment one of them might decide to eject a stream of water with no regard for whomever might be underneath. Ike used to tease Mamie about the frequency with which she was caught. "They never bother me," he said, until one night when he was waiting for the elevator in full evening dress, and a lizard let him have it right on his bald head.

Their rooms at the Manila Hotel looked out over the docks and across the lovely bay to Corregidor, swimming on its distant rim like an armored tadpole. Mamie loved to lie in bed and watch the miraculous sunsets which lighted the sky with Oriental splendor: brilliant green, fiery pink, and startling combinations of purple and gold. The business of the port made a constantly shifting spectacle of maritime activity. Ships were always unloading at the docks, naval launches and barges were dashing back and forth to Cavite, the harbor ferries beetling across the blue water, and the great ships standing in from the China Sea: the President liners, the graceful white Empress ships, Japanese Marus with the blood-red ball against white at their sterns, and the powerful gray cruisers and narrow destroyers of the Asiatic Squadron. Once the *Scharnhorst* came to pay a friendly call; heavy and menacing, she looked, with the black and red swastika flag flying from the high staff at her stern.

Ike had planned for John to attend Bishop Brent's school at Baguio. Soon after the boy's arrival, he arranged with Captain William H. Lee to fly them up. Ike was very fond of Bill Lee, who was a big man with a grin that split his face like the first slice out of a watermelon.

John, Ike and Bill crowded into the light sports plane and spiraled upward over the jungles that covered the steep irregular mountains with impenetrable green. The little plane slipped through the gap near Baguio and sat down lightly on the narrow air strip.

Ike took John over to the school and saw him through the formalities. Then he and Captain Lee had lunch at the pleasant officers' club. Afterward they sat for a while watching the golfers and enjoying the bracing air. Toward four o'clock they went back to the field. It was very narrow, and there was a cross wind.

"We'll have to wait awhile," said Lee. "The wind usually shifts at sundown."

They sat on the ground in the shade of Operations, and chatted desultorily, while they watched the wind sock. The white tube wouldn't swing, though it did droop as the wind died down. They were both very bored. Finally Lee got up, stretched and felt the breeze.

"It isn't right," he said, "but there's mighty little of it. Want to take a chance?"

"Sure," said Ike. "I've got a dinner date in Manila."

They climbed into the plane and Lee taxied to the farthest limit of the field.

"All set?"

"O.K.!"

Lee gave her full throttle and they raced along the field. Ike could see that she wasn't getting off well. The motor was small, and at five thousand feet the air begins to thin down. The plane finally lifted near the far edge of the field; beyond, the valley closed in a vee of mountains crowned by tall pines, those same pines which had plucked poor Ort's plane out of the air. Anyone could see they weren't going to clear them.

Lee pulled the plane into a steep bank and flew up another valley, fighting for altitude. As the mountains closed in again, he made a vertical turn into a still narrower defile. From this there could be no turning back.

The engine was laboring wide open, but the plane seemed unable to rise. The treacherous downdrafts over the backs of the mountains were pressing it down. Ike sighted along the fuselage and it looked to him as though they would fail to clear the trees ahead by a good ten feet. Bill Lee, with that grin splitting his face, confirmed this opinion. "Well, Colonel, we aren't going to make it."

Ike grinned back, but his stomach gave a double flip as he thought, *This is it! Aren't we a pair of fools!*

Bill Lee hauled back on the stick at the last moment and seemed to lift the little plane by main strength. The wheels danced clear of the pine trees.

In spite of this narrow escape, Ike became a flying addict. As he talked with his young friends among the pilots, he absorbed the airman's view, and the importance of aviation in war became steadily more apparent. He decided that to fit himself for the crisis, which he perceived ever more clearly just ahead, he should learn to pilot a plane. Besides, it would be great fun.

Every day Ike went out to Zablan Field for a flying lesson. By the time he was good enough to solo, his enthusiasm was terrific. There was an exaltation about being alone up there in the blue with no earthbound restrictions of roads or speed limits or lights. He said to Mamie, "If you see something interesting, you just drop down and look at it. If you don't like it, you soar up again. You can do any thing you like!"

He could hardly think about anything else. At dinner he would hold his knife like a "joy stick" under the table and pretend he was flying.

Lieutenant Colonel Eisenhower took his pilot's test in a two-seater trainer. They fastened a sandbag in the back seat for balance, but they didn't take out the dual controls. Ike took the plane up about four thousand feet and after a few lazy figure eights, he did two nice steady loops. As he came out of the second, he found that the stick was jammed.

Ike burst into a profuse sweat and looked at the seat behind. The sandbag had shifted and was hard against the stick. He couldn't get to it, but by main strength he managed to force the stick far enough back to get a little play—just enough, he figured, to land.

This was a delicate business, like walking a slack wire. It had to be exactly right, or it would be very wrong. But he managed it, coming in with a bounce that brought the Inspector tearing up with fire in his eye. Ike pointed to the sandbag and the Inspector's tone changed; he looked a little green. Ike *felt* green.

"Under the circumstances, Colonel, you did very well. Remarkably well!"

"I think so, too," said Ike, starting to climb out.

"You might as well stay there," said the Inspector, "because as soon as we secure that bag, you're going up again."

In the summer of 1938, the Eisenhowers came home on leave. They spent part of the time in Abilene, where Ike first made his usual tour of the house to make sure nothing was changed—it wasn't—and then joyfully renewed his old friendships. There were some red-hot poker games in the cluttered basement of Joner's place, which he enjoyed far more than the luxurious evenings on the Presidente's yacht.

They spent most of the rest of their leave in Denver, where Ike amused himself by driving Mrs. Doud's ancient electric all over town at its full speed of twelve miles per hour.

In September it was time to go back to the Philippines. John went down to Fitzsimmons Hospital to have the numerous vaccinations and shots in the arm to immunize him against tropical diseases. Ike accompanied his son, and between injections they had a long and serious talk about the state of the world.

That was the month of the Munich crisis, when Neville Chamberlain went to Germany with his umbrella in a desperate attempt to appease the unappeasable. When the deal was finally made which brought "peace in our time," the American people, who didn't intend to fight under any circumstances, thundered their indignation against England's "weakness." Virtually everyone with whom John had talked condemned Chamberlain's action, but oddly enough his soldier father defended it.

Very gravely, that day in the hospital, Ike explained to his sixteen-year-old son why he felt that the English Prime Minister was right in avoiding war at all costs.

"War," he said, "next to the loss of freedom, is the ultimate calamity which can befall a nation. It is worse than flood or earthquake or plague because those are natural evils and limited. Furthermore, they bring out the good side of man, his instinct to help his neighbor. But there is no limit to the evil wrought by war. The terror and horror are boundless and appalling because they are visited by man upon mankind, and the blind cruelty of nature is far less vicious than the intellectually directed cruelty of man. War is so horrible that imagination cannot grasp it in all its fearful aspects. If Mr. Chamberlain can avert it without endangering England's freedom, he is doing well by his country and by the world!"

"But has he averted it?" asked John. "Hasn't he just postponed it?"

"Probably," agreed his father, "but even at the worst, he has gained a little time. Time to build the Spitfires which are the only things that can save England from the Luftwaffe. And at the best, as long as war is not actually declared, there is always the chance that it may not come."

"How much hope do you think there is while Hitler is in power?" John argued.

His father grinned.

"Well," he said, "there's always a chance that somebody might shoot the s.o.b."

* * * * *

Tension was heightening in the Philippines when the Eisenhowers returned to Manila. As the Japanese plunged deeper into China, their mask of hypocritical benevolence slipped and they hardly bothered to adjust it. With the capture of each stronghold —Peking, Shanghai, Hankow—they became more defiant to the Western powers. Not only in the sinking of the U.S. gunboat *Panay* at her moorings in the Yangtze River but in every move and gesture the Japanese made plain their hatred and contempt for the United States, while their vast encirclement closed around the Philippine Islands. It was evident to both Americans and Filipinos that the danger from the north was close. It was only a question of time. But how much time?

MacArthur and Eisenhower, together with their staff and the Filipinos, made their plans to use to the best possible advantage what little force they had. In those three years of the ten which MacArthur had originally allotted for the Filipinos to make ready to defend themselves, he had organized a Philippine Army, but it was badly armed and insufficiently trained. It would have to be used as a second line of defense, with the Americans bearing the brunt of the fighting.

But there were very few American troops in the Islands. They consisted of all or part of the 31st, 45th and 57th Infantry Regiments, the 24th Field Artillery, 26th Cavalry and the 1st Division of Philippine Scouts. There were also some headquarters troops, a little antiaircraft, a few airplanes, and a medical regiment. It was obvious that, spread out over the vast jungle-covered area of Luzon, they would be cut to pieces by driblets. And yet some attempt must be made to defend the long coast line.

Eisenhower finally succeeded in working out a plan. The troops were to be divided into three holding forces: one for the northeast coast; one, centering on Manila, to defend the south and southeast; and one along the Gulf of Lingayen.

"That's where the main attack will come," Ike said. "Anything else will be a diversion."

No one thought for a moment that these forces could prevent a landing. The plan required that as enemy pressure increased, the three forces should retire and finally unite in the mountains of the Bataan Peninsula. It meant giving up Manila, which lay in the flatlands. Worse still—and this was the hardest decision to make—it called for abandoning Cavite, the only American naval base in the Far East. But the Americans knew their limitations. Cavite was on the wrong side of the bay, with no natural defenses. It could not be held.

In the steep mountains of Bataan, backed by the island fortress of Corregidor, they might hold out until help came from Singapore. If ever it came . . .

Ike had other ideas for the defense of the island. It could be held by air power, if they could ever get enough machines. He laid out airfields, just in case Washington someday grasped the situation and sent them planes. Then he had another scheme, which called for a Philippine Navy, consisting of fast motor torpedo boats. There were, so far, none in the United States Navy, but the Italians and Germans were said to be building them. Ike figured that a few dozen of these mosquito boats dashing out from the indented coast line at night could play merry hell with the huge fleets of transports which Japan would have to use to carry her invasion forces. But the idea was considered too fanciful.

They continued to make slow progress. American and Philippine forces held joint maneuvers, which were on the whole successful. They showed that the plan for uniting the three holding forces on Bataan was praticable, though it would require extremely skillful maneuvering in the face of enemy pressure. But they were short of matériel. It was not until 1941 that a thin trickle of airplanes began to come through. A few tanks and antitank guns arrived only just before Japan struck.

Meanwhile the men were working like moles over at Corregidor. The tunnel which carried the streetcars through Malinita Hill was waterproofed and drained. Traverses and countertraverses were built out from it until the hill was one vast honeycomb. Corregidor could hold out as long as food and ammunition lasted.

The members of the Philippine government knew of these plans, knew how desperate the situation would become before relief arrived. But they never wavered in their loyalty. The Americans had been fair and generous with them. They had cemented the alliance with the mortar of personal friendship, and the Filipinos had no thought but to be faithful to that friendship. Even the lowest echelons of the Philippine Army were pervaded by this loyalty, as they later proved with their blood in the long hopeless days of torture on Bataan.

Into the building of esprit, of this unexampled loyalty of one people to another who had, after all, held their land as conquerors, went countless deeds, small and great, and the impact of many fine personalities. Certainly MacArthur, with his dash and confidence, had much to do with it. Genial Paul McNutt, who was high commissioner from 1937 to 1939, played his part, as did Weldon Jones, Admiral Thomas C. Hart and many others who worked with the Filipinos and liked and trusted them. But it is equally certain that the loyalty of the Philippine Army was in no small measure built up by Eisenhower, through his tireless visits to every component, his infectious enthusiasm, his genuine friendship for these people, and above all, his ability to inculcate them with his own simple code of honor.

In spite of the nervous strain, the Eisenhowers' last years in the Philippines passed pleasantly. They found Paul McNutt very congenial, and they had a great many friends on the island. Conditions of life were extremely comfortable since the Manila Hotel had built an air-conditioned wing. For a moderate price they had a luxurious apartment in the new part; it had high-ceilinged rooms with great crystal chandeliers, the walls hung in damask and a huge picture window that framed the ever-changing beauty of the harbor. Their quarters struck Ike as pretty fancy—not the sort of place he could think of as home. But temporarily it was very pleasant. He had a wonderful trip with John through the wild country to the north, which brought these two closer together than ever before. How they laughed at the naked Igorotes scrambling good-naturedly for cigarettes. Never able to resist the childish appeal of these wild islanders, Ike doled out many cartons. John was bent on a military career, and as they inspected various installations, his father talked seriously with him about the problems of defending the island.

But in spite of all these agreeable aspects of life, Ike began to get restless in the summer of 1939. Four years was a long time to be away. The plans were all made; the work was going forward. It was, he thought, time to go home.

The outbreak of the war in Europe confirmed this opinion. It was the beginning of the crisis which Fox Conner had foreseen so long ago. Ike did not yet know whether we would be drawn into it. Certainly the American people were determined to stay out—if they could. But the danger was there, each day more apparent. And within himself Ike felt that tremendous sense of urgency—the absolute necessity of getting back into the main current, of placing himself in a position to serve with all the accumulated knowledge and talent which he had gathered through the years.

It was not easy to break away. Strong pressures were brought to bear to keep him where he was. Presidente Quezon was insistent and there was Ike's sense of loyalty to the Philippine people. But it failed to outweigh the inner compulsion which bade him go.

On December 13, 1939, after a series of farewell banquets, and with genuine regret at leaving their Filipino friends who themselves were almost in tears, the Eisenhowers sailed for home.

CHAPTER TWELVE

ALARMIST IKE

When Eisenhower returned to America, he felt out of touch with his fellow countrymen for the first time in his life. Their strangely complacent attitude toward the threatening aspect of events, in both Europe and the Far East, was beyond his comprehension. Ever since those days in Panama he had foreseen the impending crisis and had tried to prepare himself for it and to help his country prepare. Now that it was so plainly upon us, our willful turning of eyes to the wall seemed to him like a visitation of madness, a sickness of the spirit that might lead to catastrophe.

Americans talked about the "phony war" in Europe, and boasted about what the Navy would do to those conceited little Japs if ever they dared to challenge its power, which nobody thought they would do. Eisenhower argued and shouted and got red in the face.

"You people ought to learn what goes on," he raged. "The Japs have been preparing for twenty years. They're going to jump on us and we have nothing to fight them with. I tell you that I'm ready to retire, but I can't because this country is going to need every soldier she can scrape up."

The only result of his warnings was that people began to call him "Alarmist Ike."

Aside from these larger anxieties, and between arguments, Ike was peculiarly content. After temporary duty at the Presidio of San Francisco, he was ordered to Fort Lewis in Washington State, as regimental executive officer of the 15th Infantry. In his entire military career he had seen very little service with troops, though he infinitely preferred it to staff work. His duty with the 15th was a source of real joy to him. At the time he joined the regiment, it had just returned from a long tour of duty in China, where it had made a splendid reputation. The regimental crest was a Chinese dragon, and under it the words "Can Do." The 15th lived up to that motto. They were men after Ike's own heart.

The men of the 15th soon came to reciprocate this feeling. At first they regarded Colonel Eisenhower with the suspicious reserve which veterans always exhibit toward a new officer, but it wasn't long before word rang around that the new Exec was a right guy. Various little incidents contributed to this confidence. There was trouble about charge accounts at the Post Exchange, in the course of which Ike decided that the personnel were in the right and took drastic steps to remedy the situation. A story circulated that on his first inspection of the kitchens, Colonel Eisenhower saw mounds of freshly ground meat for hamburgers. As he passed by, he grabbed a fistful with one hand and a raw onion with the other and continued down the line munching contentedly while an astonished cook muttered, "My gawd, that must be a tough guy! Raw meat!"

Then there was the case of the feuding privates. They had been hating each other for years, and if there was one thing Ike wouldn't stand for, it was bad blood between the men. He sent for the feudists one day and ordered them to wash a window, one outside and one in. He watched them scowling at each other through the pane and finally burst into a roar of laughter. The men broke down and laughed too. It was the end of the feud.

Top Sergeant James Stack was in charge of the Inspector General's office. Since the post of inspector general was temporarily vacant, Ike had many direct dealings with Stack and liked his intelligence and integrity. An unusual personal friendship grew up between them. Then Stack found himself in a spot. He had been going with a nurse from the Tacoma General Hospital who decided that it was her duty to join the Army. In due course she was commissioned and the caste barrier rose between them. As a commissioned officer, a nurse was not permitted to associate with enlisted personnel.

Stack took his troubles to Colonel Eisenhower.

"Are you two really in love with each other?" Ike asked.

"Yes, sir. We were going to be married. I told her how it would be, but she didn't realize the way the Army thinks about these things."

"And you're sure she still wants to marry you?"

"Yes, sir," Stack said. "She wants us to go ahead and get married anyhow, but I know it would cause a lot of trouble. What does the Colonel think we'd better do?"

"Hell!" said Ike. "Love is more important than rank. I'll fix this up so you won't be embarrassed."

In these ways the echelons of the 15th found that the Colonel was on their side. He wouldn't stand for any "monkey business." Let things go wrong, and his eyes became as cold as glaciers and his voice like the lash of the wind off Mount Rainier. But you could count on him. The Regular Army men wanted leaders whom they could trust. The years of discipline had taught them to depend on their officers, just as they knew that the officers depended on them. For Colonel Eisenhower not only were they ready to do what he told them, but they tried to find out what he might want and do that as well.

After his service at Fort Lewis, Ike always felt that the 15th was his regiment, and they felt that way too, as they were to show him one day in a field in Sicily.

From a superficial point of view Ike had small reason for the contentment he felt at this time. At fifty he was only another lieutenant colonel, a rank he had held twenty-two years before. It seemed to him unlikely that he would rise much higher, except in the event of the war he so greatly dreaded. Even if it came, he'd probably be typed as a good staff man and stuck in Washington.

He voiced the reason for his inner tranquillity in one of the long confidential talks with John, in which they both took increasing delight.

"Even though I never get much higher," Ike told his son, "I shall be content. There have been certain jobs to do, and I believe that I have done them well. I know that I have the affection of my friends and the respect of the Army. I would not ask for more."

John was determined to go to West Point. His choice of a profession was not due to any urging on the part of his father—quite the contrary. When John first arrived at Fort Lewis—a lanky boy of seventeen, already taller than Ike—his Uncle Edgar, who lived in Tacoma, spent a good deal of time with him. One day when Edgar came to the Eisenhowers' quarters, his manner was unusually solemn—portentous was the word, John thought, as he greeted his uncle. It didn't take the lawyer long to get down to business.

"I know you're thinking of going to West Point, John," said Edgar Eisenhower, "but I have a proposition to make to you."

John grinned amiably, but his eyes were skeptical. "Go ahead, Uncle Edgar."

"I have a big law practice here," said his uncle. "It not only brings me in more money than I can use, but I have built it up from nothing and I think it's worth while. There's nobody to succeed me in it, nobody to whom I can leave it. What I want to say is that if you will study law, I'll take you into the firm as soon as you graduate, and eventually the whole thing will be yours."

John looked stumped, but not at all doubtful.

"Gosh, Uncle Edgar, that's a—magnificent offer, but—"

"Better think it over, John," Ike put in. "There are a lot of things in favor of it."

"I know, dad," John said, "and I'm terribly grateful to Uncle Edgar. But I don't have to think. I know what I want to do. And if, when I am your age, I can say what you said to me the other day, I'll be satisfied."

Then he bolted from the room in a state of acute embarrassment.

The following winter John went to Washington, D.C., to take Senator Capper's competitive examination for West Point. He beat the thirty-five other contestants, and incidentally, his father's mark, with an average of 92 per cent, an all-time record for the Kansas examinations. John entered the Academy in the summer of '41.

On May 10, 1940, the German armored divisions crashed into Holland and Belgium. They shattered the bow-and-arrow armies of the Low Countries so badly that the infantry, following the tanks, had only to mop them up. A surprise thrust by General Erwin Rommel went through the main French line at Sedan, isolating the whole British Army and part of the French. Meanwhile the Luftwaffe swept the skies. In a month it was all over. France was prostrate, and though England had saved her troops at Dunkerque, they had lost all their equipment.

The American people were at last frightened into action. Years before, President Roosevelt had said that the frontier of America was on the Rhine, and the country had howled him down, but when France fell, the truth of his words was startlingly apparent. Congress frantically passed gigantic appropriation bills and the Selective Service Act, but money and hastily-called civilians were of no immediate use. The necessary component was time, and no one could even guess how much of that was available.

Even though Ike had been mentally prepared for so long a time, he was appalled by the catastrophic pace of events. He had not been alarmist enough: this was far worse than anything Fox Conner had foreseen. For a time he could not pretend to map the future even for a few months ahead. His military training and special sources of information made him doubtful of England's ability to hold out; there were less than one hundred tanks left to the British Army, and practically no artillery. There weren't even enough rifles to equip an army corps. Men were guarding the beaches with shotguns. By all military logic, England was done for. If she held out, it would be by a miracle of the spirit.

By Autumn, he was more hopeful. The miracle had happened: a handful of Spitfires had turned back the Luftwaffe. American World War stocks of rifles and seventy-fives had rearmed the British—after a fashion. The President had traded fifty destroyers for the bases we needed in case the British fleet was lost. It looked as though we would get a little time.

Like nearly every officer of the Army, Ike was working day and night. The National Guard had been called out and was getting intensive training. The first of the selectees were coming in. The tremendous task of expanding a force of 165,000 men into a gigantic army of 7,000,000 was under way.

On November 30, 1940, Eisenhower was made chief of staff of the 3rd Division, of which the 15th Infantry was a component. Major General Charles F. Thompson commanded the 3rd, which was known as the Marne Division. It was a crack outfit—the only one entitled to four battle stars for World War I—and had been uniformly fortunate in its officers. General George C. Marshall had commanded one of its brigades, and Mark Wayne Clark had served with it.

Eisenhower's superior staff work with the 3rd earned him promotion in March, to chief of staff of the IX Corps of the rapidly expanding Army, under Major General Kenyon A. Joyce. He joined the corps for intensive training work at Hunter Liggett Reservation in California.

In the summer of 1941, Lieutenant General Lesley J. McNair, commanding Army Ground Forces, was casting about for a chief of staff to send to Lieutenant General Walter Kreuger's newly organized Third Army. He consulted with Mark Wayne Clark, who had been traveling all over the country checking up on maneuvers.

"We need somebody good for this job," McNair said. "You've seen them all in action. Whom do you recommend?"

"Eisenhower," was Clark's unhesitating reply. "He's one of the best."

So Eisenhower was ordered to the Third Army. He was a full colonel now.

Headquarters of the Third Army was at San Antonio. The Eisenhowers had completed the long cycle and were back at familiar Fort Sam. It was like coming home. A colonel's quarters were a lot more commodious than the little apartment in 1916, but the atmosphere wasn't so different. The Eisenhowers' was a center of hospitality for all ages, and Ike still liked to step out to the kitchen on Sunday evening to whip up one of his specialties. He was inclined to be secretive about his art; even Mamie didn't know his private recipe for potato salad.

At Fort Sam, Ike acquired the first, and certainly not the least, of his official family, the Eisenhower Invasion Team. He needed a striker, and soon after they arrived at Fort Sam, Mamie posted a notice in the barracks, according to custom, that such a job was open. She hoped someone would volunteer soon, for her couple had left and that big house was a handful.

The following morning, while Mamie, limp from the fierce June heat, was drying the breakfast dishes, the back doorbell rang. She called, "Come in!"

A cocky, friendly little private with black hair and blue eyes walked into the kitchen. He was as Irish as a green necktie, and his uniform was very resplendent for a G.I. Buttons flashed, trousers were razor sharp, and Mamie's practiced eye noted that he was wearing officers' strap shoes.

"I've come to apply for the job of the Colonel's striker, ma'am," he said.

Mamie liked his looks.

"What's your name?" she asked.

"Mickey."

"Don't you have a last name?"

"Michael McKeough is my full name, but everybody calls me Mickey."

"All right, Mickey," Mamie said. "Are you Regular Army?"

"No, ma'am," Mickey answered, a little crestfallen, "but I have had fourteen weeks intensive training."

"Do you know anything about being a striker?"

"Well, ma'am, I guess you'd say I didn't, but I was a bellboy at the Plaza Hotel in New York until I was drafted, and you learn a lot of things there."

Mamie laughed. "You'd have to help me some around the house, you know."

"Sure, that will come natural," Mickey said, grinning. "I always helped my mother with the housework."

"We pay you something extra, of course, for all that," said Mamie. "And you can have the job, Mickey, if you really want it."

"I do, ma'am," Mickey said. "I know I'm going to like it."

When Mickey reported for work he wasn't nearly so magnificent as on his first appearance. Mamie found out later that he had borrowed nearly his entire costume for that occasion. But he remained as willing and eager as he appeared at first. It wasn't long before he seemed to regard himself as a member of the family, and he developed a tremendous affection and loyalty for his Colonel. Ike inevitably reciprocated that feeling and wondered how he had ever gotten along without Mickey. Much later the little Irishman wrote to Mamie from London, "We are getting on fine here. The General is well and I try to keep the apartment the way you like it."

In the summer of 1941, the Germans smashed into Russia and seemed about to overrun that country and add its vast resources to their already gigantic empire, which embraced virtually the whole of Europe with all its industrial power. Prime Minister Winston Churchill and President Franklin D. Roosevelt met on their warships and promulgated the Atlantic Charter—brave words that lifted the hearts of men who did not realize how little armament there was to implement them even yet. We were not at war, but our ships were carrying all the matériel we could spare to England, guarded by American destroyers, which sank, and were sunk by, the wolf packs of submarines. It was war in everything but name, and everyone knew there was little time left. One hundred light tanks and the first fifty self-propelled artillery weapons delivered by our arsenals were shipped to the Philippines. Flights of Fortresses were started across the Pacific.

But with all the places there were to guard, from South America to Iceland and from the Canal Zone to Alaska, and the tenuous chain of islands to the Philippines, our resources were spread as thin as boardinghouse butter.

These imperative demands for the defense of our outer bastions sharply limited the matériel available for training our rapidly expanding army, but equipment had to be found or improvised. By July, 1941, the Army had increased to 28 partially equipped infantry divisions, the newly created Armored Force of four divisions, and an Air Force of 209 incomplete squadrons. Its total strength was more than 1,500,000 men. Maneuvers of forces up to corps strength had been regularly held, but more ambitious battle rehearsals were now possible. The divisions in training were organized into armies, and during the latter part of the summer a total of 900,000 men took part in realistic maneuvers.

By far the most important of these was the "war" between Lieutenant General Ben Lear's Second (Red) Army and General Kreuger's Third (Blue) Army in Louisiana. The Red Army was given virtually all the armor—most of it consisting of motor trucks labeled "TANK"—and was the attacking force. General Kreuger and his chief of staff, Colonel Eisenhower, had the problem of devising a defense against the Red armored columns.

This sort of thing was Ike's forte. All those years of study and constructive thinking now paid off in his complete mastery of the technique of strategy. With General Kreuger, he worked out detailed plans for a novel defense. More important still, when the Army went into action, was his ability to size up a situation almost at a glance and to form an instantaneous and correct estimate of what must be done. The training he had given himself made his mental reactions as fast and automatic as the physical reactions of an experienced pilot.

When the clouds of dust settled on the hot roads of Louisiana, and the tired troops flung themselves down in the grateful shade of trees dripping with Spanish moss, the umpires announced the result. General Kreuger, with his old-fashioned campaign hat pushed back on his head, beamed at his chief of staff, whose overseas cap was slanted at a cocky angle. The "enemy," it seemed, had lost every one of their tanks. The battle had resulted in theoretical annihilation.

Shortly afterward, Ike received official recognition of his services; it took the form of promotion to brigadier general. At Fort Sam Houston the 3rd Division held a great review in his honor, and he took the salute of the marching troops, the first star glittering with newness on his shoulder.

Ike was fearfully tired. Even two months after the strenuous maneuvers were over, he still felt the terrific pressure of work. Tension in the Pacific was building to an intolerable peak; the flash point might come at any moment, and there was so desperately much to be done. But that Sunday morning in December was comparatively quiet at Fort Sam. Ike spent the morning working at the office. After lunch he said to the two members of the staff who were on duty, "Fellows, I'm dead-beat. I'm going to treat myself to a nap. Call me if anything happens."

Ike had no sooner dozed off on a cot in the back room than it happened: the stunning news of Pearl Harbor. The reaction of his aides was a peculiar tribute to the affection in which they held their chief.

"Have we got to wake him?" asked the Captain. "He's so utterly worn out."

"He'll kill us if we don't," said the Major.

So they went in together and called him. When he heard the incredible news, Ike's weariness seemed to vanish as his latent resources of strength flowed through his body in answer to the long-awaited call. He got briskly to his feet.

"Well, boys," he said, "it's come."

CHAPTER THIRTEEN

WAR PLANS

On the morning of December 12, Ike dashed back to his quarters at ten o'clock in the morning.

"I see you've got orders," Mamie said, as he crashed through the door. "What are they?"

"Nothing exciting. I'm called to Washington. I guess they want advice on the Philippines."

"How are you going?"

"They've got a plane waiting for me at Randolph Field. I'll probably be gone only a few days. Tell Mickey to pack the small duffel bag."

In that casual fashion, Ike started on the long and tortuous road to Berlin.

Later that day, the Blue Bonnet, crack express train of the Missouri-Kansas-Texas, affectionately known as the Katy Railroad, rumbled through a thunderstorm into a small Texas town and settled back on its brakes. It was crowded with passengers, most of them rushing to Washington; in those first frantic days it seemed that the whole nation was converging on the capital. Bill Kittrell of the Lend-Lease Administration was in luck; he had a whole drawing room to himself. He sat in it, looking out the window at the lightning flaring over the plains and the slashing rain that drowned the empty main street. It looked as if the whole town had taken cover; nothing moved, and the train itself seemed dead. Kittrell looked impatiently at his watch. There was no excuse for being stuck in this flag-stop for twenty minutes.

Explanation arrived in the form of an Army car that tore up the street in winged sheets of spray and skidded to a stop beside the train. Kittrell saw an officer jump out of it and sprint through the rain.

Natural curiosity made him lounge in the doorway of his drawing room. The officer, a brigadier general, was a big man with intense blue eyes. When he took off his cap to shake the water from it, he exposed a rosy, bald head, edged with light tan hair.

"—not even an upper," the conductor was saying. "I'm terribly sorry, General."

"Looks like I have to sit up," the officer said, smiling pleasantly.

It was such unusual behavior for a general in a hurry that Bill Kittrell stared. Before he knew what he was doing, the friendliness which seemed to emanate from the big man in uniform made him say impetuously, "Would you like to share my drawing room, General?"

The General beamed. "That's mighty kind of you," he said. "Won't I be crowding you?"

Kittrell, looking at the width of the general's shoulders, thought, *Yes,* but said, "No, these things are built for three and I'm all alone."

"I'll take you up then, with profound thanks. My name is Eisenhower."

"Bill Kittrell."

The General was good company. For a West Pointer he knew a surprising amount about Texas agriculture and industry, and seemed to understand the problems of the people out there. For a while conversation ran along such general lines, but there was only one subject that anybody could really talk about that December. Soon they were discussing the war.

Kittrell was amazed at the intense feeling the General showed as he talked of what the war would mean in the way of human suffering and horror. He seemed to have a passion for peace. He spoke with quiet virulence about the Germans and their megalomaniacal military ambition down through the years. But when the Japanese were mentioned his eyes were like the blue steel of a gun barrel and his language almost took the paint off the walls.

"The one mitigating circumstance of militarism," he concluded, "is the soldiers' code of honor. In spite of their Samurai affectation, those low grade skunks have not even a vestige of honor. They represent the ultimate degradation of humanity, and they want to drag all the world into their latrine."

General Eisenhower had seen considerable service in the Philippines. Kittrell asked leading questions, some of which the General answered straightforwardly, others he parried. In spite of the rumors about disaffection in other parts of the East, Eisenhower was certain that the Filipinos would not betray us.

"I know them well," he said. "They are my friends, and I would stake my life on their loyalty."

Kittrell mentioned the landings the Japanese had made on the northern tip of Luzon.

"That doesn't mean a thing," Eisenhower said. "When they come at Lingayen the fight will really be on."

"Can we hold the Islands?" Kittrell asked point-blank.

Eisenhower parried. "It depends on the force that they have available. You can count on MacArthur to get the best out of what we have."

But later he let Kittrell see what was in his mind as he said somberly, "It will be a long and bloody job getting the Philippines back."

Another plane was waiting at St. Louis and Ike reached Washington December 13. He found that he was assigned to assist Brigadier General L. T. Gerow, Chief of War Plans. It looked as though he were going to sit out another war.

Aside from his preference for active duty, Ike could hardly have found a more congenial post. He had known Gerow ever since the early days in San Antonio, and so close had their friendship become that in one West Point questionnaire he had named Gerow and his brother Milton as the "two people who will know your address at all times." They worked together now in close harmony, and there were mountains of work to do.

On all the fighting fronts the Allies were in a desperate situation owing to lack of matériel. Deployments had to be made with regard for limited resources in troops and equipment and the terrible losses already sustained. Strengthen here. Patch there. Pray for time. In the first five weeks of the war, six hundred thousand troops with all their vehicles, guns and equipment were transported by the railroads of the country. Many of them were dispatched overseas to Hawaii, Australia, Alaska, Panama, South America. But even in these desperate days the War Plans Section of the General Staff was not concentrating solely on defense. Plans were on file for possible offensive action, but these required complete revision in the light of the present circumstances. The new plans were already on file in Ike's brain.

Only nine days after Eisenhower took his new post, the British

Prime Minister, accompanied by his Chiefs of Staff, arrived in Washington to meet with President Roosevelt. Never did two heads of state face a grimmer prospect. The American line of battle had been wrecked at Pearl Harbor. Two days later the last Allied battleships in the Pacific, the splendid new *Prince of Wales* and the *Repulse,* had been sunk by aerial attack off Malaya. The Russian lines were stiffening twenty miles from Moscow, but Hong Kong was gone, MacArthur was conducting his skillful but perilous retreat into Bataan, and a vast tide of yellow scum was lapping down the Malay Peninsula to engulf Singapore.

But Winston Churchill was a man who could not envisage failure. And the President was right with him. In the hour of defeat they called for plans to take the offensive.

The first great step toward essential unity of action was the formation of the Combined Chiefs of Staff. This assured the co-ordination of the entire Anglo-American strategy in all theaters of war, and provided for unity of command of all forces in each sector, under either a British or an American commander in chief, as best fitted the circumstances. The immediate agreement reached on this point was of the utmost importance.

Necessarily the Allied Staffs devoted a good deal of time to defensive disposition, but even these were made with an eye to the moment when the rising power of America would permit offensive action.

Eisenhower attended these conferences, and he had a plan.

It was evident that a long time must elapse before it would be possible to strike directly at the continent, but North Africa, loosely held by the Vichy French, presented an easier target. The Combined Chiefs of Staff discussed the proposition in detail and reached tentative agreements. Winston Churchill pushed the idea; he had always held the theory of the importance of the Mediterranean. The Dardanelles attack in World War I had been his baby, and in 1940, during England's hour of peril, he had dared to dispatch the last matériel in England to reinforce General Sir Archibald Wavell in Egypt. Now he coined the phrase, "the soft underbelly of Europe," and grinned like a kewpie.

While the staffs were meeting in Washington, a division of American troops was sent to the British Isles to prepare for the still distant moment of attack. In view of our perilous situation, it was only a gesture, comparable to that of the Roman Legion which marched out of the south gate of Rome to defend an out-lying province of the empire, while Hannibal's army was camped at the north gate. But if Ike recognized the parallel, he also remembered that it was that gesture which broke Carthaginian morale.

During these hectic weeks Ike found a refuge at Milton's lovely old house at Falls Church, Virginia, just across the Potomac. Often he didn't get home until eleven or twelve at night, and always he left before eight in the morning, but even these few hours of tranquillity and family association were worth the trip out of Washington. No matter how late he arrived, Ike never failed to tiptoe down the hall, as he had for so long in his own home, to peek at Milton's sleeping children.

An added burden was the sad news of the death of David Eisenhower. Ike grieved deeply over the loss of his ever gentle father; and his grief was sharpened by the fact that the urgency of war prevented his attending the funeral.

When Mamie finally got to Washington, they took up quarters at Fort Myer. Mickey brought the car on from San Antonio and the Eisenhowers were settled again—briefly.

In February, 1942, General Gerow was assigned to field duty and Eisenhower took his place as assistant chief of staff in charge of War Plans. In March, Ike got his second star, being appointed major general, and in April he was promoted to the vitally important post of chief of operations. With all the pressure of work, which never lifted for an instant, he was still maintaining a voluminous correspondence with his old friends, both in the Army and at Abilene. Sergeant Stack wrote a chatty letter about goings on in the 15th Infantry. Most of the other sergeants, it seemed, had been offered commissions, but he was still at the old grind. He closed with an appropriate quotation, "Theirs not to reason why . . ." It was in the nature of a mild hint and Ike took it like a flash. Stack was a good man, he knew.

Almost before he could say "Balaklava," Stack found himself in Washington with bars on his shoulders. He encountered General Eisenhower for the first time at eleven o'clock at night in a corridor of the Munitions Building, where the General Staff was temporarily crowded into inadequate offices, and the lights burned all night long.

"Hi, Stack," said Ike. "I see you're off to a good start."

* * * * * *

By April the situation on the different fronts was somewhat more stabilized. It is true that Bataan had fallen, as everyone knew it must. Ike grieved deeply for his friends out there and for the splendid troops with whom he had once been associated. But in other respects things looked a little better. MacArthur had been reinforced in Australia, and that great country, instead of dangling like an apple, ripe for picking, now seemed reasonably secure. In Russia the Red Armies had actually shoved the Germans back a way, while the British had temporarily chased Rommel halfway through Libya. The outlines of the future seemed to be vaguely taking shape.

In May, General George C. Marshall sent Eisenhower to England for staff conferences and a tour of inspection. Ike did not realize that he, too, was being inspected. Marshall was pleased to hear that Eisenhower got along splendidly with the English. It was, he thought, because Ike never seemed to be saying to himself, "Now these fellows are British and I must be careful," but simply ignored any national differences and was completely himself.

The North African invasion came up for further discussion and Eisenhower produced more comprehensive and detailed plans. It was all pretty tentative still, owing to the shipping situation, which was bad and getting worse. The U-boats were running riot in the Atlantic all the way from Ireland to the New Jersey beaches. Nevertheless, further dispositions were made toward an attack in November.

After Ike returned to America, General Marshall made certain inquiries of his British colleagues as to the acceptability of his candidate for Commander in Chief of the American Forces in the European theater.

He got the "green light."

On a hot day in June, Ike was summoned to the Chief of Staff's office. During a long conference, General Marshall discussed the African plans in detail. Finally he asked, "In your opinion, are the plans as nearly complete as we can make them? Do you approve of them?"

"Yes, sir," said Ike. "I consider them excellent."

"That's lucky," said General Marshall, with a twinkle, "because you're the man who is going to carry them out."

Ike was literally staggered. He had had no inkling that he was even being considered for field service. The delight with which he would have accepted command of a division was quite submerged in his sense of the tremendous responsibility which had been loaded on his shoulders.

His old friend Major General Francis B. Wilby encountered him coming down the stairs in the Munitions Building. Ike's usually ruddy face was pale and his grin was remarkable for its absence.

"How are things, Ike?" Wilby greeted him cheerfully.

Eisenhower stopped dead on the stairway.

"Brother," he said, "what do you think they've done to me now?"

General Wilby's expression changed to the solemnity proper for bad news.

"I give up," he said.

Ike sadly wagged his head.

"They're sending me over there to command the whole shebang!"

When Ike had returned from that first trip to England, he had snatched a brief weekend to visit John at West Point. It was strange to think of this tall young soldier as the boy he had tiptoed down the hall to peek at for so many years. Ike was terrifically proud of his son. This, he thought, was good fortune beyond the deserts of man, for if he had had the power to shape the boy exactly as he wished, he knew he could not have done so well as this.

At first there was a slight constraint between them; they hadn't seen each other for a year and they were both shy of the tremendous affection between them. But it was not more than a few moments before the old intimacy was restored.

They spent the afternoon walking around the post, talking of everything under the sun. Ike pointed out the spot where he had sat so long ago, thinking of the historic importance of West Point and evaluating all it had meant to him. No one was so understanding as John, because he thought the same way.

Ike saw his son once more before he left for England. John, newly become a Yearling, got a weekend leave and came to Washington. They both knew that it was the last time they would be together like this—at home—for an unpredictably long time; they made the best of it and were very gay.

Sunday afternoon came swiftly and it was time for John to go. The taxi was waiting at the curb. John came out of the house, immaculate in his white uniform. Goodbyes were said. John swept his mother off her feet in a tremendous hug and pumped his father's hand. Ike stood watching as he started down the path.

Suddenly John stopped and smartly about-faced. As he stood rigidly at attention, looking straight at his father, Ike was conscious of the slender strength of the boy, his wide shoulders and narrow body, of the high color of his face and the intense blue of his eyes. Then John's hand snapped up to his visored cap in the formality of the West Point salute.

CHAPTER FOURTEEN

ENGLAND

In General Eisenhower's first message from London he said, "The United States Army is hewing to the pattern of unqualified partnership with Britain for the common effort."

That was a direct statement of his philosophy of our relations with our ally. It was the goal he sought in every contact he had with Englishmen. No matter what vexations might arise, he ignored them serenely in the interests of unity. It was a policy that paid big dividends.

Ike's first job, when he reached England, was to form a British-American staff who could work together harmoniously on the great project now known as "Torch"—the invasion of North Africa—and on subsequent offensive actions already being planned. Before leaving the United States, he had selected his American staff, some of whom were already on the scene while others were sent over. The senior commanders under him were his old West Point friend, Major General Mark Wayne Clark, Commander of the Ground Forces; and Major General John C. H. Lee, Service of Supply; Major General Russell P. Hartel, North Ireland; Major General Charles H. Bonesteel, Iceland; guitar-playing Major General Carl Spaatz, Army Air Forces. It wasn't the Germans' first disagreeable experience with Spaatz. Back in 1918, he had taken a brief leave from his post commanding the Air Training Center at Issoudin, France, and shot down two Germans in an aerial busman's holiday. As his chief of staff, Ike took with him Major General Walter Bedell Smith, affectionately known as "Beedle," who had been secretary of the General Staff. For his personal aides, Eisenhower chose Major Ernest Lee and his old poker-playing friend of Washington days, Harry C. Butcher, now a lieutenant commander.

"Butch" had relinquished his lucrative job with Columbia Broadcasting to take a commission on the first of June. He had expected to remain in Washington as broadcasting adviser and liaison officer for the Navy, but when Ike told him that he needed him, there was no question in Butch's mind what he would do.

Eyebrows shot up all over the staff rooms when Ike put in his request for Lieutenant Commander Butcher. The objections were based on Butcher's short service and the fact that he was in the Navy and had no military qualifications. Ike settled the matter with one explosive sentence, "Dammit all, I've got to have somebody with me who isn't subservient!"

The fact was that Ike was still, as always, dependent on being surrounded by his family and his friends. More than anything else, he dreaded the inevitable isolation of high command, and he was determined to take with him one friend with whom he could relax. With Butch—and, of course, Mickey—he could make some sort of home.

Before Ike left, Mamie succeeded in snatching him out of the turmoil of preparation for a day in bed to rest up. To make sure he stayed there, she brought him half a dozen wild West books from the library. The following morning they were all stacked in the hall waiting to be taken back.

"Won't the General be reading these?" asked Mickey.

Mamie laughed. "He read them all yesterday afternoon," she said.

Ike was asked to outline Torch to the General Staff before he took off. The concluding words of his address were typical.

"That is what we are going to do," he said, "and those are the things we'll need. We're counting on you to see that we get them. Goodbye."

In accordance with the importance of his new job Ike was appointed lieutenant general. The speed of his ascent in a year from colonel to three-star general was a near record. Inevitably many people have looked critically into this sudden rise, scenting Army politics, but they were on a false trail. Before he came to Washington in December, 1941, Ike knew General Marshall only slightly; he had never met President Roosevelt. Disappointing as it was to the cynics, even the most suspicious were obliged to admit that Eisenhower's advancement was untainted. For once, at least, merit had secured its reward.

In London, Ike pitched in with his usual enthusiasm. This job meant a seven-day week and a seventeen-hour day. He kept in condition by tossing a medicine ball with Butch at seven o'clock every morning, to the peril of the bric-a-brac in his bedroom in their little three-room flat. The drawing room served as an office, where the General worked behind a huge flat-topped desk when he wasn't at American Headquarters or at Norfolk House, the secret headquarters of Torch. The whole apartment hotel—luxury flats in English—had been taken over by the military, and half the rank of the American Army and Navy in England lived there. Admiral Harold R. Stark, senior American naval officer in England, had the flat across from Ike. Lesser admirals, generals, captains and colonels swarmed through the corridors like gaudy termites. Armed sentries guarded the doors and no one could get in without a special pass. The very existence of the place was a closely guarded secret, for bombs need no credentials, and one bomb accurately aimed would have rewarded Hitler handsomely.

This extremely military ménage was far from the home atmosphere. Ike needed so much his brief moments of relaxation. In spite of all the people he saw, he was desperately lonely. Finally he went to Major Lee.

"Look, Lee, is there anything in regulations against my having a dog?"

"Not that I know of," the Major answered. "Why?"

"Because I want a dog," Ike said. "Somebody I can talk to, who won't mention the war."

Within a few days the General had his dog, a present from his staff. He was a sooty black Scottie, the son of a British father and an American mother and therefore symbolic of the Allied effort. Mickey was somewhat less joyful as he undertook the job of housebreaking the new member of the household, but anything that made the General happy was all right by him. Ike called the puppy by the enigmatic name of Telek.

"Why Telek?" asked the puzzled staff.

"That," said Ike mysteriously, "is a military secret."

And so it remains to the present time.

The fact that Ike's persistent preoccupation was to foster unity between the British and the Americans did not lead to his coddling the former or kowtowing to them. The fulcrum of his influence with men of all nations was the fact that he never concealed what he thought; if something was wrong, he went straight to the person responsible and had it out. He pursued this policy in England with everybody from Winston Churchill down, and the British liked it because they knew exactly where they stood. Nor did Ike permit the more leisurely traditions of the British to brake his dynamic impetus. Almost as soon as he arrived he said, "We should not make the mistake of thinking that morale can be improved by pampering or lowering standards to permit greater ease of living." As a step in this direction, he demanded staff conferences with British generals on Sunday. This knocked the sacred British weekend out for the only time in history except at the peak of the Battle of Britain.

Curiously enough the British liked this innovation, too, just as they liked Ike's informal ways—Lord Louis Mountbatten was Louis to him and General Hastings Ismay was "Pug." They felt that here was a fellow who was really going places, and had no pretense.

There were, of course, certain ceremonial interruptions of work, but no more of these than Ike could help. His July Fourth statement to Americans read: "There is no time for messages until we can say them with bombs and shells." By way of implementing these words, General Spaatz sent American bombers to celebrate the Fourth with the first American raid against German installations on the Continent. Only six planes went, but later the skies were to grow dark with wings.

On July 5, Ike took time off to be received by the King at Buckingham Palace, and he attended the Bastille Day ceremonies on July 14. There, for the first time, he encountered the strange personality of the leader of the Fighting French, General Charles de Gaulle, half medieval saint, half *enfant terrible*.

But the most frequent interruptions that Ike permitted himself were constant inspections of the troops. He had always much preferred to be with the men rather than to do staff work. Now, at least, he could order himself off to this or that arriving unit. The elaborate special train that the English had given him tore over the splendid railways to all quarters of the United Kingdom. Ike considered it much too fancy, but it was a great convenience.

He tried to make at least one visit to every echelon under his command. He wanted to know his men and to give them the assurance that came from seeing their commander face to face. It was heart-warming to hear them shout, "Ike! Ike!" as he drove up in a jeep.

At staff conferences in July the North African invasion was definitely fixed upon. The decision was a courageous one, for the war was going badly. U-boats still raged unchecked in the Atlantic, piling up their dismal toll. In Egypt, Marshal Erwin Rommel had turned an apparent English victory into disaster when his new 88-millimeter guns caught the British tanks in a trap and smashed more than half of them like matchboxes. Discouraged and almost but not quite broken, the Eighth Army struggled back over the weary trail to Egypt. Tobruk, which had held out so gallantly the previous year, fell in a single day with tremendous British losses in killed and captured. Back went the tired Desert Rats, back through the heat and dust, abandoning all the places they had fought so hard to win—Bengasi, Bardia, Solum, Sidi Barani, Matruh. They halted at El Alamein, almost in sight of Alexandria, and Rommel gathered his armor for the battle of extermination.

Bad luck seemed to continue. Lieutenant General William H. E. Gott, sent to take over the Eighth, was killed flying to his new command. Dubiously the British Staff hurried a substitute to Egypt. Bernard Montgomery was as temperamental as a prima donna. He seemed an eccentric choice, but he was the best they had. Hearts lifted, however, when the tale of his arrival at Eighth Army Headquarters drifted back. He found his new staff working furiously.

"What are you doing?" he asked.

"Drawing up the plans for our retreat across the Nile," they answered.

"Tear them up," said Montgomery.

Brave words, but the line was dangerously thin.

In August the great commando raid on Dieppe ended in disaster. Again the luck was out, and the Germans were too good. Half of Mountbatten's magnificent fighting men were left behind as prisoners or dead on the shot-furrowed beaches.

It seemed fantastic to think of taking the whole of North Africa in an amphibious operation, while the broken fragments of the Dieppe divisions crawled back to England and the Eighth Army waited for Rommel in a shaky line from the Qattara Depression to the sea. But the plans went forward.

While purely military preparations were being made, the psychological front was not neglected. Since the French colonies in North Africa could not exist without American supplies, the

Germans permitted a certain amount of trade. This required diplomatic representation for America there; after all, we still had an ambassador in unoccupied France. Robert Murphy, our consul general in North Africa, had supplemented his diplomatic staff with twenty vice-consuls, who were buzzing around as busy as bees, doing a number of things that were not in the book.

During 1940 and 1941, Murphy had worked smoothly with General Maxime Weygand, commanding the French Armies in North Africa. Although Weygand had been obliged to surrender France and to collaborate to some extent with her conquerors, he hardly bothered to conceal his pro-Ally leanings. He had even signed a secret agreement with the United States, in which, in return for supplies we agreed to send him, he promised never to yield North Africa to the Germans. It was certain that had Weygand remained in command, he would not have resisted our landings.

But the Germans suspected something and in November, 1941, forced the Vichy government to recall Weygand. Since there seemed to be no chance of making a general arrangement with the French, Murphy concentrated on the piecemeal undermining of possible resistance. As a binder, to hold the scattered pieces together and in some measure to fill Weygand's place, he proposed that General Henri Giraud be secretly invited to join the expedition. Giraud's dashing military record, his recent escape from the German castle of Koenigstein, and his long service in Morocco, made him a popular hero to the Frenchmen in North Africa. Murphy believed that if the General issued a proclamation to the North African Army they would follow him.

The delicate negotiations with Giraud, which were carried out by Lemaigre-Dubreuil, a member of the Algerian underground whose business interests gave him an excuse for frequent trips to Vichy, were eventually successful—except that they left the General with a startling misconception of his role in the invasion. Plans were accordingly laid for Giraud's escape from unoccupied France and for his transportation by submarine to Gibraltar.

Murphy was particularly successful in fifth column work in the north, around Algiers and Oran. In October negotiations with pro-Ally French officers reached a point where it was essential for an American general officer to meet with the French to concert action. On receiving Murphy's message to this effect,

General Eisenhower immediately started on a little inspection tour of the troops, and dropped in at General Mark Wayne Clark's headquarters in an ancient English castle.

As Ike's car turned through the high iron gates of the park, past the gray stone lodge, he saw ahead of him battlemented towers showing above the tall oaks—like the towers of West Point, he thought, with a twinge of homesickness. But the aspect was far gentler than the rugged landscape of the Hudson River Valley. Low rolling hills and peaceful meadows formed a pastoral backdrop for the ivy-covered castle. Closer at hand were putting-green lawns and formal gardens, surrounded by clipped hedges and yew trees sheared in the shapes of animals and birds. A quiet river with deep pools and flashing riffles wound through the park. The wooden huts of the American guard and the black stings of antiaircraft guns pointing skyward from the battlements were an incongruity, as startling as an igloo on Fifth Avenue. Well, the war had produced more remarkable juxtapositions than that, Ike thought. And the fantastic adventure he was about to propose to his old friend, the scholarly, reserved Wayne Clark, would just about top them all.

General Clark greeted him gaily. "Hello, Ike, have you come to look us over?"

"Yes," said Ike, "but first we've got to have a little talk."

When the two were settled in the room which Clark used as his office, Ike broached the proposition. "Wayne," he said, "you're about to make a sissy of Dick Tracy and Hop Harrigan. I wish I could go, but they won't let me."

The news was no great surprise to Clark. He had been kept abreast of the negotiations, and knowing that somebody would have to go, he wanted to be the one.

The two men discussed the arrangements: an airplane to Gibraltar, then a submarine to the coast at Cherchel near Algiers. Finally a rubber boat would take Clark through the surf when the signal lights showed on the beach.

Clark performed the mission successfully. He made contact with the French leaders and made the final arrangements for their co-operation, but it was a rugged experience. He hid on the beaches and in cellars, while suspicious French troops ransacked the house where the meetings were held. When the submarine returned to pick him up, the sea was so rough that the rubber boat capsized and Clark lost a large amount of American gold, and his pants. He returned safely to England, however. The plans were complete at last.

The invasion of North Africa was perhaps the greatest military gamble in history, for there were so many imponderables, such split-second timing was required, and so complete must be the secrecy if success were to be achieved. The forces at Eisenhower's disposal were absurdly small, owing not to any lack of men, but to an acute shortage of ships. The wolf packs of the Atlantic were dragging their victims down by the score. Seven hundred thousand tons were sunk in a single month.

On the other hand, Montgomery had inspired the Eighth Army to splendid action. They had held at El Alamein and then smashed through Rommel's lines. The Nazis were streaming back along the familiar road through Libya. Now was the time, before they got too close to North Africa. The invasion could not wait.

In the end they managed to scrape up 850 ships for Eisenhower. Torch was put off for a week while he waited for the last of them to slide down the ways, and with the workmen still welding on their decks, to steam to the docks to be loaded. The total tonnage was approximately 600,000 which at the logistical rate of six tons of shipping per man and equipment meant 100,000 men. That was the possible total in plain figures. The number of men taking part in the first attack was actually 107,000 some of them airborne.

Those were hardly enough troops for a first-class parade, and they were supposed to capture 800 miles of coast line. The original plan had called for landings in Bône and Philippeville and Tunis, but the force available would not stretch that far. Besides, there was a lack of landing boats and aircraft carriers —the *Enterprise* was the only one left in the Pacific.

Three task forces made up the expedition, two of them sailing from England and one from America. The Eastern Task Force under English Lieutenant General K. A. N. Anderson consisted of British infantry and commando units with two American regimental combat teams from the 9th and 34th Infantry Divisions and one Ranger battalion. Its mission was to take Algiers, and the American troops were ordered to land first under Major General Charles W. Ryder, because the French were supposed to like us better than the English.

Major General Lloyd R. Fredendall commanded the Second

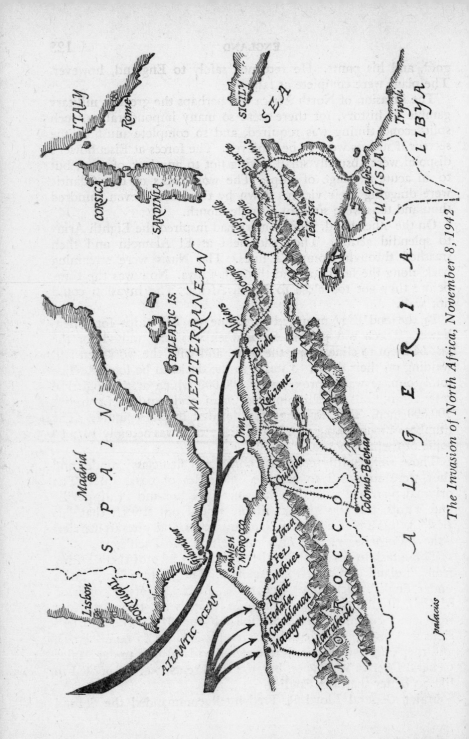

The Invasion of North Africa, November 8, 1942

Task Force, consisting of the 1st Infantry Division and half of the 1st Armored Division. They were to land at Oran and effect a junction across the northwest corner of Africa, behind Spanish Morocco, with the Third Task Force under Major General George S. Patton, Jr., which was to land at Casablanca.

This latter, which was the most powerful force, was expected to meet the stiffest opposition, since Murphy's fifth columns had got practically nowhere with General Auguste Noguès Commandant at Casablanca, and formidable units of the French Fleet were stationed there. It consisted of the 3rd Division, of which Ike's old "Can Do" regiment was a part, and the II Armored Corps. Georgie Patton had had his beloved tanks at Indio in the California desert all summer. There, where 120 degrees in the shade was a nice cool day, he had given his men—and himself—such rigorous training in desert warfare as he believed would make them even tougher than Rommel's Afrika Korps.

Battleships, an aircraft carrier and lesser units of the United States Navy under the command of Rear Admiral H. Kent Hewitt were to escort Patton's force, while the Royal Navy was to convoy those from England.

In addition to these forces, American paratroopers were to make the long flight from England, over the Bay of Biscay and slanting across Spain, to seize the airports at Algiers. Ike appointed General Clark as his deputy commander in the field.

On October 24, 1942, Admiral Hewitt assembled his force at sea and headed for Casablanca. The following day the other task forces set sail from England.

Those last ten days in England were the most nerve-racking of all for Ike. The great, irreplaceable fleets were plowing through the ocean at the snail's pace of convoys. Anything could happen now. One pinhole in the veil of secrecy, and the whole effort might be wasted. Even though the secret had been so well kept until now, the forces from England had to pass the narrow gateway to the Mediterranean at Gibraltar, where a thousand pairs of Axis eyes in Spain and Morocco would count and wonder. Was it possible that the Germans would not guess their destination?

The days were outwardly the gayest Ike had spent in London. He accepted every invitation he could find time for, and appeared everywhere, carefree and smiling. Inevitably a few rumors of an expedition to somewhere began to circulate. Ike gave them a shove in the wrong direction.

"Mickey."

"Yes, sir."

"I want you to go down to Harrod's and get me the heaviest woolen underwear they have. And a good thick sweater. If you see any fur-lined gloves, you might get them too."

"Are we going north, General?"

Ike smiled mysteriously.

"You're not to ask questions, Mickey. Just do as I say, and use your own judgment if you need anything."

"Beg pardon, General, but will Pearlie be going with us?"

Ike laughed out loud at the little Irishman's expression. Pearlie Hargrave was his second driver, a Wac, with whom Mickey was feverishly in love.

"Better let me do the worrying, Mickey," he answered.

In the first part of November, when the ships were about halfway over there, Amon Carter, the genial owner of the Fort Worth *Star-Telegram*, arrived in London. Being Amon, he wanted to meet General Eisenhower right away. All sorts of eminent people telephoned in his behalf. In the press of military and social engagements, Ike could find only half an hour, just before dinner one night.

Aman came around to the flat, and chatted with Eisenhower and Butcher. He quickly claimed Ike for his native state— anything that boosted Texas was grist for Amon's mill. He promised Ike one of his famous Stetson's, "just like Winston's."

"I hope I'll be able to wear it before too long," said Ike. "What wouldn't I give to get into a ten-cent poker game back home!"

When the General started dressing for dinner, Amon stayed on, talking with Butcher. Ike kept popping through the open door of his room in various stages of undress to make sure he wasn't missing any of the talk about things back home.

Two or three evenings later the telephone of the flat rang, and Butcher answered it.

"It's Carter," he said, holding his hand over the mouthpiece. "He wants to give a dinner for us at the Ritz on November eighth, or some other day next week."

Ike's face wrinkled in a huge grin.

"Tell him we're kind of tied up next week," he chuckled. "But if we have any free time we'll let him know."

The following day Ike left to establish his headquarters at Gibraltar.

CHAPTER FIFTEEN

"TORCH"

General Eisenhower stood in a gallery in the Rock of Gibraltar and looked through an embrasure cut in the wall of limestone. Almost directly below his feet was the inner harbor, with the naval dockyards and installations, where a couple of British destroyers and a cruiser were being repaired.

Beyond was the wide irregular circle of the bay. The convoys from England had begun passing through the strait, and anchored ships lay in the harbor as thick as logs behind a mill dam. There were British men-of-war, with the White Ensign at their sterns, and squatty merchantmen under the Red Duster. The Stars and Stripes flew from new-looking Liberty ships and the weird shapes of the American landing craft. An aircraft carrier was anchored far out; almost, it seemed, under those steep purple mountains beyond the strait—the mountains of Africa.

Looking down from that great height it was a scene of static beauty. Even the little waves appeared to be frozen in suspended motion. To Ike it seemed that for these moments time itself had stopped; it was a lapse into eternity out of the rush and worry of war. He felt swollen with an emotion that was too great to contain, for all those ships and men and machines were under his command, and many more were plunging through blue seas at his orders. His feeling was not, however, one of elation, but of a crushing weight upon his shoulders. So must Atlas, for whom those distant peaks were named, have staggered under the burden of the heavens.

One thought brought back a flicker of his old grin—the recognition that this was the wildest of all those improbabilities of war on which he sometimes pondered. Never in the furthest fancies of a daydreaming cadet had Ike pictured himself as commanding the British fortress of Gibraltar. Yet here he stood, in the most sacred citadel of the Empire, and his word was law.

The Commander in Chief had little time to dwell upon the strange quirks of his destiny; there was so much work to do. Impatiently, he snapped the spell and hurried downward toward the staff rooms.

Headquarters was in the very center of the Rock, with fourteen hundred feet of limestone piled above it. To reach it you went through the Tunnel, a gallery three-quarters of a mile long, which was so dank that drops of water dripped continually from its roof, like cold sweat from the brow of terror. The first time he went in, Ike walked sedately. After that he invariably ran the whole distance with his staff puffing along behind.

The staff rooms were air-conditioned and dry, protected by concrete casements. They had been especially prepared in advance with every possible convenience and mechanical aid. In his office, with the great maps on the wall, Ike worked unremittingly. His hours were from six-thirty in the morning until midnight; he held conferences and issued orders even while taking his bath.

It was a ticklish situation. Ships were crowded in the harbor and six hundred planes were massed wing to wing on the long narrow airfield on the flat strip of land that England owned under the sheer landward face of the rock, all within point-blank range of the Spanish guns on the hills that surrounded the fortress. And no one could be sure what Franco would do. Besides, this concentration of ships and planes was an open invitation to the Luftwaffe. Ike had steeled himself to take this essential gamble, but the risk stretched his nerves until they sang like piano wires.

He did not, however, show any sign of perturbation to the men who came to confer with him. There was a constant stream of them all day and most of the night. Mark Wayne Clark was with him a great part of the time, a tower of quiet strength. Sir Andrew Browne Cunningham, Commander of the Mediterranean Fleet, bounced in and out, wearing a white turtle-neck sweater. He was a stocky man with a quarter-deck manner. The English said of Cunningham that he was such an expert navigator that he could cut an egg in half with a battleship. He hated red tape and had been known, when in a hurry, to help coal his own ship —a man after Ike's heart.

Then there were swarms of generals: Fredendall, Ryder, and Anderson; agile little Jimmy Doolittle, commanding the new

secret Twelfth Air Force; bluff Lieutenant General Mason
MacFarlane, Commandant of the Fortress, and Brigadier General
Thomas Jefferson Davis, who was as southern as his name. Each
of them had problems which only the Commander in Chief
could solve. Ike listened and, with his lightning calculator ability
to size up a situation, unhesitatingly issued orders.

On the afternoon of November 7, less than half a day before
the hour known as H, a terrific complication arose. It was the
first of those extramilitary headaches by which Ike was to be
plagued throughout the long succeeding months. Word was
telephoned to Headquarters that General Giraud's flying boat had
been sighted.

"Thank God!" Ike said, unsuspectingly.

The tall wiry Frenchman was soon shown into the staff room
where Eisenhower awaited him with General Clark. Ike liked
Giraud at once. Although travel-worn and weary, he gave an
impression of alertness and almost youthful vigor, and there
were smile-wrinkles around his eyes. Ike thought that he was in
remarkably good shape for an old bird of sixty-three who had
escaped from Marseilles in an open boat, spent a couple of days
in a submarine and finished his voyage in a flying boat.

They exchanged greetings and a quick handshake, and then
Giraud, who spoke no English, began to talk in rapid French.
Ike's command of the language was rudimentary—he relied on
Clark to interpret—but what he managed to gather of the French
words made him dizzy.

"Wayne, is that guy saying what I think he is?" he demanded.

Clark's face was like a long exclamation point.

"I guess you've caught his drift," he said. "His exact words
were, 'General Giraud announces that he is ready to take over
command of the operation.'"

Lemaigre-Dubreuil, they discovered, had somehow allowed
Giraud to acquire the remarkable delusion that he was to command the armies of the United States and Britain. As the conversation developed, it appeared that the French General, who
always spoke of himself in the third person, had received the
further erroneous impression that an invasion of southern France
—his pet project—was also contemplated.

Ike was thunderstruck, but even in that moment he almost
laughed outright at the expression of horror on Clark's face.

"Wayne," he said, "we've got to be diplomatic about this."

Gently, as though he were facing the task of disappointing an eager child, Ike explained the real situation to the French General. It was a terrible blow. The fact that everything Ike said had to be translated was a further impediment to a meeting of minds. Giraud had come through an arduous experience sustained by his indomitable spirit and the expectation of realizing at last his cherished dream and his fond ambition to be the liberator of France. To hear that his hopes were illusory was a shattering experience.

At first he grew very angry. His eyes shot sparks and pride stiffened his back.

"General Giraud cannot accept less," he said.

Ike persisted, exerting all his tact and understanding. He expatiated on how difficult it would be for a French general, who spoke no English, to command an expedition made up wholly of American and British troops. He pointed out the impossibility of an invasion of France with the limited forces at his command. He argued and cajoled.

The processes of diplomacy extended far into the night. H-hour struck, and at selected places hundreds of miles apart, the wakes of the circling landing boats straightened out as they headed for the shores of Africa. Here and there on shadowy beaches a gun spoke, then batteries crashed in unison, and the gaily colored streamers of death reached for the charging boats. American commanders gave the signal, "Play ball!" and by the white flash of a hundred guns the "Torch" was lighted at last.

Still the three men argued in the quiet room under the Rock.

Finally Giraud, a man of sense and a true patriot, was won over. He agreed to accept the American offer of civil and military authority over the French in North Africa.

Ike had hardly bidden the exhausted General a friendly "Goodnight," and wiped the sweat from his own brow, when a startling message came from Bob Murphy. Admiral Jean François Darlan, Supreme Commander of the French Army and Navy, was in Allied hands in Algiers.

It was not until some days later that Ike heard the full story of the confused goings-on that night in Algiers. At one o'clock in the morning of November 8, Robert Murphy telephoned to General Alphonse Juin, who was the senior French officer present, in the absence of Governor General Yves Châtel, requesting an immediate interview. General Juin was huffy. Like *mon ami Pierrot* he growled, *"Je suis dans mon lit."*

"It is a matter of the utmost urgency."

"Can't it wait until morning?"

"No more than the tide."

"Come over, then."

As Murphy, with three of his faithful vice-consuls, approached Juin's villa on the hill, furtive figures in bizarre green trousers loomed out of the darkness. Lemaigre-Dubreuil had the place surrounded by boys of the pro-Ally *Chantiers de la Jeunesse.*

General Juin was incompletely dressed and completely annoyed. Murphy got to the point at once. The Americans, he said, were landing all up and down the coast. They came as liberators, to forestall a German invasion. It was to be hoped that there would be no fighting between old allies, and resistance would be quite useless. "We have half a million men," Murphy said, making his story good.

General Juin went as limp as a fatigued lettuce.

"We must telephone Darlan," he gasped.

"Darlan!" Murphy's eyebrows jumped halfway up his balding dome.

"But yes, he is here in Algiers, staying with Admiral Fenard. Yesterday he came to see his son, Alain, who has poliomyelitis."

Murphy thought fast. This changed everything. It might be either good or bad.

"We must assuredly speak with the Admiral," he said. "Invite him to come here."

Admiral Darlan stamped into the house in a fine fury. He was short and trim, and his chin jutted out like the ram of an old-fashioned warship. His bearing, manners and language were as rough as the North Atlantic.

"What the hell is this fantastic nonsense?" he demanded.

Murphy, who knew the Admiral well, suavely told his tale. Darlan was hard to convince, but when he finally accepted the truth, his rage soared to finer frenzies. A barrage of nautical oaths preceded the Admiral's opinion that "This will throw the whole damned place into the hands of the Germans."

Murphy repeated his whopper about half a million men.

"Where are they?"

The American was wondering about that too; there wasn't a sound from the port.

"Landing on beaches from here to Casablanca," he answered stoutly.

"Send for Fenard!"

A vice-consul was hastily dispatched, who found Vice-Admiral Raymond A. Fenard fully dressed, but quite bewildered.

"Admiral Darlan requests that you come to General Juin's house immediately."

"What is happening?" asked Fenard.

"The Americans are landing in great force," was the reply.

The French Admiral's bulging blue eyes lighted with pleasure and he nodded his big head energetically. "That makes me very happy."

"This is no time for you to be enjoying yourself," said the American, whose nerves had unsettled his diplomacy. "Let's get over there."

Admiral Fenard's sympathies had always been pro-Ally, and he was also inclined to favor de Gaulle. As soon as he joined the council at the villa, he exerted all his influence with Darlan in favor of reaching an agreement with the Americans. In the end Darlan was convinced and even became enthusiastic.

"I shall cable the Marshal in our secret code," he decided, "urging him to collaborate with America. I have high hopes that he will agree."

The cable was dispatched. Marshal Henri Philippe Pétain's reply was an angry order to continue resistance. However, the fifth column work had been good. General Mast and his pro-Ally officers disorganized French resistance. The Blida and Maison Blanche airfields were neatly captured by picked combat teams, and Hurricanes and Spitfires from Gibraltar landed with precision timing a few minutes later. Meanwhile Lemaigre-Dubreuil's green-trousered boys had seized the government buildings. At 5:15 on Sunday afternoon, Darlan gave the "cease fire" order, but it was effective only in Algiers. At Oran and Casablanca they were slugging it out toe to toe.

As Ike read the decoded messages that poured into the staff rooms at Gibraltar that Sunday afternoon, he knew that the operation was going well. Algiers was ours with hardly any loss. Fredendall was meeting stiff resistance at Oran, but was moving in. At Casablanca there was a hell of a fight, which had, however, been anticipated and discounted.

The situation was satisfactory from a military point of view, but Ike could never quite take that angle, and he was far from satisfied. The thought of those boys' dying so needlessly on the beaches and in the coastal hills oppressed his spirit. He had hoped, against the probabilities, that the French would make only a token resistance, but the bullets that the batteries at Oran and Casablanca were showering on our troops were certainly not love tokens. It was horrible to him that we should be fighting our ancient friends and allies. Every American and every Frenchman who died in that unnatural battle was lost without reason; every moment it continued imperiled the greater plan. It must be stopped, by whatever means, at the earliest possible moment. He decided to play his ace of trumps.

General Giraud had already issued a proclamation to the French in North Africa. Early on Monday, Eisenhower sent him in a Fortress to Algiers, at the same time issuing a proclamation of his own which embodied his hopes and beliefs. It read: "General Giraud has arrived in Algiers from France. It can be expected that his presence will bring about a cessation of scattered resistance, which is tragic between soldiers who have the same enemy. General Giraud has assumed the leadership of the French movement to prevent Axis aggression in North Africa and will organize the French North African Army, again to take up the fight side by side with the forces of the United Nations for the defeat of Germany and Italy and the liberation of France and her Empire."

It went on to state that the Allied Commander in Chief would support General Giraud and that the government of the United States had pledged itself to assist in providing arms for "this new French Army."

A few hours later Ike sent Wayne Clark and his staff in another Fortress to represent him personally.

Dispatches from Algiers quickly indicated that everything was far from satisfactory on the diplomatic front. Ike's ace of trumps turned out to be a deuce in the game as they played it in Africa. But fate had put a joker in his hands.

Giraud had to go into hiding to escape arrest by the French authorities; a proclamation from de Gaulle in London was completely ineffectual. The reason was that the officers of the French North African Army and the officers and men alike of the Navy were professional military men. Had they followed Giraud or de Gaulle, they would have imperiled their commissions, their seniority and, above all, their precious pensions. They would obey none but legitimate authority. Darlan represented that in their eyes.

When Clark, in a half-track, rumbled into the uneasy city of Algiers, he could find no one with whom to negotiate but Darlan. He cabled the situation to his chief. As Ike read the cable, he knew he was in a spot, but how hot it was he had yet to learn. Though he subscribed to Clausewitz's doctrine that war is an extension of politics, he nevertheless felt that when the issue was joined, politics must wait on the necessities of battle. He knew that Darlan was regarded as the archcollaborator by many people in America and England, but he would have negotiated with the archfiend himself if he had thought that gentleman could deliver the goods and save the lives of his soldiers. Roosevelt and Churchill, consulted by cable, also took the realistic view, and Clark was given permission to try to negotiate with Darlan.

Ike's cable ordered Clark to demand an immediate armistice on all fronts, on pain of a total attack by the Americans in tremendous force. The bluff worked. A French officer said to General Clark, "When I think of the enormous forces you command, I tremble."

With a face like a totem pole, Clark replied, "It even frightens me."

There were only 10,000 Allied troops in Algiers.

Carrying out the bluff, Clark, contrary to his gentle nature, took a high tone with Darlan at their meeting on Tuesday, November 10. The military situation strengthened his hand: Ike had cabled to Patton that morning:

Dear Georgie:
   Algiers has been ours for two days. Oran defenses are crumbling rapidly with naval shore batteries surrendering. Only tough nut to crack is in your hands. Crack it open quickly.   Ike.

Clark laid the armistice terms on the table—liberal they assuredly were—and in effect said, "Sign or else!" He had angry words with Darlan, whose pride was touched. Fenard trotted from one to the other, pouring soothing-syrup words. Reports from the fighting indicated that Oran was indeed crumbling and Patton was mounting an offensive at Casablanca. In the afternoon Darlan signed the armistice. Almost as his pen traced the letters, Oran fell. Noguès at Casablanca obdurately refused to accept oral orders to cease firing, and a French airplane sped through the night, anxiously dodging Luftwaffe and Allied planes alike, to carry the written word. On Wednesday morning Ike sighed his relief as resistance ended.

But the trouble wasn't quite over. Befuddled old Pétain reacted violently to the news from Africa. He fired Darlan and ordered him to turn authority over to General Noguès of Casablanca. The Admiral sent for Clark, and said, "In the face of this, I must revoke the armistice."

"I shall not allow it," Clark said.

"Then you must arrest me," Darlan declared, with a twinkle in his eyes.

Clark saw the point and obliged him.

At this time Giraud popped out of his hole and demanded that authority be turned over to him. Realizing that to do so would precipitate civil war, Clark refused.

Darlan was not long under arrest. About noon, word came that the Germans were marching into unoccupied France. The Admiral immediately decided that Pétain was acting under duress and declared that he would collaborate with the Americans. He issued an order to the French Fleet at Toulon to sail to join the Allies. From Gibraltar Eisenhower also sent an appeal to the French Navy to join his forces.

Neither of these appeals had any effect. Perhaps the French naval officers delayed too long, or perhaps their peculiar sense of honor led them to scuttle their ships rather than join either side.

For three days Ike had been reading contradictory dispatches from Algiers and trying to make sense out of the kaleidoscopic shifts of French politics. Then one definite fact emerged; Darlan had thrown in with the United Nations. On receiving this news, Ike's mind turned to the possibility of completing the original design. He needed Tunis, the nearest port to Italy through which Axis troops would pour to defend the remains of their African empire and reinforce Rommel's army retreating across Tripoli. If he could secure it, the enemy would be blocked and Rommel caught like a fox between two packs of hounds. It was worth a tremendous gamble, and he took it.

Darlan was persuaded to order General Barré, Admiral Esteva and Vice-Admiral Derrien at Tunis and Bizerte to resist the expected German attack. Eisenhower directed the British First Army, at Algiers, with some American units, to re-embark and occupy Bougie to the eastward. General Anderson acted promptly. He took Bougie that same day—Wednesday, November 11—and in a wild overland dash, units of his army reached Bône, nearly two hundred miles east of Algiers, on November 12. The race for Tunis was on.

Meanwhile it was absolutely essential to have a stable French authority in North Africa. The safety of our tenuous lines of communication demanded it, the whole success of our enterprise depended upon it. Since we came, not as conquerors, but as liberators, the French had to set up their own government. But, Ike thought, for God's sake let them hurry.

With the cessation of hostilities most of the ranking French officials had hurried to Algiers. Yves Châtel, the Governor General, had returned. Noguès arrived from Casablanca on Thursday, November 12. But they seemed unable to do anything but wrangle. In exasperation Eisenhower wired Clark that the French must choose a leader or he would set up a complete military government. He also sent a message to the French officials in which the strength of his feeling burst the conventions of official language and produced an impassioned appeal to their patriotism:

"Valuable moments have been wasted trying to bring Frenchmen together. What do these men want? Are they not content with leadership in the great movement to raise France from bondage? . . . They have the opportunity to achieve immortality in the hearts of their countrymen by uniting in the common aim. . . . They must not abandon France in her moment of despair by engaging in selfish fighting. . . ."

On receipt of this message, the French leaders desired to hold a secret conference. Clark agreed, provided they would admit General Giraud, who had been kept on the outside looking in. He was accepted and the conference room doors closed on the embattled Frenchmen.

But though the doors were shut they could not drown the angry voices within the room. The sounds of that epic argument echoed through the sleeping city to arouse the wondering Arabs in the crooked alleys of the Kasbah. Morning came, and still no decision had been reached.

On that day, November 13, Ike decided that it was time to take a hand in the game. With Admiral Cunningham, he started for Algiers in a Fortress.

Down the long, narrow field at Gibraltar the great plane raced. Ike, looking upward, saw the sheer face of the great Rock cutting off the sky. Then they were airborne, and the Fortress swept out of its shadow over the brilliant bay, still crowded with shipping. The incredible blue of the Mediterranean opened before them. Softly exquisite was the shining veil which concealed the engines of death beneath it and bore the battered ships on the highway of victory. They flew high over it, skirting the southern coast, where the foam made a gleaming white border between the blue of the sea and the gold of the sand. To the right the purple mountains of Africa rolled in gigantic waves to a mysterious horizon.

It seemed quiet in the plane—despite the roaring engines— quieter by far than the guarded staff rooms deep underground, where the telegraph messages clamored ceaselessly. Ike was glad to have these few hours for thought. It seemed too soon when he saw the white city of Algiers, like a great marble amphitheater on the curving hills around its bay. But those moments in the air had restored serenity.

They tell of the almost miraculous effect of General Eisenhower's presentation to the Council. General Clark, forced by circumstances to play a conqueror's part against his inclination, had riled the French and set their pride on edge. Eisenhower came to them in a different role, with a glow of genuine friendliness. That engaging grin of his needed no translation; surprised, the French surrendered to his charm. They resumed their secret deliberations in a more reasonable mood and before the day was done came up with a proposition. Darlan was to be High Commissioner, representing the French State, and Giraud would be Commander in Chief of the Army, under Darlan. There was to be an Imperial Council composed of the governors and residents of French Africa and the ranking military and naval officers.

So it was to be Darlan again. However sensible the arrangement seemed in Africa, Eisenhower knew that there would be trouble in the outside world because of the Admiral's reputation as a collaborationist. He sent urgent telegrams to Washington setting forth the situation, and before he made the agreement, the American State Department and the British Foreign Office approved it.

Whatever one may think of the poker-faced French Admiral, and however dubious his past conduct, from that moment forward Darlan played straight. He gave the Allies the benefit of his technical knowledge by making the dispositions for the unloading of the innumerable ships bringing supplies and reinforcements. Fifty of Eisenhower's original armada had been lost, the majority by bombing in the congested harbors, but many times that number had to be unloaded. On November 15, two days after the settlement and only a week after they were fighting the Americans, Darlan ordered the French Army to march into Tunisia to protect the right flank of the advancing Allies.

Perhaps the most important service he rendered was on the very day following the agreement. Governor General Pierre Boisson of Dakar had arrived in Algiers. Boisson was a tall, one-legged veteran of a hundred battles, who in 1940 had knocked de Gaulle's expedition against his province into a cocked hat. So long as he held Dakar, it would be a costly job to take it. He was a tough customer, and he came in a skeptical mood.

Eisenhower, Cunningham and Darlan gave a joint luncheon party for the peg-leg general. They plied him with food, argument and charm, and by the force of these powerful persuasions they brought him around. Thus was the most important port on the Atlantic coast of Africa, that cannon pointed at the heart of America, delivered to the Allies free of cost, with the magnificent French battleship *Richelieu* and numerous smaller vessels thrown in.

Not all of Ike's first days in Algiers were harassed by the intricacies of politics. There were pleasant interludes. Beaming from ear to ear, he pinned the third star of a lieutenant general on the shoulder of his old friend, Mark Wayne Clark. Georgie Patton blew in flamboyantly from Casablanca in his private Fortress, escorted by six Lightnings. Patton stamped into Eisenhower's headquarters with the pearl-handled six-shooters swinging against his thighs and spurs jingling on his cavalry boots. His bald dome fringed with white hair shone like freshly waxed parquet.

"Hello, Ike," he roared, "I guess I'm one of God's most favorite people. When I got to Casablanca I found the French had all their navigation lights on to guide a convoy in from Dakar. They showed us exactly where we should go!"

Patton had been in the thick of things. When one landing boat had been shot out from under him, he got ashore in another and led his beloved armor in a tank, shooting his head out of the hatch like a turtle and bellowing orders. His men called him "Flash Gordon" or the "Green Hornet."

"Say, our tanks are a hell of a lot better than anything I've seen so far," Patton went on. "And that new 105-millimeter self-propelled gun is a honey. It knocked a hole in the fort at Lyautey big enough for a company to march through."

"That's good to hear," Ike said. "I'm glad you didn't get hurt, Georgie."

Patton laughed.

"It was a real nice fight," he said, "and now French and Americans are getting on damn friendly."

That night the Germans came over Algiers. Their bombs crashed along the docks and among the ships with great flashes of white light that were followed by the crimson glare of fire. Flak rose to meet them from the tiered circle of the city, concentrating toward a point in the sky. The bright lines of tracer bullets and the colored balls of the 37-millimeter shells looked like streamers from a gigantic Maypole, while the flashes of shell bursts from the five-inch guns danced all over the sky.

As Ike watched the show from the balcony of a hotel in the hills, his ears vibrating with that vast cacophony of explosions, the earth-shaking crash of the bombs, the ear-splitting crack of artillery and the spasmodic chatter of automatic weapons, he had an ironic grin for himself. He had served in the United States Army for thirty-one years during two wars, and he was Commander in Chief of a great and growing Allied army engaged in the business of conquering a continent, and yet—this was the first time he had ever really been under fire.

On November 16 it became necessary for Eisenhower to return to his headquarters at Gibraltar. The Flying Fortress, *Ramblin' Reck,* with Lieutenant A. E. Aenchbacker, recently of Georgia Tech, as pilot, waited on the muddy field at Blida under an angry sky. Lieutenant Aenchbacker paced up and down under the nose of his ship, glancing alternately at his wrist watch and at the heavens, and deriving no comfort from either. The General was damned late.

The copilot, sitting in the open door with his legs hanging out, advised his superior to take it easy.

"He's held up somewhere. We probably won't get off at all."

"We sure won't if he doesn't come soon," Aenchbacker agreed. "That field at Gib is bad enough on a nice clear day, but doggone if I want to try it on a misty evenin'."

"Don't worry, they won't take any chances with General Ike."

At the last possible moment a muddy jeep shot between the gates, wallowed across the field, and pulled up under the wing of the plane. A big, bundled-up figure jumped out and splashed through the standing water. Aenchbacker formally saluted the three stars on the rakish overseas cap.

"Sorry to keep you waiting, Lieutenant," General Ike said genially. "Think we can get through?"

"I reckon so, sir," said the pilot dubiously, "if you want to take a chance."

"I don't want to," said Ike, "but it looks like I'll have to."

The Fortress waddled across the slough of the field, heaved itself clear of the mud, and headed out over the water. There was nothing gentle about the Mediterranean that day. Slate-gray waves snapped fangs of foam at the dark bellies of racing clouds. The northwest wind roared down the funnel of the sea, cutting the speed of the plane by forty miles. After two hours daylight began to fail.

Aenchbacker turned the controls over to his copilot and made his way aft to where the General sat, studying reports. He saluted, grabbing the back of a seat as the plane heaved to a gust.

"It looks lousy ahead, sir. Do you want to turn back to Oran? We won't have sufficient fuel after this."

The General looked keenly at him, and Aenchbacker noted the intense blue of his eyes.

"What do they say at Gibraltar?"

"We can't raise them on the radio, sir."

The General's eyes seemed to get bluer; he was weighing the chances against the vital things he had to do. At Oran he would be more or less out of touch. He thought of Anderson's frail spearhead on the road to Tunis, which had reported contact with enemy patrols. Would the French and their few elements of American armor get there in time to protect the flank? Did Anderson need reinforcement and where could it come from? There were a thousand things to do at Gibraltar. Communications were bad at Algiers, the cables choked by outgoing messages. Oran might be worse.

"What would you do if I were not aboard?" he asked.

"I reckon I'd try it, sir."

"Then go ahead," the General said.

The sky came down toward the sea and dirty gray shreds of

cloud ripped past the gun blisters. Then they were in the fluff, their wingtips lost in the darkening mist. Aenchbacker took her "upstairs" to get above it, but the stratum of clouds was very thick. He decided to come down and try to fly contact. When the altimeter registered five hundred, he still could not see the water. He took her back up as the navigator reported that they were approaching the strait—"if I am on the beam."

Aenchbacker imagined the sea narrowing to the gate. He could almost feel the mountains shouldering through the clouds, and his hands were wet on the wheel. Glancing over his shoulder, he saw a tall figure at the entrance to the navigator's cabin. With an apologetic smile, he said, "I'm afraid we're in a spot, sir."

The General grinned back and said in a steady voice, "Just do your best."

But Ike didn't feel steady inside. He remembered Bill Lee grinning at him in the cabin of the little plane at Baguio, saying, "We aren't going to make it, Colonel." Now, as then, it seemed a silly way to die.

Suddenly Gibraltar came in strong on the radio. They were mad with anxiety down there.

"Proceed back to Oran."

"Not enough fuel. What have you got?" Aenchbacker asked.

"Ceiling one-fifty, visibility four hundred yards."

"Light up. I'm coming in."

Then he spoke curtly over his shoulder. "General, strap yourself in."

Ike obeyed.

He heard the engines slow and the wind whistle free as the plane glided down in a steeply banked spiral. He thought of the narrow field, a forty-mile wind quartering it, and the sheer face of the Rock cutting off the sky. It didn't seem possible that they could make it. There were all sorts of jumbled pictures in his head: Mamie in a gay print dress, John saluting as he said goodbye, the maps on the wall of Headquarters in the Rock. He wondered if Wayne Clark could handle this business if anything happened. Or whom else they'd pick.

Then he saw a glow of light and realized that they must be almost down. He braced himself for the smash. That limestone would be a lot harder than the pines at Baguio. There was a vibration through the plane, a rumbling of wheels on tarmac . . .

As the Fortress stopped rolling, men swarmed toward it. An irate colonel climbed aboard and went for the pilot.

"What the hell do you think you're doing?" he roared. "Why didn't you obey orders to set down at Oran?"

"Didn't get them in time," replied Aenchbacker, scowling.

The kid looks all in, Ike thought.

"Lieutenant Aenchbacker was obeying *my* orders," he said. "And what's more, he's a helluva good pilot!"

The boy from Georgia Tech grinned gratefully at his general. "Well, anyhow we made it," he said.

CHAPTER SIXTEEN

CHAIRMAN OF THE BOARD

On November 18, 1942, nearly three weeks ahead of schedule, General Eisenhower moved his headquarters from Gibraltar to Algiers; he could no longer stand being that far from the fighting. It seemed to him that things could be more easily handled on the spot, that everything would be less complicated. He soon learned he was jumping out of the skillet into the flame, for the next three months in Algiers were the most difficult and nerve-racking of his entire life so far. Even Ike's equable disposition could not throw off the cares that piled up on him; he began to show signs of strain.

Fortunately, his physical environment could hardly have been better. Headquarters were established in a comfortable little hotel on a steep-terraced hillside behind the city. Ike's own office was in a small room whose windows looked out over the white houses of Algiers to the port, where the ships were crowded behind the long breakwater. Beyond was the wide curve of the bay surrounded by gentle green hills with white villas gleaming between the trees; and farther still was the sea with all its exquisite tones of blue, like a changeable-silk coverlet. Ike called his office "Grand Central Station" because so many people kept pouring through its three doors.

The General's living quarters, which were in a house still farther up the hill, consisted of one of two Moorish villas enclosed by a high white wall, the second villa being occupied by Mickey and Admiral Cunningham, who had become Ike's close friend. The first house, where Ike, Butcher and Telek lived, had plenty of servants' rooms but only two master bedrooms. When important visitors like General Marshall came, Ike had to give up his room to them.

The lower floor, however, was magnificent. There was an elaborate salon with a big fireplace and, by happy chance, a piano. The hall was even more flamboyant, with Saracenic arches, a tessellated marble floor and a grand staircase. Ike said that this pseudo-Moorish splendor gave him the willies, and he always used the back door.

Though the appurtenances of his life were comfortable, Ike maintained almost as strenuous a schedule as he had in the first days at Gibraltar. He got up at seven, and things began to happen immediately. Usually two or more of his generals were with him for breakfast—Clark and Patton, and perhaps Fredendall or Jimmy Doolittle. By eight he was at the office. He lunched at 12:20 at the officers' mess, talking earnestly all through the meal, trying to find out what the junior officers thought.

If he was lucky, Ike got back home around a quarter of seven, but did not find much relaxation. Usually he brought more generals home with him: General Sir Harold Alexander, from Egypt, and Anderson, back from the front. On other evenings it would be a French Admiral, Darlan or Fenard, accompanied by Robert Murphy. On rare and wonderful evenings, "Toohey" Spaatz was the only guest, and then for a little Ike could sit quiet while his old West Point friend strummed out favorite tunes on his cherished guitar.

Bedtime came theoretically at 10:30, and Ike's saving attribute was that he could go to sleep instantly, no matter how charged with tension. But even this refuge was subject to capricious interruption. Frequently an urgent call would get him up for an hour or more of telephone conversation.

When General Marshall came to stay at the villa after the Casablanca conference, he was troubled by Eisenhower's strained appearance.

"You're to take more time off," he said. "Get in some horseback riding, take some exercise. Don't go to the office until nine-thirty, and leave at five. That's an order."

Ike followed this régime for just one day. Then General Clark came in from a tour of the front and the new schedule was forgotten. One of his aides, Major Meecham, gloomily said to a member of Marshall's staff, "I wonder what General Marshall will think of this breach of orders."

"Think nothing of it," said the other. "General Marshall makes up nice schedules for himself and never sticks to them."

It was not the long hours or the hard work that plowed the new furrows in Ike's face; it was the nervous strain of his vast responsibilities. The military matters he could have coped with, though he was in a difficult position, never before having held command of an army in the field. But it is probable that no commander has ever faced so complex a task since Napoleon attempted simultaneously to conduct his campaigns and govern all Europe.

It is the American tradition that our generals shall not dabble in politics, and Ike had kept singularly free of such entanglements. Now he had to learn to be a politician in a hurry.

In those turbulent days, the civil administration of that great, heterogeneous population of Arabs, Berbers, Frenchmen, Spaniards, various European refugees and Jewish residents, not to mention the semi-independent state of Morocco, was a problem that might have stumped Machiavelli. Darlan and his Council were charged with this task, but they needed firm guidance and lots of help. In the first place, not all the French were sincerely co-operative. Darlan did his honest best, but by the necessities of the situation his administration had been saddled with a number of hang-overs from the Vichy régime, some of whom tried to play a double game. Yves Châtel was a questionable character, and Noguès pretty intractable. Other lesser men were secretly pro-Axis. The American Commander in Chief kept a firm grip on the situation, but it was contrary to his nature; he liked to trust men, not to spy upon them.

Another harassing factor was the violent criticism of the "Darlan Deal" from partially informed sources in England and at home.

In London, General de Gaulle viewed with alarm and the press criticized cautiously; but the most violent reaction was in America. Owing to the fact that all lines of communication were jammed with outgoing messages, little news from home reached Ike. He had no idea of the intensity of the storm until his brother Milton arrived in Algiers.

Ike's youngest brother had become deputy director of the Office of War Information in the summer of 1942. Early in December the President sent him to Algiers on a confidential mission, though for his own agency he was there to help establish the machinery of psychological warfare which was to be used especially against the Italians. His coming was a source of great comfort to Ike—it was great to have Milton in the adjoining bedroom. They could visit even after they had gone to bed. In the evening Milton would sit at the great piano and play the tunes which carried them back to the little music room in Abilene: the March from *Tannhäuser*, "Bells of St. Mary's," "I Passed by Your Window." As he sat in his deep chair with his eyes closed, humming, Ike seemed to see his mother sitting at the old upright piano in the light of the oil lamps; he could almost smell the sweetness which an evening breeze brought through the open windows from the summer fields of Kansas.

But the news Milton brought was far from soothing. Back home they were accusing Ike of political bungling because he had made a military agreement with Darlan. Even the President's reassurance that the agreement was purely a temporary military one had not checked the criticism. The newspaper *PM* had been particularly virulent, and other "liberal" papers had joined in with the ill-considered criticism.

Inasmuch as news was not reaching Algiers, this was Ike's first knowledge of the public reaction to the Darlan arrangement. He was deeply hurt. More than any of his multitude of cares, this mistrust by his own people oppressed him.

"What is the real trouble?" he demanded. "Are people suspicious of my motives? How can they be? All my life I've been utterly devoted to our American free system. Why wouldn't I be? Democracy gave me the best education in the world and a chance to use whatever talents God gave me. What in hell is this war for, but to beat fascism and the autocracy that now threaten our own freedom? Don't you suppose every man at the front knows that?"

Of course Ike didn't have to tell Milton, who was steeped in the same democratic philosophy and who now heads a great midwestern college that typifies the American free system. But in all honesty Milton was compelled to report that many back home thought that even temporary dealings with a man like Darlan were a betrayal of principle.

"I'd never compromise the principles for which my country stands," Ike shot back.

And then Milton opened Ike's eyes still further. He reported that most of the news reaching the United States was coming via Radio Maroc, a station at Rabat, which was still in the hands of pro-Axis sympathizers. Direct communication from Algiers to the United States was not yet functioning.

Ike issued a quick order. "Get that radio station under American control at once," he told an aide. "See to it that it reports the truth. The people in the United States and Great Britain are entitled to the truth—and the whole truth, too!"

Then for a moment he leaned back in his chair. He thought of the gamble he had taken when he set out to conquer a continent with 107,000 men. Facing him had been 100,000 French troops, who might have been either enemies or allies. Besides, Spain had 145,000 picked men in Spanish Morocco. If Franco had thrown in with Hitler, there were at least six German divisions behind the Pyrenees, ready to move quickly down through the Iberian Peninsula. Rommel was retreating toward Tunisia, and Axis troops were speeding for Bizerte and Tunis by air, surface ship, and submarine. The danger of a great pincers movement had been tremendous.

"I was bluffing a flush on two pairs," Ike said aloud, "and it worked through a great stroke of luck. I drew Darlan, a joker that filled my hand. Only *he* had the authority to order the French to stop fighting, and he was the only man on whom the others could agree to form a civil government. You see, this country has suffered an intellectual blackout ever since the fall of France; the people have heard only what the Germans and Vichy wanted them to hear. Hence, they have believed in the inevitability of an Axis victory. They were therefore—the military, I mean—not prepared to accept any but the constituted authorities. Contrary to all our advance information, Giraud could develop no following. The army would not accept de Gaulle. Chaos threatened at every turn, and only Darlan could prevent that."

Ike leaned forward and pointed his finger at Milton for emphasis.

"Do you realize that our lines of communication stretch from Casablanca to Constantine and beyond? There are viaducts, bridges, telephone and telegraph lines, and hundreds of other essential things along that route. Who guards them? Frenchmen! Who maintains order in the cities, towns, villages? Frenchmen! If we had been compelled, first, to slug it out in entering the country and, second, to use our own troops to maintain internal order and keep our lines of communication open, we could have been set back in this war at least six full months and it would have cost us thousands and thousands of lives. All these things and a hundred more had to be taken into consideration when we made the military agreement with Darlan. Do you call this betrayal?"

"Of course not," said Milton. Then he added, "My only suggestion is that at the earliest possible opportunity the Signal Corps make it possible for all the American and British correspondents to get their dispatches directly to the two countries. People want the truth, all of it."

"That's right, and they'll get it if we have to work night and day to get the communication stations functioning," Ike said. "Every correspondent here, representing the free press and radio of the two free countries, will have every facility put at his disposal so that he can get his stuff out as fast as he can write it! After all, this war is a war of all our people and the facts belong to them. You can depend upon their judgment if they have the truth!"

That night Radio Maroc was placed under American management. Ten days later, a new communication station was opened and put at the disposal of news correspondents and radio commentators. All censorship was lifted, except what was essential to protect military operations.

Where the French needed the greatest amount of help was on the economic front. The Germans had gutted the country through their trading association, which used barter, false rates of exchange, and every possible form of economic exploitation to strip it of everything portable that they could use. By the time the Americans arrived, the whole economy of North Africa had bogged down. Normally a food-exporting region, it faced starvation.

Eisenhower's biggest extramilitary job was to help the French get things going; in this his experience with industrial mobilization in Washington in the 1930's proved invaluable. Sufficient American food had to be distributed to hold hunger at bay until the African farms began producing again. Machinery repair parts had to be provided and technical advice given to restore agriculture. Certain essential consumer goods had to be brought in. This was not philanthropy, but enlightened self-interest; if North African economy could be restored, it would pay big dividends.

It was lucky that Ike had never succumbed to the narrowing influence of military specialization—that he had kept the civilian

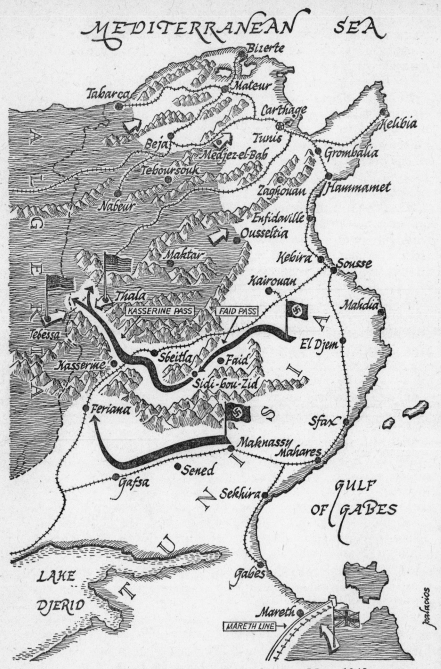

The Tunisian Campaign, February–May, 1943

point of view—for the job he faced required the utmost tact and firmness and a sympathetic understanding of social problems. No man who was insensitive to the feelings and needs of the people could have been successful. And successful Ike was.

It is a matter of record that within a year of the occupation, North African production was 85 per cent of normal, and by the middle of 1944 was running well above prewar figures. Our money and food and goods were well invested. This is one place where lend-lease has cost us nothing. We have been fully repaid by imports of phosphate, cobalt, iron ore and other precious products of the country, and by sixteen million dollars in cash.

These remarkable results were not, of course, the work of any one man. The French labored zealously to repair their shattered country, and under the Commander in Chief was a staff of American experts and technicians, headed by Robert Murphy. What Eisenhower did was to hold things together. He welded men of different and antagonistic nationalities into harmonious teams; he soothed injured feelings and settled disputed points with justice and decision. His personality gave French, British, Arabs and Americans alike a sense of confidence in the future and a faith in the fairness of his administration. He didn't try to run things himself, but he inspired others to do their best.

While the Commander in Chief was acting as mediator for the acrimonies of French politics and as receiver in bankruptcy of a prostrate national economy, he was faced by a deteriorating military situation. All through November and December, 1942, while the persistent rain turned the whole country into a dismal swamp, the race for Tunis continued. By November 25, the British First Army with American reinforcements was at Tebourba and Medjez el Bab, only thirty miles from Tunis. Three days later they took the airfield at Djeida. Farther south, a light Allied mechanized spearhead reached Pont-du-Fahs, while Giraud's French Army, reinforced by American parachute troops, skirmished through the rugged mountains around Sbeitla and Gafsa, guarding the right flank of the thin Allied line. But this was as far as we got.

Ever since Admirals Esteva and Derrien, preferring Pétain's orders to Darlan's, had thrown open the great ports of Tunis and Bizerte to the Germans, enemy reinforcements had been pouring in by ship and plane across the narrow straits from Sicily. German tanks roared out against the light Allied spearheads and drove them from Tebourba. The First Army clung to Medjez el Bab by its fingernails. We had lost the first heat of the race.

The contest now became one of supply and reinforcement. As rapidly as possible, Eisenhower was sending men and matériel to the front. Fredendall's armor and the 1st and 34th Infantry Divisions were being shipped up from the Oran area, but logistics favored the Germans. Their line of supply was only eighty miles long, across the straits from Sicily. Our main port was Casablanca, a thousand miles away. The narrow-gauge railway which ran from Casablanca to Tunisia via Algiers could handle only 1,000 tons of supplies a day—the army needed 10,000—and Algiers, like all our other Mediterranean ports, was open to aerial bombing and blockading by submarines, while Philippeville and Bône, the ports nearest Tunisia, were small and inadequate. The roads leading to the front were built for light traffic and in a short time were completely pulverized by the heavy military vehicles. In fact, this logistical difficulty plagued the Allies through the whole campaign. Eventually we did have 500,000 men in Africa but inasmuch as we were never able to supply more than 250,000 at the front, until the very end, we were outnumbered by the enemy.

The worst feature of the situation, from Eisenhower's point of view, was our lack of decent airfields. The Germans were operating from the splendid, all-weather fields at Tunis and Bizerte, while the persistent rain drowned our temporary fields under three feet of standing water. Those fighter planes which did manage to take off looked like flying boats as they raced through the water in clouds of spray. For this reason it was impossible to give our troops adequate fighter protection.

Christmas Eve, 1942, was for Ike one of the blackest days of the campaign. He had ordered a grand attack on Tunis to start that morning. It was the last chance of a quick victory, for the Germans were getting a thousand men a day across the straits, and building up stocks of matériel much faster than the Allies. The rain and fog, which bogged down Eisenhower's transport and grounded his planes, were an advantage to the Germans; for bad weather enabled their convoys to slip past the British Navy and their Junkers transport planes to hide in the clouds until they reached the permanent Tunisian airfields. Already the First Army was outnumbered by the enemy and one-third of the entire

Luftwaffe had been transferred to the Mediterranean Theater.

Each day now Eisenhower's position grew worse; he knew that any delay would make attack impossible. This was the final heat of the race.

Ike—and Telek—came to General Anderson's headquarters at Souk-el-Khemis to observe the attack in person. Ike was almost gay in his relief at getting away from the politics of Algiers and being once more with troops. Though the rain had held off for a few days, it was cold and dreary. Ike wore what he called his "goop suit," which consisted of overall-like trousers with bottoms that buttoned around his shoes, a heavy battle jacket and a knitted helmet. Looking a little like a teddy bear, he drove in a jeep all over the front on the eve of the attack. He inspected the Coldstream Guards and the Grenadier Guards in the hills at Medjez el Bab, and the units of Fredendall's 1st Armored Division waiting by the roadside to charge the deadly German 88s. On the airfield at Souk-el-Arba, he saw Spitfires, Hurricanes and Lightnings taking off in clouds of spray and he visited the jaunty British parachute troops, whose battle cry, "Yo Ho Mohammed!" had the hair-raising quality of the Rebel yell of our Civil War. As the troops cheered him, he grinned and waved, and wished them luck. But the luck was out.

That night the rain began again—a tropical downpour that turned fields, roads and airstrips into bogs. Mechanized equipment was stalled; trucks could not go through, and even the infantry could hardly lift their feet from the sticky mud. In Anderson's tented headquarters, where the rain beat like muffled drums on the canvas roof, the generals met, and each read in the other's eyes the knowledge of defeat. With a heavy heart, Ike countermanded the order to attack: his daring gamble had failed, and ahead lay weary months of fighting. He knew the chance had been worth taking, though he had never underestimated the difficulties. Bad weather, bad communications and bad luck had weighted the odds against him. The race for Tunis was lost.

On that dismal Christmas Eve, Ike still lingered at the front, driving through the rain to those sectors he had not yet inspected, and visiting the wounded in the field hospitals. When he got back to Anderson's headquarters, another blow fell. Admiral Darlan had been assassinated.

Back to Algiers he went quickly, before the pot of French politics could boil over in the heat of this new flame. Air transport was impossible—not even a gull could take off from Souk-el-Arba. The only vehicle that could travel was a jeep.

For a day and a night Ike slammed through the rain over the pitted, muddy roads in the little car, taking turns at the wheel with Butcher and a sergeant. During those weary hours he had plenty of opportunity to think, and his thoughts were grim. It was a time to try his resolution.

The Germans, firmly established at Tunis, had to be driven out by a major campaign, and now his rear was threatened. Whatever anyone might think of Darlan, he had given North Africa a stable government. What the repercussions from his death would be no man could say. It might plunge the country into civil war and wreck those long, dangerous supply lines by which the First Army lived, leaving it helpless before the rising German power. The very circumstances of the Admiral's death were unknown to Eisenhower. Perhaps his assassination was part of a vast conspiracy, and even now the forest fire of revolt was sweeping across Africa. Perhaps the pot had not waited to boil. . . .

Once during the drive the thought of an historical parallel brought a grim smile to Ike's face. Sheridan galloping his charger to save a lost battle was certainly a more glamorous figure than his modern counterpart, tearing through the rain in a mud-spattered jeep to join a political affray.

When he arrived in Algiers, battered and weary from his bucking jeep, Ike found the situation not so bad as he had feared. Darlan's assassin, a young university student named Fernand Bonnier de la Chappelle, had apparently acted on his own in a fit of mental instability. Possibly he had been encouraged by others with ulterior motives, but it was certain that there was no general conspiracy back of him. Chappelle was hastily tried and executed by the French.

General Clark had handled the situation with firmness and tact. A meeting of the Imperial Council had been called and they were debating when Eisenhower arrived at the uneasy city. Upon their decision rested the fate of the whole campaign and of the greater designs being formulated; for if they chose badly, the resulting confusion would delay all operations.

For a while the Council seemed to lean toward the intractable Noguès, but wiser advice prevailed. Without doubt the confidence that Eisenhower inspired in the members of the Council helped to bring them to a choice they knew he would prefer.

They remembered gratefully that he had held out, against the advice of his staff, for rearming the French troops with American weapons. In the end, General Henri Giraud was unanimously elected high commissioner, while retaining his position as commander in chief of the French military and naval forces.

Giraud's administration got off to a good start. He released political prisoners and fired Yves Châtel, the pro-Vichy Governor of Algiers. Even General Charles de Gaulle, the leader of the Fighting French, had a friendly word for Giraud, though he was much disappointed at not being summoned to Algiers to take charge himself. Such an assignment was still impossible as he had not yet secured sufficient support from the people of North Africa.

Under clearing political skies, Ike was able to relax a little. He even went so far as to acquire a hideout in the hills, where he could occasionally spend a peaceful evening. All he had to do now was to direct a major military campaign and make arrangements for the Casablanca Conference.

This latter task should have been enough to bring gray hairs to any commander's head. If President Roosevelt and Winston Churchill had got out a map and tried to find the most dangerous spot to meet, they could hardly have picked better. North Africa was still full of Axis sympathizers and out-and-out spies—the authorities were rounding up batches of them every week. Casablanca had been bombed and could be attacked again. And it was close to dubious Spanish territory. It was, Ike thought, just the place those two lovers of adventure would choose, but he recognized the tremendous lift to Allied morale that the news of such a dramatic meeting would cause. If it came off safely, it might be worth the risk.

Casablanca proved a dream conference. There was not a single incident to mar the sunny scene; everything ran as smoothly as a new Rolls-Royce. While Churchill and Roosevelt agreed on the larger aspects of global warfare, the British and American High Commands, not at all daunted by the precarious position of their armies in Tunis, worked out the details of the invasion of Italy and formulated plans for the greater invasion to come. In the general atmosphere of harmony, President Roosevelt was even able to get the two temperamental French leaders, Giraud and de Gaulle, to shake hands with each other for the benefit of the photographers—evidence of a purely phony friendship, which nonetheless had tremendously beneficial results.

One immediate decision of the conference was of great moment to Ike. It was to create a North African Theater of Operations with Eisenhower in command. It was an impressive demonstration of confidence for such veteran generals as Alexander and Montgomery to consent to serve under a comparatively untried American. Ike appreciated the compliment and hoped he might deserve it.

A by-product of the conference was the addition to Ike's Invasion Team of perhaps its most important member. Air Chief Marshal Sir Arthur William Tedder was an impish little man, as air-wise as a gremlin. He had commanded a reconnaissance squadron in the last war, and had been shot down once and thrice mentioned in dispatches. As director of research and development for the RAF in 1938, he had pushed the Spitfire program which was to save England, and as head of the Middle East Air Command he had cleared the skies for Montgomery's victory at El Alamein. He stopped off at Casablanca en route to England to take over his new job as vice-chief of the Air Staff in London.

Ike liked the wiry, talkative little Englishman immediately, because he didn't pull any punches. Chance gave them an opportunity for a long conversation, and they found that their minds meshed like precision gears. First it was on the subject of the Luftwaffe.

"Not all they're cracked up to be," Ike opined.

Tedder grinned. "The only trouble with the Germans is that they haven't enough imagination to succeed in the air. Their planes were designed as flying artillery and that's the way they use 'em still. They got away with it in Europe because nobody else had an air force. Now they can't change their tactics and concentrate their force to defeat the enemy in the air before they go beetling around after ground objectives."

"The classic military principles hold for the air as well as the land," Ike agreed. "The main object is to disarm the enemy. That's what we must do, and now that the operations of the Middle East Command are beginning to overlap with mine, they should be placed in a single air command."

"I've been saying that for some time," Tedder remarked. Then a little shyly he added, "I don't know how you'll like this, but because we've had so much experience with desert operations, I think the air commander should be British."

"You're absolutely right," Ike exclaimed.

In the course of that conversation Ike made up his mind; it was a hunch, like the one he had had about P.A. back at West Point. In his usual direct way he went straight to Winston Churchill.

"I want Tedder," he said, and explained the proposed amalgamation.

"You've got him," Churchill said.

When the conference broke up, General Marshall came to visit Eisenhower in Algiers. Marshall's brilliant mind and wide understanding gave him an immediate grasp of the local situation, and he not only made valuable contributions to the tactical planning, but he left Ike with a renewed assurance that the General Staff would back him to the limit.

February, 1943, began deceptively well. French politics were unwontedly serene. Assistant Secretary of War John J. McCloy arrived to look things over, and brought with him Jean Monet, a Frenchman of rare ability and understanding. For the past two years Monet had been living in America, first as purchasing agent for the British Government and later in an advisory capacity on war purchases to the United States government. He was respected by Americans, British and French alike, and almost immediately he acquired great influence over Giraud. This was evidenced by a sudden accession of reasonableness on the part of the French. Monet continued to increase his influence among his countrymen and was soon accepted as a member of the Council. He did more than any other single person to promote Franco-American unity.

On February 4, the formation of the North African Theater of Operations was officially announced, and when the British Eighth Army finished chasing the Afrika Korps out of Tripoli and arrived at the Mareth Line in Tunisia, where Rommel had decided to stand, it came under Eisenhower's command. In the new setup, General Alexander became Ike's deputy in the field with direct command of the Eighteenth Army Group, consisting of the British First and Eighth Armies, the United States II Corps and the French XVII Corps in Tunisia. Tedder took over the newly formed Mediterranean Air Command with Carl Spaatz under him at the head of the Northwest African Air Force. In accord with Tedder's ideas this command was divided into a strategic air force under Doolittle and a tactical air force under Major General Lewis Hyde Brereton. Admiral Cunningham became naval commander in chief in the Mediterranean under General Eisenhower's direction.

As in England, Ike's guiding principle was unity. He was determined to form a single force from these diverse elements. There were to be no British, French nor Americans: only the Allied Forces.

For technical reasons, such as differences in national customs of eating and in the types of arms carried, the units of this new army were to be no smaller than a division and might preferably be as large as an army corps. But this would not be allowed to make any difference in essential unity. At Headquarters, an American and an Englishman faced each other at every desk, and worked out their problems together.

Such an amalgamation had never been carried out before. In World War I the armies of the different nations had been sharply separate entities, united only by being under the over-all command of Marshal Foch. Now they were to be merged so completely that they would even *think* of themselves as one great army dedicated to a common victory.

That he succeeded in this seemingly utopian project is, perhaps even beyond his military genius, Eisenhower's finest achievement, his first claim to greatness. He did it by being fair and frank, ready to trust or praise a good man of any nation, devastating in his wrath against incompetence, no matter who was the culprit. In his own mind he allowed no national distinctions. Once he was praising the gallant action of an officer to General Hastings Ismay, who was a visitor at his headquarters.

"Was he British or American?" General Ismay asked.

Ike thought a moment, and then grinned. "I honestly don't remember," he said.

The attitude of the Commander in Chief permeated through all the echelons. The Allied Forces began to take an enormous pride in their unity. An ardent esprit de corps inspired them. Let a newcomer arrive and begin to make distinctions between British and Americans, and his ears were pinned back so fast he hadn't time to blink.

Ike was equally successful in forging his commanders into a smooth working machine. Their personalities were as sharply defined as their abilities were great. Here were Alexander, conservative and precise; Montgomery, flamboyant, intense, dramatic in his black beret; Clark, intellectual and reserved; Patton, rip-roaring and headstrong; Tedder, casual and humorous; Spaatz, loving the sky and his music; Cunningham, hearty and bluff. What a diversity of men to handle as a team! But a team they became, pulling together for the good of all. They were hardly conscious of the hand that guided them; indeed, at this stage, still not quite seasoned in command, Ike preferred to suggest and then weigh opinion, rather than to exercise authority. He referred to himself as the "Chairman of the Board."

Things were quiet at Headquarters on the afternoon of February 11, 1943, and when a French jeweler arrived to see the General, he was shown to Butcher's office. Butch talked with him and brought him in to Ike.

"I thought you might like to see this fellow," he said. "He's got some really beautiful little trinkets."

The jeweler proudly displayed a set of twelve hand-wrought silver stars. Ike examined them, smiling.

"They're pretty snappy," he agreed, "but I've got no use for so many. You should have come when General Marshall was here."

They were still looking at the stars when there occurred one of those wild coincidences which no writer of fiction dares use: a British naval officer dashed into the room.

"General," he said, "I've just got a rather interesting piece of news on my wireless. Washington has announced your promotion to full general."

Confirmation arrived in a cable from Mamie next day.

General Eisenhower celebrated his new rank by taking Telek on a visit to the front. On February 12 he started for Tébessa where General Fredendall, commanding the II Corps, had his headquarters. As always when he went among the troops, he was gay, not knowing that the next few days would bring his army to the brink of disaster and tear his heart by the toll of death and suffering. Nor did he sense the personal peril that awaited him.

But though he did not foresee the immediate event, he was far from satisfied with the disposition of the American forces. During the race for Tunis, it had been necessary to throw every unit into battle the moment it reached the front. For this reason the American divisions—the 1st, 34th, and 9th, and the 1st Armored—were broken up into combat teams and intermingled with their Allies. Ike was determined to regroup them as soon as possible.

Meanwhile these mixed combat teams were disposed in the valley between the two mountain ranges which run parallel to the coast of Tunisia. They also held the passes to the coastal plain. To the east of the mountains along the coast, the Afrika Korps had united with Colonel General Juergen von Arnim's army coming down from Tunis. Rommel, secure for the moment in the Mareth Line, was gathering his armor for a charge through the mountains, which he hoped would smash the Allied forces before they could unite with the Eighth Army moving up from Tripoli.

Generals Alexander and Fredendall knew that an attack was preparing, and faulty intelligence reports led them to believe that it would come through Pichon Pass and strike down at Sbeitla. Fredendall's largest combat team, Combat Command B, had been ordered to guard this section with 200 tanks of the 1st Armored Division and strong infantry and artillery contingents. Two other combat teams were stationed far to the southward near Sidi bou Zid, watching Faid Pass. At the extreme end of the line—which wasn't a line but a series of strong points—mixed French and American infantry held Gafsa. Planes of the Allied Air Force were operating out of Thelepte airfield in the Sbeitla Valley.

As soon as Ike reached Fredendall's headquarters at Tébessa, he gave orders for a shifting of strength. The 1st Armored Division and the 1st and 34th Infantry Divisions were to be concentrated in a powerful striking force just east of the main mountain range. Thus they would be able to meet a German dash through any of the passes with overwhelming might, instead of being in danger of being picked off piecemeal. Unfortunately Rommel was too fast on his feet.

On the 13th, Ike started out on an inspection tour. Leaving Tébessa, which was just across the Algerian border, he went through Kasserine Pass in the main mountain range, and inspected Combat Command B, concentrated in the snowy mountains. Then he went on down the valley to Sbeitla where the Roman ruins and the Arch of Diocletian reminded him of other conquerors who had passed that way.

It was a brilliantly clear day, so crystalline that objects ten miles away were sharp against the horizon. The great tawny plain was dotted with small green irrigated fields, where white native houses stood, and patches of the thorned cactus that was raised for camel fodder. Arabs were working in the fields and guarding their humped herds. When he reached Sidi bou Zid, Ike could distinguish individual pinnacles on the mountain rampart that stood between the Allies and the Germans on the coast.

Ike went on to inspect the smaller combat commands—CCA at the mouth of Faid Pass on the very slopes of Essouda Mountain, and CCC, which was camped in a gigantic cactus grove.

The troops shouted "Ike! Ike!" as they always did when he came among them. In spite of their long stretch in the desert he thought they looked fit, and very young and gay. They were standing by for an alert, for something was moving behind the mountain wall.

The morning of February 14 found Ike at Brigadier General Paul Robinett's headquarters at Sidi bou Zid. At dawn an alarm came through, and soon Stukas were diving at the slopes of Essouda Mountain. That something was moving with a vengeance. Like an enormous mechanical serpent, the 21st Panzer Division of the Afrika Korps crawled through Faid Pass, brushing aside the light defending units. As they reached the lower slopes of the mountain, the tanks fanned out and tore across the valley, spitting fire from their guns, each trailing a great column of dust. Behind them came more tanks and yet more, with self-propelled 88s and mechanized infantry in half-tracks. Although the Arabs went on herding their camels and working their fields, apparently oblivious of the appalling spectacle, the whole plain was alive with armored monsters.

Some of the tanks charged straight at Sidi bou Zid, while others swept around in a great encircling movement. The Allied artillery went into action. Here and there a Mark IV tank stopped and a tall column of black smoke rose to mark its funeral pyre. The Sherman tanks of CCA charged out against the enormous odds, their 75s cracking spitefully. The Americans were inexperienced, but they were valiant. Tank after tank was smashed and began to burn, but the guns kept firing long after their interiors were a molten hell. Instead of escaping, their crews fought on until the whole machine blew up.

The action of CCA was as magnificent as the Charge of the Light Brigade, and almost as futile, for behind the 21st Panzer Division came the 10th Panzers, veterans of the Russian front, newly equipped with the terrible Mark VI Tiger tanks. Shells from the 75s burst against their armored snouts like snowballs on a wall.

Meanwhile the soft-shelled vehicles—the trucks and half-tracks and mobile kitchens—were retreating in long columns across the plain, making for the Sbeitla road. CCC came out of its cactus grove and crossed to defend Sidi bou Zid against the German frontal attack.

"General, you've got to get out of here."

It was Colonel Williams, chief of staff to General Robinett, speaking.

Ike put down his field glasses reluctantly.

"I sure hate to go," he said.

But he knew his place was at Tébessa, where he could get full reports and plan countermeasures against the disaster that threatened to engulf his armies.

"Better get going, sir," said Williams urgently. "We may be cut off any minute and it would be a fine thing if you got captured."

With a heavy heart, thinking of those boys in CCA who were dying on the mountain slopes, Ike climbed alone into a jeep with a sergeant at the wheel, and took the road to Sbeitla.

All that afternoon they drove down the long road of retreat. The soft-shells, hurrying to the rear, jammed the right side of the highway and raised great choking clouds of dust, which the wind swept across the plain. Behind him, Ike could see more and more of the dismal columns of heavy smoke that marked the burning tanks. The gunfire was incessant, but it seemed to him that the heavier boom of the German guns was more frequent.

The wind was rising. It scooped up the surface of the plain in swirling clouds of dust which mingled with the smoke of battle and the dust of retreat to give a sick pallor to the sky. Ahead of them the setting sun was a pale-orange ball.

In the windy darkness they passed through Sbeitla. Men were working feverishly to load and save what matériel they could from the great dumps among the Roman ruins; others were preparing to destroy what must be left behind. Diocletian's Triumphal Arch looked ironic in the wan moonlight.

The sergeant was worn out and Ike took the wheel. It was hideous driving on the narrow road. The massed vehicles were moving slowly, nose to tail. The plain trembled with the thunder of motors, and occasional flames from exhausts gave a flickering infernal blue light. Ike edged the little car forward, sometimes getting a clear run up the left side of the road, squeezing back somehow into line to dodge a convoy racing toward the front. Once in a while he took the jeep right off the road and bumped across the plain past traffic jams.

But the strain of driving was nothing compared to the heartbreaking sense of defeat, the mass impact of those hundreds of machines and thousands of men, laboriously inching down the weary road of retreat. He knew, now, how Napoleon must have felt as the Grande Armée shuffled back across the Russian plains.

Toward morning they got clear of the traffic; the road was empty ahead, rising toward Kasserine Pass. Being infinitely weary, Ike turned over the wheel to the sergeant and instantly went to sleep in the back seat. *Asleep in his chair at 8:30 P.M. inspection —8 demerits.*

The next moment—so it seemed—Ike crashed with terrific violence on the rocky ground. He lay there for a moment gathering himself. The foothills were gray with dawn and empty of human life. The jeep lay like a beetle on its back, partly in a ditch, and Ike saw the sergeant's helmeted head sticking out from under it. He got quickly to his feet. A sharp pain shot through his back, but disregarding it, he ran limping toward the jeep.

"Sergeant, are you hurt?"

"I don't think so, sir, but I'm stuck under here."

"Keep still then, and I'll try to get it up."

The car was lying at an angle, and Ike, with his strained back screaming protest, managed to lift one side. The sergeant scrambled out completely intact, and joined his strength to Ike's. Together they rocked the jeep until it bounced back on its wheels.

"I'm terribly sorry about this, sir," the sergeant said, as they climbed into the car. "It was all my fault. I went to sleep at the wheel."

Perhaps the generals of long ago, who had passed this way— Hannibal and Scipio, Caesar, Tamerlane, or even Lyautey— looked down in amazement at the Commander in Chief and his sergeant toiling alone in the wilderness. If so, their jaws fell wide open at the reply of the American General to a man they would have executed.

"Don't worry about it, boy," said Ike. "If I'd been driving I'd have done the same."

Back at Tébessa, Eisenhower and Fredendall took rueful stock as the tired men and broken machines poured back through Kasserine Pass. The whole long valley was lost. German columns ranged throughout its length from Ousseltia to Gafsa, and lunged viciously at the Allied rear guard, which was fighting valiantly to give the retreat time to get through the pass. CCA was shattered, nearly all its tanks lost, its infantry prisoners or fighting their way back through the mountains. CCC was but little better off. Only CCB, fortunately the most powerful, was still intact, battle-scarred but grimly determined.

The generals decided to try to hold Kasserine Pass. If the Germans burst through and swept the Algerian plateau, they would cut the supply lines of the First Army and either force the evacuation of all Tunisia or, at the worst, trap the Allied force in complete disaster.

The pass was at once mined, and infantry was stationed in the hills. CCB was concentrated near Tébessa. Anderson had rushed a British Armored Brigade down from the north, and supported by artillery from the American 9th Division, it guarded Thala and the vital road which cut across the First Army's communications. Meanwhile, engineers swarmed about the great supply dumps of Tébessa, burying TNT in them in case they had to be blown up.

The Germans expertly swept up the American mine fields and the Panzers poured down through Kasserine Pass on February 21. Their column divided as it reached the plateau, one section attacking Tébessa and the other turning north against Thala. Ike went out to Thala to watch the action.

This was a different sort of day: gray clouds obscured the mountaintops and hovered low over the plain. It was bad weather for planes, but Toohey Spaatz had everything in the air that would fly. Lightnings, Spitfires, Marauders, Mitchells, Bostons, and even great Fortresses swept low overhead, their wings brushing the clouds as they poured destruction on the long German columns. But the Panzers came on, fanning out. When they were only four miles from Thala, the American artillery opened fire and the new English Churchill forty-two-ton tanks charged out to meet them.

Ike, watching through his glasses, saw that this would be no walkover for the Panzers. Those 155-millimeter guns from the 9th Division could check a Mark VI when nothing else could. German tanks began to stop and burn. Churchills were burning too, but not so many of them. Soon the Germans had enough;

their tanks turned around and beetled back for the hills. In front of Tébessa it was the same story. CCB, grim veterans now, smashed the German spearhead with tanks and 105s.

The next day the Allies attacked, moving their big guns up to within range of Kasserine Pass. The planes roared low under the clouds and the tanks ran around snapping at the enemy's heels, as the whole German mass swirled back through the gap in the mountains, leaving a trail of wreckage to mark their route.

Retreat was ended, and Rommel had been stopped. Thala was the high-water mark of Germany in Tunisia.

Back in Algiers, Ike digested the bitter lessons of the battle. The near-catastrophe had been due largely to inexperience—his own and that of others. The Allies' use of mines had been faulty; they had hardly any at Faid Pass, and at Kasserine Pass the mine fields were beyond range of the artillery. The Allies had allowed themselves to be defeated piecemeal and there had been losses due to lack of battle technique. But the courage of those untried troops had been magnificent beyond praise, and in the end the Germans had been held. No irreparable damage had been done. The General felt that he, like all the echelons of his command, had gained infinitely in wisdom. The strength of his confidence in his troops and the depth of his admiration for them shone through the official wording of his message to General Marshall:

"Our present tactical difficulties resulted from my attempt to do possibly too much, coupled with the deterioration of resistance in the central mountainous area . . .

"You would have been impressed could you have seen the magnificent display everywhere by the American enlisted men. I assure you that the troops that come out of this campaign are going to be battle-wise and tactically efficient."

Ike set furiously to work to restore the situation. He had no intention of permitting the setback to upset the schedule or delay the next great move. The first step was to retake our lost ground, and that had to be done mainly by armored divisions supported by infantry. Fredendall, an infantry general, didn't have the technique or the feeling for tank warfare. What Ike needed was a man who could handle his armor with wariness and audacity. After all, they were meeting the Old Master, Rommel himself. This was the big league and what he wanted was a damn good tank man.

There was one ready to his hand. Georgie Patton was sent forward to command the II Corps.

Georgie did what was expected of him. Within less than a month, he cleared the Sbeitla Valley of the enemy, and by March 21 the lines were restored to their original positions. The stage was now set for the final phase. The American troops were veterans, knowing defeat, but made confident by victory.

On March 20, Montgomery had begun the grand assault that cracked the Mareth Line. As he fought his way up the coast, British, French and American forces stormed the coastal range, and on April 7, patrols of the American 9th Division, sweeping down the mountain slopes, met advance units of the Eighth Army.

Either because he was wounded or because he knew the jig was up, Rommel relinquished command to von Arnim and went back home. The new German commander pulled his troops back to the mountains that guarded Tunis and Bizerte, and waited for the last assault.

As his armies closed in for the kill, Eisenhower found himself in a far different position from the one he had occupied during that first dash for Tunis. Logistics were now all in his favor, for he had succeeded in rebuilding roads and organizing transport lines so that a huge volume of supplies flowed toward the front. More important still, numerous fine airfields had been built, and the fighter planes at the front were supplied by ten new pipelines, gushing gasoline. Von Arnim's supplies, on the other hand, were cut to a mere trickle by the blockade of the British Navy and the power of the Allied Air Force, which now had complete command of the air. After the Germans lost a whole convoy of twenty six-motor, 120-man transport planes, they gave up attempting to reinforce by air.

Nevertheless, it looked as though von Arnim's position would be a tough nut to crack. He still had nearly 300,000 troops, including the crack armored divisions of the Afrika Korps, and he was entrenched among the precipitous mountains that guarded Tunis and Bizerte. If there weren't to be a costly frontal attack, something tricky had to be worked out. Eisenhower devised a daring tactical maneuver, which in football language might be called a backfield shift.

First of all, since the II Corps would now be fighting in the mountains, he took Patton out and sent him to activate the

Seventh Army for the invasion of Sicily. In February General Marshall had sent Omar Bradley to serve on Ike's staff, and to that expert infantryman Ike entrusted the II Corps with as much confidence as he had once predicted a brilliant future for Bradley in *The Howitzer*.

The II Corps was next to the Eighth Army on the extreme right of the line. Figuring that von Arnim would expect the strongest attack from that quarter and concentrate to meet it, Ike ordered Bradley to cross his army over to the left wing and carry the attack against Bizerte.

It was an extremely difficult maneuver, for it meant that the thousands of vehicles and men of the II Corps would pass behind the whole front, crossing the roads over which the supplies for the First Army must maintain an uninterrupted flow. Bradley, Anderson and Alexander worked out an elaborate timetable, and the tremendous operation went off without a hitch and in complete secrecy.

Von Arnim was tricked. By the time he found out what was happening to him, it was too late to shift his forces.

During the latter part of April, Bradley's troops, which included units of the French Army and Goums (the native African troops), fought along the crest of the hills toward Bizerte. It was a bitter, step-by-step advance, which finally succeeded in clearing them for the armor that came through the valleys and pierced the German line at Mateur. Meanwhile Alexander, following Ike's shifting tactics, switched most of the Eighth's armor to the First Army for a plunge through center at Tunis. On May 5, General Ike reported to Marshall: "Tomorrow morning we start the big drive which we hope and believe will see us in Tunis in a day or so. I believe we can clear up the Bizerte angle very quickly, but the Bon Peninsula may be a difficult matter."

Ike's hopes were justified. With thousands of planes and massed artillery blasting the Germans, and the infantry fighting over the hilltops, the way was cleared at last for the tanks. The 1st American Armored Division tore into Bizerte at 4:15 P.M. on May 7, 1943. Six and a half minutes later, British tanks clanking down the last straight road and plunging through the poppy fields and wheat, rolled into Tunis.

The broken Axis troops retreated into the mountainous Cap Bon Peninsula, which was geographically something like Bataan and might have been stoutly defended. But they had had enough.

They streamed toward the Allied lines by platoons, companies, regiments, and finally by divisions—thousands and tens of thousands of enemy soldiers—with no other thought than to find somebody who would accept their surrender. On foot and in motor trucks and driving their own armored vehicles, they swarmed out of the hills, almost engulfing their conquerors in that vast tide of beaten men. The final returns showed that 252,415 German and Italian troops, with uncountable quantities of equipment, yielded themselves to the Armies of Democracy.

General Ike of Kansas came down to Tunis to review his conquering legions. He hated to spare the time from planning the greater things to come, but he wanted to mark his victory for a larger reason than mere glorification, or even recognition, of the men who had fought so well. This time the Germans must never doubt that their armies had been broken in the field.

So Ike stood on the dais in the blinding sunshine, among the broken buildings of the white city of Tunis, and took the salute of that vast company of men from different nations whom he had welded into one great victorious army. His generals stood beside him—Alexander, Giraud, Montgomery and Bradley. But it was not of the generals he thought as he waited there in the sunshine, looking down the flag-draped street to where the head of the procession would appear. He was thinking about the men who were marching toward him and the men who wouldn't march any more.

The heart-lifting skirling of the Scottish pipes heralded the procession. Their wild music seemed strangely appropriate to the Oriental aspect of the crowd which surged against the line of khaki keeping the roadway clear; sheiks of the desert and Arabs of the town, men in flowing white robes and women in multitudinous chiffon veils peering with dark excited eyes above their yashmaks. The Europeans were conspicuously few in that throng, which for a brief moment made Ike think of a scene from *Beau Geste*.

Then he forgot about the people, for his army was coming. Its bright banners were the Tricolor, the Union Jack, and the Stars and Stripes, but it was *his* army.

The French came first, with their long polelike rifles, a forest tipped with steel. Then came the Goums in flowing robes, who had taken the hills near Bizerte with naked knives. There was another band, playing "The Stars and Stripes Forever," and the II Corps swung by. They were lean, tough veterans, but they looked so young and so like home that Ike swallowed hard as his hand snapped up in salute to the flag.

They were followed by the British divisions of the First Army, among them the Coldstream and Grenadier Guards, marching as at Whitehall, and the British paratroopers swaggering in their green berets. Then came the Eighth Army, the proud Desert Rats, who had traveled all the way from Alamein, fourteen hundred miles across the arid sands.

There were no more bands after that, only the discordant symphony of mechanized war—roaring motors and backfiring exhausts, like the parade before the start at the Indianapolis automobile races magnified a hundred times. There were scout cars, antiaircraft guns, half-tracks, tractors towing 155s like enormously elongated sewer pipes, mobile kitchens, jeeps by the hundreds and the trucks and mobile machine shops of the Supply Corps, who worked and died without glory. Finally came the tanks, hundreds of them, roaring and clanking, choking the roadway with a monstrous torrent of potential destruction. But their hatches were open and their crews rode on top, smiling and holding the spring flowers which had been thrown to them by the liberated people. Again Ike thought how young they were . . .

When it was over, this new kind of conqueror stepped down from the dais with his heart filled to bursting, not with pride in achievement, but with humility at the thought of these men of many nations, who had put their trust in him and fought and died so well at his command. He was filled with a kind of exalted love for every one of them and with a fierce determination to bring about a swift victorious end to the war which kept them from the homes they longed to see.

CHAPTER SEVENTEEN

"WE FOOLED 'EM AGAIN"

The next operation will be the invasion of Sicily."

General Eisenhower stood at the end of the crowded room, smiling broadly at the soughing sound of amazement that swept through the massed correspondents. He knew that their surprise was due not so much to the news itself as to his telling it to them so far in advance. That was his way with the press—tell them everything and put them on their honor. In this manner he forestalled dangerous speculation based on what the correspondents could see going on. He was a great believer in the honor system.

One reporter close to him gasped, "Sicily?"

"Sure," said Ike. "Why do you think we took Pantelleria and Lampedusa?"

It was the obvious move. The huge triangular rock at the toe of Italy's boot cut the Mediterranean in two; the time had come to neutralize it so that the supply lines would run freely down the length of that vital artery of conquest. Also, Sicilian airfields were essential for the next stroke at the "soft underbelly."

The difficulty was how to achieve any element of surprise. All through the months of May and June, Eisenhower had Doolittle's strategic air force pounding Sardinia, Sicily and Crete impartially. That might at least arouse doubt in Nazi minds; they couldn't be sure of his real objective—it turned out they thought it was Sardinia. Meanwhile, the preparations went forward as fast as possible.

The invasion of Sicily would be no walkover against half-hearted defense, like the landings in North Africa. The Axis was reported to have about 350,000 troops crowded into the island. Among them were such tough outfits as the Hermann Goering

Division, made up of air force ground troops, veteran infantry and tanks; the reconstituted 15th Panzers; the 29th Motorized Division; and the Italian *Ariete* Division, who were hard-boiled in spite of their nationality. Ike recalled very well what had happened at Dieppe, where half the attacking force was left lying on the beach. He was determined that there should be no such failure here; but he was terribly aware of the danger.

While people in America wondered why he didn't do something, the Commander in Chief gathered his forces and made his plans. There would be no lack of shipping this time—three thousand vessels were assembled for the invasion armada—but Ike was still short of landing craft.

"What beats me," he said, "is why we designed such a land-bound army in the first place, knowing that it must always fight on the other side of water!"

Patton was rehearsing the new Seventh Army in landing operations along those African beaches which most nearly resembled Sicily. Meanwhile, the II Corps were resting at Oran and General Clark was readying the Fifth Army for a later adventure. The 1st Division, however, was soon yanked out of its comfortable camp at Oran to learn the latest tricks of amphibious warfare. Their final practice was an assault against a beach defended by the British 46th Division. Under their dashing leaders, Terry Allen and Theodore Roosevelt, they stormed it with such élan that the British general announced that he had theoretically held out only two hours.

Afterward the 1st was given leave in Algiers, and there was nothing theoretical about the way they took the city. When Ike drove through town in his staff car with the flags of all the Allies flying from its fenders, the celebration didn't even pause.

"They're sure having fun," he said. "God knows they deserve it!"

The weary Eighth Army were going to Sicily too. And there was no rest for General Ike, either. His schedule was as strenuous as ever, though those who knew him well and loved him best were delighted to see that the signs of strain were vanishing. Although Ike had studied the technique of war intensively for thirty years, the actuality was inevitably different from theory. But he had learned fast, and his confidence was mounting. He looked well and seemed serene.

However, his determination to exterminate the enemies of his

country burned with the fierce heat of an oxyacetylene torch. He
wrote to a friend concerning the small peace party in America:

I doubt whether these people, with their academic or dogmatic
hatred of war, detest it as much as I do. They probably have not seen
bodies rotting on the ground and smelled the stench of decaying
human flesh. They have not visited a field hospital crowded with the
desperately wounded. But far above my hatred of war is my determination to smash every enemy of my country, especially Hitler and
the Japs—

The papers have already told you of the very satisfactory technical
victory we achieved in Tunisia. One chore is out of the way, now we
must all catch our breath, redouble our efforts and steel ourselves to
a continuation of the task . . .

There were certain necessary interruptions of work. The shy
English king came to Africa and conferred on Ike the Grand
Cross of a Knight of the Order of the Bath. Giraud gave him
the Grand Cross of the Légion d'Honneur, with a kiss on each
cheek. Churchill paid a friendly visit, and General Marshall and
General Sir Alan Brooke, British Chief of Staff, came to go over
the plans with Eisenhower, Alexander, Montgomery and Patton.

General Charles de Gaulle finally arrived in Algiers to negotiate with Giraud for a real union between the two factions of
French opinion. De Gaulle had been invited to come sooner
but had refused, appointing General Georges Catroux as his representative. In April he had changed his mind, but Eisenhower
had advised him to wait until Tunis fell, for he didn't want fire-
works in his rear while the guns were still shooting in front. Now,
at last, the two Frenchmen really got together to work out the
plan for a united French Committee.

On July 8 General Eisenhower flew to Malta, where secret
Invasion Headquarters had been established. Cunningham,
Alexander and Tedder were at the airfield to meet him. Ike was
much touched by this manifestation of their regard. He drove
through the streets of Valetta—that indomitable city, battered
but not broken by 3,300 Nazi raids—and on into the perpendicular countryside. His command car climbed a final craggy hill and
stopped before ancient Verdala Palace, where Field Marshal the
Viscount Gort, Governor of Malta, had invited him to stay.
Lord Gort, who had friendly blue eyes under bushy brows,

was on hand to greet him, and could hardly wait to show off the wonders of his palace, which had been built in 1586 by the Knights of Malta. He conducted Ike through the great hall, and the frescoed salons and banqueting room. They peered into oubliettes, with rusty chains eloquent of prisoners who had languished there, and Gort demonstrated the incredible thickness of the massive stone walls which had been built proof against the ordnance of the time.

"I guess they come in darned handy now," Ike ventured.

"They assuredly do," said Gort.

After the tour of the palace, the Marshal took his guest up the spiral marble staircase, and showed him into an enormous bedroom with a ceiling thirty feet high.

"I hope you'll be comfortable here," Lord Gort said anxiously.

Ike could think of a lot of rooms where he would have been more comfortable, particularly a 10 by 12 bedroom in a little house in Kansas, but he reassured his host.

"It's grand," he said, which was no less than the truth.

Ike spent the next day, D — 1, at Invasion Headquarters. Like those at Gibraltar, they were in a tunnel in the rock. The Knights of Malta believed in preparedness, and in blasting sure shelters in the mountain, they had prepared so well that their defenses were proof against an onslaught of which they never dreamed. But they had not considered comfort.

Ike stepped from the blinding sunshine of the street, where thermometers registered a hundred degrees or more, into a chill that had been gathering for four hundred years. It struck into his bones and seemed to congeal the innermost organs of his body. Even the oil stove burning in his underground office could not dent that timeless cold. After sitting at his desk for ten minutes, Ike's teeth began to chatter and he sent for an overcoat.

For the first time in months—almost, it seemed, since he could remember—Ike had little to do. The plans were complete and the orders given. There remained only the long anxious wait.

At 11:30 he received John Gunther, representing the combined American press, and Ted Gilling, observer for the British papers. Ike had not wanted any correspondents attached to headquarters.

"Let them go to the front," he had told Butcher. "I hate this goldarned personal publicity."

Butcher was firm. "You've got to have them," he said, "if only for the historical record."

"Well, if that's how it is, all right," Ike agreed. "I always liked history, but doggone if I thought I was going to be it!"

Once he accepted the idea, the Commander in Chief was extremely helpful, according to Gunther. Ike had never quite got over that yen for journalism which he had acquired in the stuffy, exciting little office of the *News* at Abilene, and he listened with sympathetic interest while Gunther and Gilling described the woes of a reporter under triple censorship.

That afternoon Butcher astonished the two correspondents by recalling them to Eisenhower's office.

"I've been thinking about you fellows," Ike said, "and I believe I've worked things out for you. But you've got to promise not to write any more about me than you can possibly help."

After that interview, Ike took off his overcoat and went out. A blast of superheated air hit him at the mouth of the tunnel. The wind tore like a sirocco through the streets, lifting miniature whirlwinds of dust; it turned the sea to a sapphire blue confusion of tumbling waves with angry white crests. Force 5, the reports said, but it seemed stronger. If the wind continued to blow like this, the landing operations tomorrow would be appallingly difficult; if it increased, they would be impossible.

"It will probably go down with the sun," Butcher said reassuringly.

But as the sun sank, the wind rose; forty miles an hour, they figured it now.

There was still time to postpone invasion. Major General Matthew Ridgway's 82nd Airborne Division had not yet taken off from Africa; the thousands of ships converging over the uneasy sea might yet be halted. Ike weighed the odds as he might assay a hand at poker. To postpone meant inevitable confusion: some units might fail to receive the order and be massacred on landing. Any delay would almost eliminate the chance for the tactical surprise on which so many lives depended. On the other hand, a gale would cost thousands more lives by making it impossible to land artillery or tanks and by upsetting boats and drowning countless troops.

While he was thinking it out, a cable arrived from General Marshall, who had been apprised of the weather conditions: "Is it on or off?" The Chief of Staff requested an answer in four hours. By the time the cable arrived, Ike had half an hour left to make up his mind.

He went out and climbed a little way up the hill. The wind was booming over the cliffs and hissing through the leaves of the olive trees, yet the sky was clear and the edge of a fat red moon was lifting from the western horizon. Ike tried to sense the pressure of the gale. He watched a Maltese windmill whirling wildly, and thought of others spinning above the Kansas plains on just such nights. The wind very seldom continued to blow like this all night when the sky was so clear. Already it seemed to him that the windmill was turning less frantically. Abruptly he decided, and went in to write a cable to General Marshall:

"It's on. A high wind but I think we'll be able to report success in the morning."

Then the Commander in Chief went out to keep his vigil on the beach.

When the last of the airborne troops had gone down the tumultuous sky, Ike returned to his little headquarters room. There was a period of comparative calm while he waited for reports and thought about all the things that might go wrong.

He had taken another of his considered gambles, a daring attempt to achieve that precious element of tactical surprise. There were only two obvious places to invade Sicily: the good beaches on the southwestern side from Gela west to Marsala, and the strip of beach on the eastern coast from Agosta to Catania. But the best Axis troops would be massed at these danger points, ready to blast the beaches and smash down with their tanks before the Allied armor could get ashore. The rest of the coast had natural defenses of rocks, reefs and cliffs.

Ike played the long shot. He chose the rocky southeastern corner of the island. The Seventh Army and a new Canadian division were to land from Licata and Gela *eastward* on the west side, while the Eighth Army was to take the eastern coast. The precipitous shores might cause the loss of matériel, but if the German commander had made orthodox dispositions, there would be only inferior opposition and the Allied troops would run less risk. Thousands of lives might be saved.

Over and over again, as the night went slowly by, Ike wondered if it was possible that he had fooled the Germans. For if there had been a leak or they had guessed his plans, then the slaughter on the difficult rocks would be far worse than on the easier beaches. That thought was like an icicle boring into his brain and sending its paralyzing chill throughout his body. If such a catastrophe occurred, his would be the responsibility, his alone the blame. It would mean the end of his military career; but it was not of that he thought. What mattered was all those young men on the transports and landing craft who had put their faith in him and who would die if his great gamble failed.

In the glimmer of dawn the fighter planes roared off the Malta fields by squadrons to give air cover to the men on the beaches; and a little later word began to trickle back from the beachheads. The British and Canadians were ashore, having met feeble opposition from the Italian coast defense troops. The wind was dropping, but up to ten o'clock, when the sun was high overhead and half the scheduled day was gone, there was no message from Patton.

It was just like Georgie, Ike thought, not to send one word until he had something big to tell. Meanwhile, Malta was so close to the Gela beachhead that tantalizing scraps of radio conversation between men ashore and men on ships and planes came over the air waves; an officer calling to a cruiser to "get that gun behind 56"; one pilot shouting at another, "Stukas at eleven o'clock"; confused jumbles of words, voices hoarse with tension . . .

When the news came from Patton it *was* big. Terry Allen had taken his 1st Division up the beach even faster than in the sham battle in Africa. They had pushed inland toward Ponte Olivio Airfield and had been thrown back by tanks of the Hermann Goering Division. But the cruisers *Boise* and *Savannah* had picked off the tanks, sharpshooting with six-inch guns, and the 1st, with Colonel Darby's Rangers, had gone in again and taken the airfield. The 2nd Armored Division was landing its tanks; the 3rd and 45th Divisions were going strong against feeble opposition. General Bradley of the II Corps had established headquarters ashore. The Eyties were surrendering in droves.

By nightfall Ike was grinning like a happy jack-o'-lantern.

"By golly!" he said to everyone he saw. "I can't believe it, but we've fooled 'em again."

Jubilation lasted no longer than overnight. The next day Ike heard news that literally made him ill. C-47 transport planes, carrying reinforcements of the 82nd Airborne Division, had come over the beachhead just as a German bombing attack began. In the confusion, with bombs dropping out of the night sky, American anticraft batteries on ships and on shore had shot down

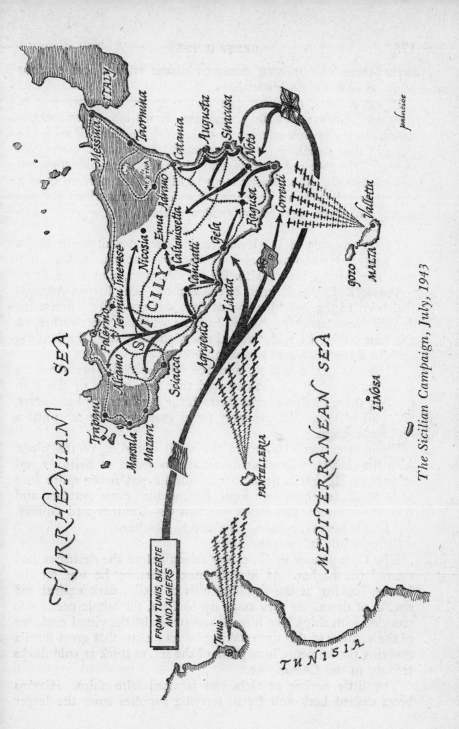

The Sicilian Campaign, July, 1943

palacios

twenty-three of our own transport planes with a loss of four hundred and ten American lives.

It was a freak accident, due to the incredible mischance of German bombers mingling with the formation of transports; nevertheless the Commander in Chief tortured himself with the thought that somehow he might have foreseen and avoided this disaster. He gave orders to revamp the entire recognition system and to take the most drastic steps to obviate the possibility of a repetition of such an accident. But for months afterward the thought of those wasted lives saddened him.

By the evening of D+1, Ike couldn't stand waiting in Malta any longer. He had to go and see what was happening. Cunningham lent him a low, rakish British destroyer, and came down to the docks in the darkness to see him off. The British Admiral had been to the beachheads that day, and was full of praise for American seamanship. "They had the worst of the weather on the west coast," he said, "and the way they handled the landing craft in those big waves was magnificent."

That was praise indeed, and Ike felt especially proud of his countrymen when he remembered that nine-tenths of the men guiding those pitching boats through the breakers were amateurs, and half of them had probably never even seen the sea until a few months ago.

Eisenhower went aboard to the shrill squealing of the pipes, with the side boys lined up in all the formality of British naval etiquette. He felt a little foolish, for he was never quite sure what to do on these occasions. Behind him came Butcher and then those inseparable twins, the two Gs—Gunther and Gilling.

"This is history, I guess," Ike said to Butcher.

"It certainly is," was the reply.

The Commander in Chief was asleep before the destroyer had cleared the harbor. At five the next morning he was on the bridge, looking at the tumbled hills of Sicily, dark against red streaks of dawn. As they came up to Gela, the whole ocean was crowded with ships. Ike himself was struck by the visual evidence of the vastness of this undertaking, when he saw that great flotilla covering the immense blue plain of the sea, as thick as wild ducks feeding in the Chesapeake.

The little harbor of Gela was jammed with ships. Higgins boats dashed back and forth, ferrying supplies from the larger vessels. The white beaches beyond were littered with wreckage and swarming with men working like ants. Burnt-out LCIs and LSTs lay at cockeyed angles with the breakers boiling around them; others, more fortunate, were spewing supplies through their gaping bows, from which huge steel pontoons made a bridge to shore. Black clouds of smoke towered above recently bombed equipment, and the debris of war gave a disheveled look to the clean sand.

Above the harbor, the apparently undamaged town climbed the hills. Except for the wreckage, it looked as peaceful as a picnic until a British cruiser moved lazily past the farther headland. There was a flash and crack from her forward guns as she searched for a hidden enemy battery, and through his binoculars Ike saw the yellow smoke of the shell bursts spurt upward from a distant hillside.

Patton's headquarters ship, the *Monrovia*, was anchored off "Red Beach No. 2." Ike and Butcher went aboard her in a small boat to breakfast with Patton and Admiral Hewitt. Georgie was in rare form. He was as well-turned out as though he were going to ride at Madison Square Garden, and no one could guess from the shine on his cavalry boots that he had marched through the breakers in them under enemy fire on D-day morning.

After breakfast, Ike returned to the destroyer. She got under way and tore along the coast at better than thirty knots. Ike and Butcher stood on the bridge, watching the peaceful hills and busy beaches flow past like an old-fashioned cyclorama. As they swept by a lighthouse just beyond the American right flank, there was a series of sharp cracks and white fountains spouted out of the sea four hundred yards to port.

"Action stations!"

The crew of the destroyer leaped into position. Their sun-burned bodies were stripped to the waist, and many of them wore ragged beards and had towels wrapped around their heads. Looking down on them as they passed the shells up to the guns, Ike thought that Sir Harry Morgan, the buccaneer, would have felt at home on this quarter-deck.

"Will you take cover, sir?" suggested the captain.

"I'd rather stay here, if I'm not in the way," Ike answered.

"The Commander in Chief is never in the way," was the reply.

The destroyer reeled to the crash of her guns and the smell of cordite was sharp in Ike's nostrils. The enemy battery fired again, a little closer this time.

The executive officer, black-bearded and stripped like his men, came forward with a helmet.

"I suggest you put this on, sir," he said.

Ike tried it, but the strap dangled above his nose. "I'll need two men to hold it on," he laughed. But he saw that his presence was making the English nervous, and, anyhow, the excitement was almost over. "Come on, Butch," he said. "Back to our gilded cage."

Presently the destroyer dropped anchor among the vessels lying off Correnti, where the Canadians had landed; this was the primary objective of the trip. A duck was signaled alongside. Ike boarded it, and in a few minutes the unwieldy craft heaved through the hissing breakers and rolled up the shore on its wheels. The beach was a scene of enormous activity. Men were feverishly unloading supplies, putting up green pup tents, laying down wire mats, cooking and digging. Others were swimming in the flashing surf or just lying in the sun. Right here, war didn't look so bad.

An English colonel of the "sahib" type approached the duck. Ike climbed out.

"I'm General Eisenhower," he said.

"I say, not really!" gasped the Englishman.

"Really," Ike said, laughing, "and I want to speak to the senior Canadian officer."

"These are Canadian troops, but there are no officers present just now. They're all farther in."

"Then, will you be good enough to lend me a jeep?"

"Of course, sir," said the colonel, "but there are still a lot of snipers around."

"I've got to find a Canadian officer," Ike repeated.

He climbed into a jeep, and, with a goggle-eyed Canadian boy at the wheel, started inland. The way led along a narrow dusty lane that wound through pleasant summer meadows in which the grass was deep and green and ancient trees stood grandly. This was a lovely land, Ike thought; and sadness filled him as he sniffed the sweetness of flowers and foliage. Somehow death seemed more bitter here than on the harsher plains of Africa.

Once the jeep had to pull over and stop to give way to a painted two-wheeled cart, pulled by a tiny donkey and driven by a dark-skinned peasant girl, who waved gaily. Farther along, the peaceful countryside was disfigured by the wreckage of war—a smashed German tank, with its long gun drooping forward and the tracks blown from its juggernaut wheels, an 88 minus its muzzle, and an American half-track lying on its side. There were broken helmets half hidden by the sweet grass.

In places the lane cut into the countryside like a canyon, so deep that Ike could not see over the sides. He was itchily aware that this was fine country for snipers, but he had no intention of turning back from the mission he had come so far to perform.

At last Eisenhower found a company of Canadians in charge of Captain G. E. Moore. He introduced himself and then in tones so warm that they lent sincerity to the formal words, said, "Through you, captain, I welcome Canada to the Allied Command."

General Eisenhower returned to Malta and then to his permanent headquarters in Algiers. The campaign wasn't easy; no fight against veteran German troops could ever be that. To the American and British echelons fighting their way from hill to hill and watching their comrades die, it seemed bitter and harsh. But as a military operation it was brilliantly successful.

While the Eighth Army fought its way down the east coast, taking Syracuse and Agosta, Americans and Canadians secured the airfields near their beachhead and the 3rd Division headed west to capture Canicatti and Agrigento. At this point Eisenhower's tactical plan called for another tricky and daring play.

The Germans had as usual pitted most of their best troops against the Eighth Army. They figured further that the Americans would move west along the coast in an attempt to capture the fine ports of Marsala and Trapani, where it would be easy to unload heavy equipment and from which good roads led to Palermo, the leading port and capital of Sicily. They therefore deployed their strongest remaining forces along the west coast. But Ike fooled them again.

While the British and Canadians pinned down the German armor, he sent the Seventh Army straight inland, despite the Axis threat to his left flank. In hard fighting the Americans captured Enna, cutting the German supply lines to Palermo and to the troops on the west coast. Then the fighting 3rd Division, the 82nd Airborne and the 2nd Armored turned west. Under Major General Geoffrey Keyes of the 2nd Armored, this force cut straight across the rugged country to Palermo. In some places mountains three thousand feet high barred their way, but nothing halted their swift progress. In two days they marched seventy-two miles from Ribera to Palermo. The capital fell and the enemy forces massed in the southwestern corner of the island were cut off; 100,000 Axis troops surrendered.

On July 31, Ike paid another visit to Sicily. Coming this time in a Fortress, he landed at Palermo. Georgie Patton was there to greet him, looking extremely warlike in his three-starred helmet, which he apparently never took off. Knowing how Ike felt about the 15th Infantry, Patton had ordered them to the airport as the Commander in Chief's Guard of Honor. Their former Colonel Ike, with the four stars on his jaunty overseas cap, stepped from his plane and walked through their rigid lines. Under Georgie's strict discipline the 15th was very stiff and military, but Ike stopped to greet many an old friend in the ranks. When they got the order "At ease!" the 15th broke into a near riot, yelling, "Ike! Ike!" That was the sort of thing which moved Eisenhower; he was a "softy" for the men he had been close to. Between British and American troops he could be completely impartial, but the 15th was his own outfit. *Can do,* he thought. Well, they had certainly proved that they could!

From Palermo, Ike flew over to Syracuse to confer with Alexander. The Eighth was, as usual, having the toughest time, fighting the pick of the German Army on the slopes of Mount Etna. Ike stopped for an inspection at an airfield, where his Fortress burned out a brake, and he got aboard the C-53 transport *Time's a-Wastin'*. Since the enemy air force was all over the island, Patton gave him a squadron of P-38s to guard him home.

From the taking of Palermo, the campaign continued to its logical conclusion. The British were held up by the strong defenses around Mount Etna, but that was according to plan: their part was designed as a holding operation. It was impossible for the Axis leaders to restore their position on the west; the best they could do was to put up a bitter defensive action against the advancing Americans to gain time for an evacuation of Sicily. The Germans, according to their custom, let the Italians hold the bag while they carried out a "Dunkerque" across the Strait of Messina.

The end came on August 17, when the 3rd Division beat the 2nd Armored in the final race for Messina. The conquest of Sicily was complete.

At his press conference when the campaign ended, Eisenhower gave the accolade to the Seventh Army: "I can only say this," he told the correspondents, "today the Seventh Army is worthy to fight alongside the Eighth. I can offer no higher praise . . ."

But the victorious conclusion of the campaign brought little satisfaction to General Eisenhower, because of an unhappy incident that caused him acute distress. Georgie Patton had driven his troops to the limit of human endurance, and he had driven himself beyond it. In the last days of the campaign, he committed an act which could be excused only on the ground of complete nervous exhaustion.

The first notice of the incident came to Ike in the form of a report from the colonel commanding the evacuation hospital at Sant' Agata di Militello; then Merrill Mueller of the National Broadcasting Company and Demaree Bess of the *Saturday Evening Post*, who had visited the hospital the following day, came to Algiers and told him the whole story as they had heard it from eyewitnesses.

General Patton was visiting the wounded in the evacuation hospital, as was his almost daily custom. He walked through the wards, calling greetings to men he had known, asking new patients about their wounds. There was nothing out of the ordinary until he stopped beside a cot where a young soldier sat weeping with his head between his hands.

"What is the matter with you?" he asked kindly.

"It's my nerves, I guess," the boy said. "I can't stand the shelling."

Patton's fetish was personal courage and this reply seemed to snap his own overwrought nerves. He roared a corrosive stream of abuse and profanity in which such printable epithets as "coward" and "yellowbelly" were the moderate exception. Finally he struck the boy with the back of his hand, sending his helmet liner rolling under the beds.

There was uproar and confusion in the ward. A spunky nurse made a dive for the General, but a doctor and an intern intervened. Patton went on through the hospital, shouting out his sympathy for those who were really wounded, but continuing to rage about the man who had temporarily lost his nerve.

What made the incident more distressing was the fact that the soldier was a Regular Army man, who had served with gallantry all through Tunisia and Sicily. He had been diagnosed as a medical case and sent to the hospital against his will. As a Regular Army man, with pride in his record, he felt that he was forever disgraced. "Don't tell my wife," he moaned. "Please don't tell my wife!" That his trouble was only temporary was proved by the fact that he soon returned to the front and fought as bravely as before.

Ike was virtually heartsick when he heard the full story. For the first time in his life that wonderful ability to restore himself by sleep deserted him. Through two long nights he lay awake, tossing on his bed in his hot room in Algiers, trying desperately to determine the right thing to do.

His primary consideration was to see that the unfortunate soldier received whatever amends were possible. His second problem was to decide whether the incident had been so damaging to Patton's standing with his army as to render him unfit for further command. With all his faults—and Ike was well aware of them—Patton was a great leader of assault forces. He had dash and energy and unquestioned courage. These qualities, combined with the great technical knowledge which he had acquired in his long years of study, made him perhaps the only American general who could match Rommel in handling armored divisions. Furthermore, he had just led his army to a brilliant victory; and, however the echelons might regard him personally, they had that trust in him as a commander which is the essence of morale. To deprive the Allied cause of the services of such a man would delay the hour of ultimate victory.

Then, too, Ike knew how hard George Patton had driven himself during the campaign. He had rested not a moment, but had forced himself beyond his strength. When he was not actively engaged in directing operations, he had gone among his men, exhorting and encouraging, deliberately exposing himself to danger for the sake of his theory that those soldiers fight best who are inspired by their commander. In thousands of instances he had personally supported, encouraged and sustained individuals.

There was no hesitation in the way Ike met the first problem. He wrote Patton a blistering letter. As one officer who saw it said, "General Ike certainly took the hide off him." The letter directed Patton to apologize to the soldier he had struck, to everybody in the hospital and to the whole Seventh Army. It further stated that the question of relieving Patton of his command would depend on the effect of his corrective action.

To a man of Patton's temperament, humbling himself in public must have been a bitter experience; but there was nothing niggardly about his apology. He carried it off in the extravagant manner which was his way, for whatever he did he did wholeheartedly.

First he gathered all the witnesses of the incident together and apologized to his victim, to them, and to the commandant of the hospital. He then ordered that as many officers and men as possible should be assembled at the headquarters of each division under his command, and went before each in turn to repeat his apology.

Before making his final decision as to whether Patton should be relieved of command, Eisenhower went to great lengths to ascertain whether any resentment against their general existed in the Seventh Army. He sent two generals to investigate the situation; and finally went himself to Sicily and talked in his characteristically frank way with the men. All reports and his own experience led him to the conclusion that the rank and file themselves felt that Patton had done a splendid over-all job, and that no irreparable harm had been done.

Finally, Ike discussed the whole affair freely with the correspondents in Algiers and found that in their opinion the measures taken by himself and General Patton were amply sufficient. On these grounds he decided to retain Patton in command of the Seventh Army.

In his report to General Marshall, Eisenhower concluded as follows: "Summing the matter up: it is true that General Patton was guilty of reprehensible conduct. Following exhaustive investigation I decided that the corrective action, as described, was suitable and adequate. Eventually it has been reported to me many times that, in every recent public appearance of Patton before any group composed of his own soldiers, he is greeted by thunderous applause."

The facts of these unhappy occurrences did not become public in America until November. When Drew Pearson, the columnist and radio commentator, broadcast the story, there was bitter criticism of Eisenhower for suppressing the news so long. The truth is that he did nothing of the kind.

According to Quentin Reynolds, in his book *The Curtain Rises*, he said to Eisenhower at the press conference, "This would be a nasty story to get out. Goebbels could do a lot with it. Every mother in America would think that her son was being subjected to this sort of treatment."

Eisenhower replied wearily, "I know, I know. But I will not impose any censorship on the story. No security is involved."

The correspondents all assured Eisenhower that they believed it was up to the Army to handle the story as it saw fit.

"I appreciate that, boys," Eisenhower said, "but I still won't order any censorship ban."

According to Reynolds, the sixty-odd correspondents then agreed among themselves that they were satisfied with Eisenhower's decision, and that it would be playing into Goebbels's hands to publish the story. They imposed a censorship on themselves for what they believed to be the good of their country, and loyally observed their own ban until Drew Pearson broke the story.

On August 30, two generals stood by a stone wall, looking through binoculars across the Strait of Messina. One of them was a big man with smiling eyes who wore an overseas cap at a cocky angle; when he turned his head the four stars on the cap flashed in the afternoon sunshine. The other, small, dark, and vibrant with nervous energy, wore a curiously shaped black beret. In the field behind Eisenhower and Montgomery, Sicilian farmers were swinging long-handled scythes. Hay lay in fat golden swaths on the stubble, and the sweetness of it filled the air. The calm blue of the water added to the apparent tranquillity of the scene. But the windless, crystal air shook to the concussion of "Long Toms," the great American 155-millimeter rifled guns, and on the soft green hills across the strait in Italy sulphur-yellow flowers of death bloomed and faded, while the dull boom of the bursting shells echoed the cannon's thunder.

The time had come for the first assault on Hitler's Fortress.

CHAPTER EIGHTEEN

THE COMMANDER IN CHIEF

The invasion of Sicily and the bombing of Rome on July 19, 1943, had cracked the thin crust of Fascist officialdom which held down the seething lava of Italian discontent. On July 26 Mussolini was deposed and imprisoned; and Field Marshal Pietro Badoglio was appointed by the King to head the new government. Nobody was more surprised than the Marshal, who had known nothing of the conspiracy.

On the fall of Mussolini, Eisenhower ordered all bombing of Italian cities to cease temporarily, and began to broadcast proclamations urging the Italians to make peace with the Allies. Badoglio, like the vast majority of his fellow countrymen, wanted to do just that; but, since the Nazis were in virtual occupation of the country, it wasn't so easy. The resulting diplomatic maneuvers involved General Eisenhower in a drama of international intrigue that outdid the efforts of the writers of lurid fiction.

It was August before Badoglio managed to slip two envoys out of the country. They were General Giuseppe Castellano and Signor Franco Montellari, who reported to the British Embassy in Madrid to discuss an armistice. They were terrified for their lives if the Gestapo should find them out, but their credentials were in order. A secret meeting was arranged in Lisbon and Eisenhower sent Major General Walter Bedell Smith and a brigadier general of G-2 to represent him.

The Italians had hoped to come in on the winning side, but they got the unconditional surrender formula; and the envoys left for Rome to place the terms before Badoglio and the King. The Americans presented them with two tiny radio outfits with which to communicate with Allied Headquarters.

Meanwhile Badoglio, who was in a fearful hurry for peace, sent another envoy, General Giacomo Zanussi, accompanied by a captured British general, Adrian Carton de Wiart, as evidence of good faith. Zanussi was taken straight to Algiers to see General Eisenhower.

Faint signals from the little wireless sets indicated Badoglio's acceptance of the Allies' terms; and word was sent that the Italian envoys were starting that night by plane for Sicily. They met with Smith and the G-2 representative at Advanced Headquarters in an olive grove near Catania.

There was more quibbling and Castellano made another secret trip to Rome, while Eisenhower came over to Sicily. On September 3, the armistice was finally signed in the conference tent at Catania, to take effect on September 9—D-day for the Italian attack.

In Catania, Castellano put forward a proposition which Ike quickly accepted; he suggested that an airborne division be sent to seize Rome in conjunction with Italian troops. The 82nd Airborne was hastily alerted for the adventure. Meanwhile the Eighth Army had already landed on the foot of Italy, seizing the naval base at Taranto.

The Sicilian campaign had gone so well that Eisenhower knew that the luck could not hold forever. He was right.

The first hitch occurred during the planning of the airborne attack on Rome, when the Allied Staff found that they could not get sufficiently exact information. Brigadier General Maxwell Taylor and Colonel W. T. Gardiner volunteered to risk their lives on a secret trip to Rome. They reached the Italian capital on September 7, which was D-2. But their personal safety was of less concern to them than the disconcerting news that the German garrison had been heavily reinforced. Fourteen fresh Nazi divisions had been hurried to Italy. As a result of secret conferences with Badoglio, Taylor decided that the American airborne division would be slaughtered on landing. Atmospherics made the transmission of this message over the tiny radio senders extremely difficult, and Eisenhower did not receive it until the paratroopers were actually standing by their planes on the eve of D-day. He immediately canceled this phase of the operation.

Still hiding in the Palazzo Caprara in Rome, Taylor and Gardiner were having a difficult time with Badoglio, who was in a funk. The Marshal contended that if he carried out his agreement to announce Italy's surrender that evening, simultaneously with a broadcast by Eisenhower, the Germans would shoot him on the spot. When Eisenhower got the message to this effect, he sent back a red-hot wireless to Badoglio, stating that he intended to announce the armistice anyhow. This put the Marshal in the position where, if he did not follow suit, he would lose the friendship of the Allies and be arrested by the Germans anyway.

At 6:30 on the evening of September 8, a calm, confident voice spoke over the air waves: "This is General Dwight D. Eisenhower, Commander in Chief of the Allied Forces.

"The Italian government has surrendered its armed forces unconditionally. As Allied Commander in Chief, I have granted a military armistice, the terms of which have been approved by the governments of the United States, Great Britain and the Union of Soviet Socialist Republics . . .

"Hostilities between the armed forces of the United Nations and those of Italy terminate at once. All Italians who now act to help eject the German aggressor from Italian soil will have the assistance and support of the United Nations."

An hour and a half later, Badoglio found the courage to speak. He told his people that the Italian government had sought an armistice from General Eisenhower, which had been granted. He ordered the Italian forces to cease all acts of hostility against the Anglo-American armies, and added the significant command to "oppose attacks from any other quarter."

Then the tall old Marshal and King Victor Emmanuel got into a black limousine and left town. They appeared the following day at Taranto, which was held by the Eighth Army.

The subsequent arrangements between the Badoglio government and the United Nations have been likened to the Darlan deal and subjected to the same adverse criticism. There were, however, two important differences. The first was that it was not an improvisation, but a considered plan laid down by three countries—England, Russia and America. The second was that Eisenhower did not have the responsibility for these arrangements; they were decided by the regular political representatives of the three nations concerned.

The agreement did, however, follow the pattern of dealing with the responsible authorities until someting better could be evolved. Later, Fascists were removed at all levels as in the case of the Vichy partisans at Algiers. It becomes evident that such an arrangement is essential in an occupied country where fighting is still going on, if military operations are not to be hamstrung by internal chaos. Even General de Gaulle has followed this procedure with all but the highest officials in France.

Meanwhile, Ike was able to devote himself to military matters, which, in view of ensuing events, was extremely fortunate.

General Eisenhower stood with Admiral Cunningham on the bridge of a British battleship and watched the spoils of victory come up over the horizon. The long line of gray ships steamed slowly over the deep-blue water of the sea they had once called their own. There were battleships and heavy cruisers, six-inch gun cruisers, destroyers and submarines—all that was left of the fleet which once had bluffed the British Navy.

They had suffered defeat and humiliation in this war, and gained no glory. Indeed, a gap in the line, where a few hours earlier the great battleship *Roma* had steamed, spoke mutely of their most gallant action: Nazi planes had attacked the Italian Fleet on their way to surrender, and they had fought their way through, leaving their finest ship sinking from the torpedoes of their former allies.

As Ike watched the Italian line of battle wheel in obedience to the orders of the British Admiral, he knew that this was the first great vindication of his strategic design. Though they had accomplished so little, as long as the Italians had a fleet in being, it was a menace against which twice its strength in Allied warships must guard. Now those British and American ships could sail away to the North Atlantic or the South Pacific wherever their strength was needed most, while down the vital Mediterranean highway to the east the argosies of victory sailed unchallenged.

The voice of their Commander in Chief, telling of Italy's surrender, reached the Fifth Army as their ships converged on the Gulf of Salerno on the evening of September 8. Their cheers rang across the quiet sea from transports and landing craft and warships; for they believed that this meant that there would be no fighting when they landed in the morning. Their officers went among them to tell them not to be too hopeful, but this did not dampen their enthusiasm. Even General Mark Wayne Clark was grinning like an amiable gargoyle.

"There are Italian divisions at Salerno," he told the correspondents. "This armistice may mean that we will at least get ashore without a fight."

Eisenhower had chosen Clark to command the Fifth Army under Alexander because of the nature of this operation. He picked his generals as a golfer might select a stick from his bag, according to whether the shot was a drive, an approach or a putt.

This Italian invasion was designed to be a holding operation on a large scale. Its immediate and minimum objectives were the capture of the splendid port of Naples and the great Foggia airfields. If Rome could be taken as well, so much the better, for its sentimental significance; but Ike did not want his men wasted by all-out attacks when the design was mainly to tie up as many Nazi divisions as possible. On this premise, and considering that the fighting would be in mountainous country where the armor would be handicapped, Ike had long ago weighed his generals and made his choice. Patton was too impetuous and his special talent for tanks would be wasted; Bradley was reserved for another occasion; Wayne Clark, scholarly, cool and skillful at infantry tactics, was the man to conserve his forces and make the most of opportunity, while refraining from attempting too much with too little. And yet—Wayne Clark was destined to fight the bloodiest battle of the Mediterranean war.

The rejoicing aboard the invasion armada was decidedly premature. Unknown to all on board, Rommel had outfoxed them. The Italian divisions at Salerno had been replaced only the day before by crack German troops. This time they were ready at the right place; this time it was going to be different.

At 3:30 A.M. on September 9, 1943, the first wave of landing boats started for the beaches. Making the attack were British commandos, the 36th American Division, formerly the Texas National Guard, and the 46th and 56th British Divisions. Raw troops they were, never before under fire, but they became veterans in about eight hours.

As the Higgins boats and the ducks heaved in the creamy breakers, the coastal batteries opened with a crash. Then the German 88s began to fire down from the hills and the automatic weapons that enfiladed the beach sprayed the attackers. It looked as if the entire strip of sand were laced by white and red and purple streaks of fire; it was impossible to conceive that a man could stay alive there for five minutes.

But men did. They tumbled ashore from the boats and ran,

crouching for a few yards, then flopped in the sand and dug feverishly with their helmets or answered the enemy with the light weapons they carried. Behind them the cruisers *Boise, Savannah* and *Philadelphia* began to search for the coastal batteries with long fingers of fire from their guns. More men rushed ashore as the LCIs began to come in and the LSTs maneuvered for position. Ever so often a blinding flash of light and a tall column of fire, streaked by the sparkle of exploding ammunition, indicated that a landing craft had blown up.

There was an unexpectedly broad belt of mines in front of the beach where the commandos and the 36th were landing; their heavy stuff had to wait until the field was cleared by mine-sweepers under enemy fire. Meanwhile the Texans hung on by their eyebrows and fought the German armor and artillery with tommy guns, rifles and bazookas.

With the dawn things got worse. The Beaufighters of the night patrol turned back, and Seafires, Spitfires, P-38s and P-51s wheeled in formation at different altitudes to hold the sky. But, except for the carrier-based Seafires, these Allied fighters were operating from Sicilian fields at extreme range and could not remain over the beach for more than a short time. This incomplete coverage gave the Luftwaffe plenty of opportunity, which they took.

Messerschmitt 109s skipped over the crests of the hills and dove at the beaches, raking them with machine guns and light cannon. Squadrons of bombers went after the crowded shipping, while Stukas dove screaming at the supply dumps. The German air force was only a few minutes' flight from its main Mediterranean base at Foggia; the planes could make a round trip every two hours. Meanwhile, from the hills which commanded the strand, German artillery fired downward on the unprotected Allies.

It was a miracle that we were able to establish a beachhead at all—a miracle of courage and desperate tenacity shown by men who had never before been in battle. Somehow supplies were brought ashore, and men fought and crawled forward until the lines were advanced a short distance inland.

At his headquarters Rommel heard of the advance and smiled. Let them come a little way if they liked; then he would unleash the power of his crack divisions which were pouring through Rome and down the main-line railway to Naples.

When the German counterattack did strike, it looked as though Rommel would be avenged for El Alamein and Tunisia. The

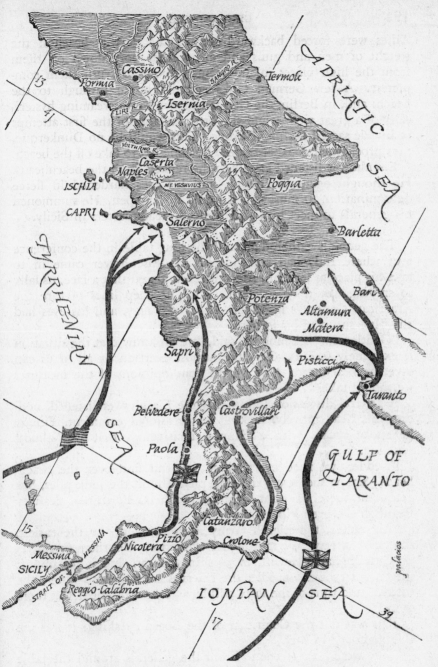

The Invasion of Italy, September, 1943

Allies were forced backward toward the narrow beaches; the weight of men and guns and armor that bore down on them from the high places inland seemed about to crush them completely. A few German tanks actually broke through to the beach; and, in Berlin, the German papers were screaming hysterically of a great victory and the utter collapse of the first attempt to invade sacred *Festung Europa*. This would be no Dunkerque, they proclaimed, for there would be none left to take off the beach.

Eisenhower listened grimly to the reports from the beachheads. He thought again of Dieppe, and his eyes hardened in fierce determination. It must not, it would not happen. He summoned his generals to meet him at Advanced Headquarters in Sicily.

The generals gathered around the long table in the conference tent where Italy had surrendered. As Eisenhower came in to take his place at its head, Alexander wondered that a face, usually so smiling, could be so stern. With its deep lines of care the American General's face looked almost craggy, and his eyes had the blue sheen of an iceberg.

"Gentlemen," Eisenhower said, "we all know that the situation is extremely serious. Only the utmost exertion by all of us can save the beachhead. May I have your opinions of the measures we should take?"

A general discussion followed while Eisenhower listened, nodding his head gravely, making an occasional comment. Finally he spoke again, with a clipped incisiveness that was almost startling.

"Tedder, we need every plane you can find over the beachheads. Scrape the desert airfields, pick 'em off the junk piles, but get them there! I want fighters, bombers, Fortresses, Seafires, Beaufighters, even Piper Cubs.

"Alexander, the Eighth Army must come up by the easiest, the *quickest* way. We must effect a junction. Get them there!"

"Cunningham, Hewitt, every ship you can find is to support the troops ashore! Beedle, the reserves must get up faster, the turn-around time of the ships will have to be shortened. Get them there!"

This was not the Chairman of the Board speaking; it was the Commander in Chief.

They were a great team. From the generals around the table to the cooks of the Texas Division shooting at German tanks with revolvers, they did all that men could do, and when that was not enough, they did twice as much. American planes darkened the sunny Italian skies. Great flights of Fortresses smashed enemy communications and wrecked the network of railways around Naples as a broom sweeps down a spiderweb. More troops and tanks and guns poured into the narrow beachhead. Ashore, British and Americans stood off the dreadful power of the Panzers, and when the enemy gave them a breathing spell, attacked against the heavy odds.

The Eighth Army was racing up the coast, and Texas boys who last year might have sneered at the "limeys" clasped their red-hot guns and whispered, "God, make the English come."

The wind of fortune veered, and the first weathercock to swing was the German press, cautioning its readers against expecting too much. "The fierce resistance of the enemy . . . Fresh landings in overwhelming force . . ." The Panzers crawled back into the hills, licking their wounds, and an advanced patrol of the Fifth Army met up with some Desert Rats in a scout car. It was an auspicious meeting.

On September 19 Eisenhower, with Butcher and Admiral Hewitt, visited the Salerno front. Those steep green hills were quiet now; and the little waves lapped undisturbed on the beaches. But the fearful force of the fire had left them scarred and pitted, desolate with the redolence of death.

Ike borrowed a jeep and started for the front. The way led through the Hellenic ruins of ancient Paestum, now reduced to rubble by the surge and ebb of the armored tides. A little Greek temple which had stood there for twenty-five hundred years was no more than a few broken columns and a drift of marble dust.

From there the wreckage-littered road rose steeply, winding through gorges, climbing in hairpin turns. Even Ike, who had planned it, could hardly understand how his men had gained these heights against such odds. And still farther beyond them, he saw the mountains, ridge on ridge like angry green waves, blocking the road to Naples. The troops would have to fight their way across the spiny range which ran out into the Sorrento Peninsula before they looked down on the easy littoral around Naples. They'd do it, he knew, but the going would be tough.

Near the front the weary Texans roused themselves to yell

for Ike, and Wayne Clark showed off his men with a pride his reserve could not conceal.

"They got to be veterans quicker than any troops you ever saw," he said. "They'll match the Seventh any day."

Clark was optimistic about getting to Naples.

"The Jerries are softening up," he said. "You can feel it. The bombing has wrecked their communications so badly that I doubt if they dare make an all-out stand here for fear of being trapped."

Clark was right. It took fierce fighting to get to Naples, but the Germans did not make a last-ditch stand. They had left their Sunday punch in the wreckage at Salerno, and their defense of Naples was a delaying action to give them time to wreck the port.

Naples fell and the Eighth Army took the Foggia airfields. This latter action not only deprived the German air force of its principal Mediterranean base, but also enabled the Allies to keep their fighter planes in close support and gave them a springboard from which the heavy bombers could attack those parts of the German Fortress which, by reason of distance, were inaccessible from England.

So were the prime objectives of the campaign accomplished. The Italian Fleet had been subtracted from the German strength and added to that of the Allies. We had gained a magnificent port and the best airfields in all that theater of operation. More important still, at least twenty Nazi divisions, many of them drawn from Russia, Yugoslavia and the defense of France, were tied up in Italy.

There remained the taking of Rome. For a time Eisenhower believed that this, too, might soon be accomplished; but the Germans threw in still more reserves for a desperate stand in the mountains north of Naples, and the Allied attacks were stopped at the key fortress town of Cassino. With the forces at hand it was impossible to break through, and for a little time yet Rome had to be left in German hands.

Nevertheless, the Allied Commander in Chief could view the results of his strategy with confidence. The governments under which he held command seemed well-satisfied, and there may have been a hint of things to come in the carefully chosen wording of the citation with which President Roosevelt at this time awarded to General Eisenhower the Oak Leaf Cluster to the Distinguished Service Medal. After stressing the General's "outstanding contribution to the war effort of the Allied Nations," his service in organizing the occupation of North Africa and in handling the internal situation there, his skill in co-ordinating the British, American and French naval, air and ground forces for the great victory in Tunisia, and the brilliance of the Sicilian campaign, the citation concluded:

"Throughout these operations, in preparation and execution, General Eisenhower has displayed conspicuous ability to secure complete unity of command of action of a great Allied force, with disastrous consequences to the enemy."

(Signed) Franklin D. Roosevelt.

CHAPTER NINETEEN

"YOU'D BETTER BEGIN PACKING..."

While Allied military affairs had been moving so favorably, the United Nations had been making what was probably even more important progress on the political front. The objective of their statesmen had long been unity between the British Empire and the United States, on the one hand, and Russia, on the other. During the summer and fall of 1943, this end was forwarded in a series of diplomatic exchanges and conferences. Russia's participation in the settlement in Italy was evidence of some progress, and a definite basis of agreement was reached at the Moscow Conference in October. There remained, to crown these diplomatic labors, the long-desired meeting between Roosevelt, Churchill and the enigmatic ruler of Russia. This was finally set to take place at Teheran from November 27 to December 2, 1943.

On November 19, General Eisenhower was in Oran to meet *his* Commander in Chief, and the following morning he accompanied the President to the airport for the long flight to Cairo. A big four-engined transport awaited them, piloted by Major Otis F. Bryan, formerly vice-president of Transcontinental and Western Air Lines, Incorporated. Behind it, the fighter escort of P-39s and Spitfires sat on the field with their propellers turning. A fuzzy gray overcast scudded no more than two thousand feet overhead, which meant that the flight must be made at low altitude if the fighters were to hold formation.

Though the plane was light with weight, it was heavy with honor, and heavy was the responsibility on its pilot and crew; on Colonel Covington, who commanded the fighters; and most especially upon General Eisenhower, who was ultimately accountable for the security of all. Aboard the transport, in addition to the President and the General, were Admiral William D. Leahy, Harry Hopkins, Major General E. M. Watson, Rear Admiral Ross T. McIntire, Rear Admiral Wilson Brown and Lieutenant Franklin D. Roosevelt, Jr.

Not wishing to put all the rank in one airplane, it had been arranged that General Marshall, General Henry H. Arnold and Admiral Ernest J. King should travel in other transports with their respective staffs.

As soon as the President was comfortably settled, Major Bryan taxied the great transport onto the runway and revved up its four motors, each in turn. Just as it was poised for flight, a little Piper Cub came brazenly in for a landing despite red flares of warning. When it was out of the way and its pilot had been verbally skinned alive, the presidential plane took the air.

Ike, sitting beside the President, looked down as they banked around the field to see the fighters scooting across it in formation. A glance upward showed him the P-38s wheeling overhead to give local cover for the historic take-off.

Holding barely below the clouds, Major Bryan headed out to sea, for the low ceiling made it impossible to fly contact over the mountains. Ike got a tremendous sense of speed from the gray masses of vapor sliding past just above the wings and the trailing wisps of fog that flashed past the windows. The escort closed around them, rising and falling on the invisible inequalities of the air; the ocean beneath them looked as flat as a pewter plate.

When he was not chatting with the President, Ike rode in the copilot's seat beside Bryan. As they approached Djidjelli, where the second relay of fighters was to relieve the first, he felt the back hair rise on his scalp. He had spotted a twin-engined French bomber heading for them. He pointed it out to Bryan. At the same instant a P-39 broke formation and dove at the stranger. The Frenchman paid no heed, and three more fighters peeled off and went screaming down on the slow bomber, like stooping hawks.

Orders were to shoot down anything approaching within three miles of the President's plane, and Ike expected to see the guns open at any moment. But just in time, the Frenchman realized his danger and wheeled away, shepherded by the watchful fighters.

The President spent that night at Tunis. He was supposed to proceed the next morning, but decided that he would prefer to spend the day looking over the battlefields, and make a night flight to Cairo. The fighters, which would be useless in the darkness, were sent on ahead with orders to rendezvous with the President's plane when it reached the Nile at dawn.

The big transport with its irreplaceable cargo flew unescorted across the Libyan Desert. Ike was naturally concerned for the safety of those in his charge; but once the plane was airborne there was nothing he could do about it and, summoning his invaluable resource, he slept until the sky ahead lightened with the dawn. Then he went forward and took his favorite place in the copilot's seat.

The colors of morning flowed into the sky and were reflected in the tumbled immensity of sand seven thousand feet below them. Ahead, Ike saw a strip of verdant cultivation stretching across their course from horizon to horizon, and in the middle of it a winding ribbon of delicately tinted water. The Nile was really Nile green.

Major Bryan hit the rendezvous at El Minya right on the nose and on the minute; but there was no sign of the fighter escort. For what seemed to be a long time the transport circled in the empty sky like a lonely condor. After perhaps a quarter of an hour, it was patent that something had gone wrong. It was discovered afterward that the fighters had understood the rendezvous to be at 6:00 A.M. Egyptian time, whereas it was really two hours later at six o'clock Greenwich time. They had circled in that same sky until their fuel began to run out, and then returned to Cairo.

The question now was whether to break radio silence and ask for an escort, or to bring the President into Cairo unprotected. Bryan put it up to Eisenhower. Weighing the odds, it seemed to Ike that secrecy was a surer shield than air cover.

"Take us in," he ordered.

The plane flew along that narrow strip of irrigated green fields, which, Ike knew, split the desert for twelve hundred miles from Khartoum to the sea. On either side of it, a wave of tawny sand seemed about to break over and obliterate the thin strand of civilization. As they approached Cairo, Bryan gradually brought the plane lower, so that they could distinguish the irrigation ditches, the ox-turned water wheels, and the fellaheen laboring in the small vivid green fields outlined by dikes of chocolate-colored mud.

Ike went aft to talk with the President, who was as excited as any tourist. He was particularly interested in the Nile boats, with their lateen sails carried high on their masts to catch the wind above the level of the embankments.

Presently three triangular shadows appeared against the golden sand, and Bryan swung off his course to show the delighted President what the Pyramids and the Sphinx looked like from above. Then the plane headed up the straight black ribbon of a road toward the jumble of flat-topped roofs, domes, and dainty minarets of Cairo.

General Eisenhower attended the Cairo Conference, but he took little part in its political arrangements. He spent every possible moment in conference with Generals Marshall and Arnold and the British Chiefs of Staff, working on the great plan that for so long had been the focus of his thoughts and the object of his will. Abstract and general it had been when they talked at Casablanca nearly a year ago; now it was finite and defined to the point where detailed decisions were being made. But it would continue to lack purpose and essential clarity until a commander was appointed.

When the Cairo Conference was ended and the statesmen pushed on to Teheran for the grand climax, Eisenhower went back to Algiers to attend to business. He was to meet the President afterward to learn firsthand the decisions of the conference.

In a white villa by the sea at Carthage they met again. The President was to stay there with Ike for two days of relaxation before going on to Sicily and Malta and home.

On the afternoon of the first day they sat alone together in the pretty, modern drawing room of the villa, overlooking the vivid blue water of the Gulf of Tunis. The tumbled mountains of the Cap Bon Peninsula looked fierce and rugged against the delicate colors of the evening sky. The broken columns and roofless walls of the town the Romans had built on the grave of their great enemy were warmed by a rosy light.

The President was in high humor, the resilience of his spirit rebounding from the strain of the great events which he had recently concluded. He looked at his General, of whom he was genuinely fond; there was a twinkle in his eye and the famous cigarette holder went up at an acute angle.

"Well, Ike," he drawled, "you'd better begin packing your duds. You're going to London."

CHAPTER TWENTY

SUPREME COMMANDER

The surge of emotion started in Ike's brain and lodged in his stomach. The President's casual words meant that he was to be Supreme Commander of the Allied Invasion Forces. On the surface of his mind, he was not particularly surprised, for it was in the cards that an American general would command the armies, and he realized that he was a logical choice. But deep in his soul Ike was astounded.

It was such a long way from the little white house in Kansas to this villa at old Carthage, with the President sitting there in the companionable way of friendship. The odds against that Kansas boy's attaining the position now offered to him were enough to make a poker player's head swim. Getting a pat royal straight flush was nothing compared to it, for, Ike realized, he was to occupy a post such as no American had ever before held. Even General Pershing had commanded only an American army, while Eisenhower was to be entrusted with the direction of the greatest military enterprise in the history of America and Britain; and under him would serve not only the armies of those great countries, but the navies which were designated for the invasion and the troops of all their smaller allies. His opportunity was magnificent; and his responsibility was crushing.

If a man let himself dwell on that, he might well be frightened; but Ike found he could face this tremendous job serenely. Two years ago he would have been appalled; even a year ago he might have been nervous; but since then he had been tested and proved. He was prepared to accept this greater responsibility, not with conceit, but with full awareness that now all his years of arduous training and study and the fullness of experience which he had gained in Africa, Sicily and Italy would be integrated to help him meet the most tremendous trial of military leadership yet assigned to one man. Within himself he felt the power to do the job. As at last he found words to thank the President, he faced the future confidently.

The appointment of General Dwight D. Eisenhower to the Supreme Command was one point on which the United Nations were completely united. The people of his country had absolute confidence in him, which was reinforced by their genuine affection inspired by his simple, friendly personality and their tremendous pride in the fact that he was so completely American. Joseph Stalin, who should know a good general when he saw one, had pressed for Eisenhower's appointment at Moscow and Teheran. The British, too, headed by Winston Churchill, had long since given him their confidence, and, what was more rare, their friendship.

The press of the entire free world acclaimed the choice made at Teheran, without a single sour note—a unanimity even more remarkable than that of the United Nations. The London *Times* Weekly Edition lost its sober conservative tone in an enthusiasm that was symptomatic of editorial opinion everywhere. Its comment read in part:

"The charge entrusted to the Supreme Commander, which is nothing less than the liberation of the continent, has no parallel in history since the great Duke of Marlborough assumed the leadership of the armies of the Grand Alliance. No choice could have been more acceptable to all the Allied Services than that of General Dwight Eisenhower.

"Since he was nominated to the command of the combined services of the United Nations, based on Africa, he has presided over operations which have proceeded with unbroken success. His most individual contribution of strategy has been his gift of drawing together officers of divers nationality and professional training into a harmonious brotherhood, thereby generating a spirit of comradeship which has been communicated to all the ranks in the field."

The great transport slid down the hill of the air toward the spokes and wheels of light which were the streets and circles of Washington. The black band of the Potomac with its stitching of brilliants passed beneath the unfolding wheels, and the fivefold circle of the Pentagon Building slipped under a wing tip. Ike was so excited that he could hardly speak. In a strictly personal way this brief home-coming, this chance to see again the people he loved so much and had missed so sorely, meant more to him than all the honors he had received and the victories he had won.

The fat tires rolled gently down a concrete runway and, as they stopped turning, a limousine with its curtains drawn dashed under the spreading wing. Ike stumbled down the little ladder from the plane and hopped into it, followed by Butch, Ernie Lee and Mickey.

At the Wardman Park Hotel, where they had lived in adjoining apartments ever since their husbands had gone abroad, Mamie Eisenhower and Ruth Butcher were waiting in a state of expectation which bordered on frenzy. It was long past midnight when they heard a muffled laugh in the back hallway, and their husbands walked in. The men were smiling broadly, and each carried a tiny Scotty puppy in his arms. Instantly the kitchen was filled with laughter and the hysterical yapping of the puppies. As soon as she was able to speak, Mamie demanded an explanation of the dogs.

"They're a son and daughter of Telek," Ike said. "One is for Ruth's daughter and the other for Milton's children."

The puppies were put in a spare bathroom, and the reunited couples talked the night out, while Ike, who had had short rations of his favorite food for a long time, ransacked both kitchens and ate every onion he could find—raw.

The days of Ike's leave were spent in fast and furious dashing from place to place in curtained limousines and dodging in and out of back doorways. This furtive behavior was necessary because the presence of the Supreme Commander in America was the topmost of top secrets.

The first two days, Sunday and Monday, January 2 and 3, were spent in Washington. On Monday night Ike and Mamie boarded a special car in the railway yards for a brief visit to John at the Military Academy. Only a physical peculiarity of the terrain at West Point enabled Ike to make this trip with the essential secrecy. The station is under the bluffs and cannot be seen from the Academy. Ike's car was put on a guarded siding, and nobody at West Point knew of his presence there, except General and Mrs. Wilby and six cadets.

Almost before the car stopped moving, Ike sent an aide to fetch John; and before the officer was even out of sight, he began pacing the floor and going to the door to look expectantly up the hill.

John was working in the machine shop when a messenger arrived with an order to report to the Superintendent's office immediately in whatever uniform he had on. He was startled, for no boy's conscience is clear enough to face that sort of thing calmly, but when John in his dirty denims, saluted the Superintendent, General Wilby was beaming like the sun on Midsummer Day.

"General Eisenhower is down at the station," he said. "He seems to want to see you."

John had not even guessed that his father was in this country. He saluted and was off like an antelope, followed by the badly winded aide.

But when the father and son who cared so much for each other met, they were very casual.

"Hi, dad!"

"How goes it, John?"

Then they fell into earnest conversation about such unimportant topics as the Tunisian campaign and whether John should elect the artillery or choose his father's branch, the infantry. Mamie, watching them, wondered if John could really be as cool as he seemed. Then, as he passed her walking through the car, she noticed that his hand was quivering.

"So you are kind of excited," she whispered.

"I'm practically boiling," he answered.

The Wilbys came for lunch, and in the afternoon John made a brief trip to the Academy to change his clothes, and to buy some of Ike's favorite pajamas, which could be purchased only at the Cadet Store.

"How would you like to have some of your friends down for dinner?" Ike asked, when John got back.

"I'd like it," John said, "and they'd go crazy."

John named five cadets, and then the question arose as to how to get them away from evening mess without attracting attention, for no cadet eats out on Tuesday evening. The problem was solved by General Wilby's ordering them to dine at his quarters.

The fortunate five arrived promptly and were greeted by the Superintendent, who said, "I regret, gentlemen, that I am unable to have the pleasure of your company this evening. You are to dine with General Eisenhower in his private car at the station."

Even West Point discipline isn't equal to a shock like that. Military formality cracked up badly under the strain, and the five were barely able to give the feeblest of salutes. But they were very rigid and official again as they sat down to dinner in the General's car.

That wasn't the way Ike liked his parties to be, and he went to work on his guests. His friendliness, aided by a superspecial steak, put them so completely at ease that before the evening was done they were offering well-considered advice on how to win the war.

That night Mamie and Ike returned to Washington, and the following evening they went to White Sulphur Springs, where General Marshall had lent them his house. There Ike spent much of the time visiting his wounded men at the great military hospital, and the rest of it cursing the weather, for as soon as the skies cleared he was to fly home to Kansas for a family reunion. Milton was now president of the Kansas State College of Agriculture and Applied Science at Manhattan, and the plan was to gather the Eisenhowers together at his house on the campus rather than in Abilene, lest the great secret of the General's presence in America get out.

Bad weather delayed Ike's take-off until Saturday, and even then his big transport had to battle winter storms halfway across the continent. It was after dark when the plane was set down on the icy field at Fort Riley. Ike stayed on board, while Colonel McCarthy, who was acting as his aide, went to Operations to telephone for a car. As McCarthy was putting through his call he saw two soldiers peering through the window at the huge shadowy wings of the General's plane.

"I wonder who came in by that big ship," one of them commented.

"Don't go and tell me that's Eisenhower," his companion said. "Every time a plane like that's come in for the last year and a half, they say it's Ike."

An Army car drove up close to the transport and Ike got into it alone, carrying Telek II in his arms. As it dashed through the windy night, the Supreme Commander pressed his nose against the window, trying to see all he could of those bleak prairies, which were so familiar and so dear.

Milton's gray stone house stood among trees in a corner of the campus. Ike saw lights glowing behind the drawn shades of every window as his car followed the curve of the driveway. When it stopped, the front door of the house swung wide, as though all the warmth and light and love that awaited him had burst it open. Milton came to meet him, smiling, and pumped his hand, and when Ike stepped into the living room, he found his mother waiting there, alone.

"Why, it's Dwight," she said in thrilling tones.

Then there was a sound of scuffling and laughter in the hall. Milton's wife, Helen, came running down the stairs with her children, Buddy and Ruth. Ike caught them up in his arms, hugging and kissing them in turn, and gleefully presented Ruth with Telek II, who promptly licked her face. More of the family were coming downstairs: Arthur, beaming like an effulgent moon, and his wife, Louise; the Douds, who had come on from Denver, and Helen's mother, Mrs. Eakin.

Those few hours in Kansas were the happiest Ike had known for more than two years. He soaked in that happiness, trying to store it, as one would charge an electric battery, against the long, lonely months ahead. His mother seemed alert and gay despite her nearly eighty-two years; Arthur was in grand spirits; and as for the youngest brother, Ike had the feeling that he had at last come into his own. Milton had cherished the ambition to be president of Kansas State all through his adult life; it was good to see people as happy as he and Helen were, with their lovable children and their beautiful house, and, above all, their busy and useful life.

For dinner the Eisenhowers had rare roast beef—a wartime scarcity—which was testimony to the importance of the occasion. Afterward the brothers talked until long past midnight. When at last they reluctantly started for bed, Ike said to Milton, as he always used to, "I think I'll just tiptoe down the hall and take a peek at the kids."

Because weather reports warned of storms closing in, Ike had to leave early the next morning, and Milton planned to go with him. They had mush and chicken gravy for breakfast—it had been impossible to procure puddin. The two brothers took off about nine and flew directly to White Sulphur, where Ike had two more days with Mamie before he had to go back to Washington for the final conferences.

Ike was to leave for England on Thursday evening. That day

General Marshall invited those of his old Army friends who were in Washington to a farewell luncheon in the Chief of Staff's office at the Pentagon. Very few of them knew whom they were going to meet. As the Supreme Commander greeted them with his familiar grin and a strong clasp of the hand, they felt he was the same old Ike they had always known; and yet, in that radiant, confident personality they sensed a subtle difference, a new quality, to which more than one, considering it afterward, put the word "serenity."

All of them knew that this man would not dawdle on the road to victory.

After lunch Ike had about two hours left to spend with Mamie in her apartment at the Wardman Park. All through his leave she had been as gay and flashing as when she was a girl, and they had laughed a great deal. Now she was subdued; and at the end she clung to him.

"Don't come back again till it's over," she cried. "I can't stand losing you again."

SHAEF—pronounced Shafe and meaning Supreme Headquarters Allied Expeditionary Force—was a cluster of small brick buildings set in a wooded park at the end of an English lane. Other sections were scattered throughout England and Scotland, but the heart and brain of SHAEF were there. Its very existence was an inviolable secret. The houses were roofed with tin, over which camouflage netting was spread; and they were anything but imposing. They contained, however, all the intricate apparatus necessary to conduct the greatest military enterprise in history. There were guarded war rooms in which the great wall maps showed the latest information on enemy dispositions; a huge telephone exchange through which communication could be had instantly with thousands of units on land and sea; and deep underground, the operations center.

When Eisenhower was there he lived in an elaborate trailer which he called his "circus wagon." His office was a room perhaps twenty feet square in the main building. Its windows looked out on a tranquil scene of park and woodland. Two easy chairs cozily faced the fireplace, and Ike's big walnut desk, with a battery of telephones on it, stood near the window. The only visible indications of the business of war were a huge globe at one side of the room, a stand of Allied flags behind the Supreme Commander's chair, and, on one wall of the room, a silver screen which could be rolled up like a window shade to reveal a large-scale war map.

The forces of destruction controlled from that small room were so tremendous as to distance the imagination. The Widow at Windsor with her "ships on the foam and millions at 'ome" never had at her command one-tenth the power that was deployed at the end of an intricate system of electrical communications by General Ike of Kansas.

The men of Eisenhower's carefully chosen Invasion Team worked in offices close by. Tedder, whose mind meshed so precisely with his own, was Deputy Commander in Chief. As commander of all the ground troops, Ike had picked Montgomery, the inspired leader whose military genius flashed more brightly than that of any other Allied general. Under him, less brilliant but nevertheless keenly intelligent and a rock of steadfastness, Omar Bradley directed the American Ground Forces.

There were new faces on the team. Air Chief Marshal Sir Trafford Leigh-Mallory commanded the Allied Air Forces, but under him were Toohey Spaatz, Brereton, with the enormously enlarged Ninth Tactical Air Force, and Doolittle with the heavy bombers of the veteran Eighth. Other additions were Admiral Sir Bertram H. Ramsay, commanding the Combined Naval Forces, and his American subordinate, Rear Admiral Alan Kirk; backing them up was Ike's old stand-by, Admiral Cunningham, who was now First Sea Lord. Finally, there was Lieutenant General Walter Bedell Smith, Chief of Staff, of whom Ike said, "Beedle is the most nearly indispensable man."

In a lowly capacity, but perhaps hardly less indispensable, Sergeant Mickey McKeough still looked after his general, and in his spare time continued to court Ike's second driver, Pearlie the beautiful Wac.

Ike regarded his Invasion Team as comrades, not subordinates. They worked together, pooling their intelligence under the skillful co-ordination of the Supreme Commander, who bent every effort to weld this new and greater Allied Force into a single army, inspired by one great purpose. Ike sent one subordinate home for referring to an Allied officer as "a British s.o.b."

"I don't mind your calling him an s.o.b. if he is one," said Ike, "but I'm damned if you shall call him a *British s.o.b.*"

The plans for the invasion went forward fast. Compiling them was an undertaking of astronomical magnitude, which might well be reckoned in light-years. Long before Eisenhower took command, rough drafts had been made of several possible methods of attack; and when the decision was made, the chosen plan became a template to guide the work.

The basic conception of the first assault had the simplicity of sensible military practice. It was to seize beachheads on the north side of the Cotentin Peninsula of Normandy, within fighter range of England. The next step was to drive across it, isolating the peninsula and the port of Cherbourg from the rest of France. Finally Cherbourg was to be taken from the rear, thus providing the Allied forces with a great port through which essential supplies and reinforcements could be landed. Meanwhile the enemy forces at the base of the peninsula were in turn to be isolated as far as possible by the bombing of all supply routes to prevent them from obtaining reinforcements and supplies.

The beauty of the plan was its flexibility. If the enemy sat back and waited, reluctant to throw his full weight against the Allies in Normandy for fear they would strike elsewhere, they could then exploit the landing to the full, as in actuality they did. If, on the other hand, the Germans hurled in everything they had, lessening their strength elsewhere, the Allies, with great forces as yet uncommitted, could strike at the weakened link in the chain of defense. Whatever the enemy did would be wrong, because the Allies had mobility, the initiative and a fluid plan.

But to implement this simple conception required detailed planning of infinite magnitude. First, Army Intelligence, G-2, collated all obtainable information concerning enemy dispositions and made it available to the Chief of Staff. He allotted small sectors to individual officers, each of whom had to work out the details for his particular position. The next step was to fit these plans together like an extremely intricate picture puzzle, and revise them in the light of available troops and matériel. The action of naval and air forces, the disposition of transport ships and landing craft, and the supply problems had to be co-ordinated. Special equipment had to be procured to take care of peculiar enemy defenses, such as the mines fastened to stakes, the underwater obstructions and the ingenious barriers on the beaches. Finally there was the preparation of the huge floating harbors which enabled the Allied Armies to land so much faster than the Germans thought possible.

As the plans were worked out, they were submitted by the

Chief of Staff to the Supreme Commander for his approval. Even after that they had to be constantly revised in the light of changing conditions and new enemy dispositions. The drawing up of the orders for each of the tens of thousands of units on land and sea and air was in itself a task of great magnitude. For instance, one complete set of naval orders weighed three hundred pounds, and the total number of maps used by all arms was 125,000,000.

In all our previous wars the staff work of the American armies had left a good deal to be desired. This time it has been superb; and it is worth a footnote that Eisenhower is the only Commander in Chief in our history who came up through the Staff. All the others were field officers.

Despite the enormous burden upon him, Ike was able to spend a third to a half of his time with the men of his armies. He could do this because he chose his subordinates carefully and then trusted them to solve their particular problems, not cluttering his own mind with lesser matters or drowning himself in a sea of detail. His elaborate special train roared around the British island faster than ever as he went from one cantonment to another. On these trips he always took a special jeep equipped with radio, so that even when he was actually on the ground with the troops, he could be in direct contact with Supreme Headquarters and carry on his staff work.

Another trip took Ike to Belfast in Northern Ireland to inspect units of the combined fleets gathered there. It was a blustery day with a cold, penetrating rain, and he was wearing a long Army raincoat over his uniform. As he was piped over the side of an American destroyer, the sailors stood in rigid lines awaiting his inspection. Noticing that they wore no protection against the weather, the Supreme Commander stripped off his own raincoat, saying, "I'll be damned if I'll wear a coat while I inspect men who aren't wearing 'em!"

Ike's preoccupation with weighty matters did not prevent him from keeping in close touch with his family and friends in America. His one real relaxation and his greatest pleasure was still to write letters and receive news from home. Mamie got several long letters every week and his mother nearly as many. Ike's brothers and old friends heard from him frequently—not short notes, but long, thoughtful epistles in which Eisenhower unburdened his mind and philosophically discussed world affairs, as well as individual problems. In addition, he answered every serious letter he received, from requests from school children in Abilene for his help in selling war bonds to notes from complete strangers.

A typical example of his consideration for the individual is an incident which occurred during the early stages of the Italian campaign. Ike received a letter from John saying that an Italian tailor who worked in the Cadet Store at West Point was much concerned for the safety of his daughter, who lived in a small town in southern Italy. John wanted to know if there was any way in which he could be reassured. The Commander in Chief took the time to see what could be done; and within two weeks of the day the tailor spoke to John, the grateful Italian had word that his daughter was safe and well.

It sometimes seemed to the Allied Staff that the Supreme Commander had more time than anyone else; they knew he did more things. He could find leisure even to chat with an enlisted man from Abilene, who dropped in at London Headquarters to see his fellow townsman.

Once or twice a week, Ike had a pleasant leisurely lunch with Winston Churchill. These two had become great friends. The Prime Minister called the Supreme Commander "Ike," and Eisenhower addressed him as "Sir" or "Prime."

"The reason I like you, Ike," Churchill said on one occasion, "is because you ain't no glory-hopper."

Ike laughed delightedly, for Prime had borrowed one of his own favorite phrases.

As the time approached for the great trial by battle, tension rose under the tin roofs of SHAEF, in the offices, cantonments and barracks throughout the British Isles, in ships and at flying fields, and throughout the whole world. But nowhere was it so painfully acute as within Hitler's beleaguered fortress. This was no accidental circumstance, but part of the plan.

It was obvious that strategic surprise was impossible to achieve. The marshaling of millions of troops, thousands of ships, and untold quantities of matériel could not be kept a secret. Eisenhower therefore decided to capitalize on the knowledge which the enemy must have of the mounting power of destruction threatening him. A war of nerves became part of the softening-up process which the Allied Strategic Air Force was carrying out in the more concrete form of thousand-bomber raids on the vital centers of the enemy. The press and radio were encouraged to put out stories of the vast preparations being made, and allowed to hazard guesses as to where the Allied Force would strike. German nerves were worn down by loss of sleep and frayed by incessant reminders of that gathering potential of destruction.

In addition, Eisenhower kept in close touch with the leaders of the underground in the occupied countries, and an American radio station was opened in England for the purpose of communicating more directly with the subjected peoples. As the hour neared, Eisenhower prepared instructions for D-day, which spokesmen broadcast in appropriate languages to the European underground. Not only were these short treatises on revolt and sabotage instructive to thousands of Europeans who were ready actively to aid the Allied cause, but they added immeasurably to the German jitters.

A final instrument in the process of needling Nazi nerves was the huge invasion exercises held at frequent intervals. Though the practice landings were made on British beaches, the hundreds of warships, transports and landing craft involved invariably started out straight for the European coast and did not turn back until they had produced alarms and excursions among the enemy. After crying wolf a great number of times the German watchers became careless.

Though the strategic fact of impending invasion was completely publicized and exploited, Ike was grimly determined to achieve tactical surprise; the moment and place were secrets guarded by every precaution that could be taken, and the utmost severity was adopted toward careless conversationalists.

Another element of surprise, in addition to the floating harbors, was the new landing technique that Eisenhower had personally decided to adopt. The orthodox method of seizing a beachhead was to have the first assault waves attack in the darkness before dawn at high tide. In the English Channel, where the tide rises eighteen feet, this latter point would seem particularly important. Instead, Eisenhower ordered the attack to take place in broad daylight, at a time when the tide was starting to flood, not only for the sake of surprise, but so that the landing craft could see and avoid the obstacles which the Germans had sown between high and low water.

Even with all possible precautions, there remained, to haunt Ike's mind, the acute danger of a leak. So many thousands of men must of necessity know where the Allied Force would strike, and so many hundreds had to know approximately when, that it seemed almost impossible that there should not be a breakdown somewhere in the line. It was, Ike thought, imposing a terrific strain on human nature.

But the secret was well-kept.

CHAPTER TWENTY-ONE

THE BIG D

Monday, June 5, 1944, was to be the Day. By Saturday night most of the troops had poured down from the marshaling areas onto the transports and landing craft that were to carry them on the great crusade, symbolized by the flaming sword and rainbow of Eisenhower's chosen shoulder flash. Many of the ships were already at sea, converging on the Baie de la Seine from ports in Scotland and Northern Ireland, while in English harbors thousands more awaited the appointed hour.

But it seemed that the weather, that ancient ally which had served these islanders so well in the past, from the storm that wrecked the Spanish Armada to the fog at Dunkerque, had turned traitor. Meteorologists produced increasingly gloomy prognostications: Monday, they said, would be a day of storms and high winds. Low-lying clouds would make air cover impossible, and the Channel would be at its familiar worst, with big breakers smashing on the invasion beaches.

Eisenhower read the reports and took counsel with his team. Then he decided to accept what seemed the lesser risk, and arrest that avalanche of men and guns and ships. The order went out over the wires and through the air to thousands of units. It was a triumph of organization that the tremendous mass movement could be halted.

Far at sea in the rising storm, the dripping ships swung slowly around, wallowing in the trough of the waves, staggering back to England, while the seasick troops crammed in their holds, cursed and wondered. In the harbors other men, crowded drearily in the rain on the decks of LSTs and LCIs, cursed too, as the word was passed; and settled themselves to the misery of waiting for the inscrutable will of authority. And on the beaches of Normandy, the enemy at their radar and observation posts relaxed and muttered, "Another feint."

On Monday morning at 4:00 A.M., around a long table in the library of an old country house were gathered the Invasion Team —Tedder, Ramsay, Leigh-Mallory, Montgomery and Beedle Smith. At the head of the table sat the Supreme Commander, smoking innumerable cigarettes—in spite of Monty's dislike of them—and chatting casually with the generals. The meteorologists were due to make another report; it was all up to the weather at this point. When the report came, it spoke of clearing skies, as far as any man could predict the fickle climate of those parts. Tuesday would be windy but not stormy, with a reasonably good ceiling; the clouds might break by noon; the lessening wind would start at twenty knots.

Of each man in turn, the Supreme Commander asked a question; each told what his Service could do under the expected conditions and offered an opinion. Monty's was "Let's go!"

Then Eisenhower summed up what each had said and calculated the odds. On one hand was the grave uncertainty of the weather, to which the howling wind gave point; on the other, the falling morale of the troops held on crowded ships with their nerves tense. At the end he spoke a quiet sentence, which in its simple, unheroic words and its vast import became, as it was spoken, a part of American tradition.

"Gentlemen," said General Eisenhower, "*WE* will go ahead as planned."

So were launched four times a thousand ships, and many more thousands of smaller craft. Half a million troops, with millions to back them up, faced outward across the stormy sea. There could be no turning back this time; the Hour was too close. Come wind or storm or the fair perfection of a June day, the beaches would be stormed.

D–1, with ragged clouds scudding overhead on the wet salt wind: a dozen times an hour in his walled tent at Advanced Headquarters, Eisenhower cocked his head to look upward between the flaps, trying to read by his weather sense something the meteorologists might have missed. Outwardly he seemed so casual and confident that one reporter asked, "Aren't you at all nervous, general?"

"I'm so goldarned nervous," Ike laughed, "that I'm practically boiling."

Eisenhower spent most of the day visiting the troops. In the morning he was on the quays, chatting with British soldiers who were boarding their landing craft. Late that afternoon he made a round of the fields where the airborne divisions and paratroopers were mustering to take their places in transport planes and gliders. The men were all ready for their perilous task, loaded down with cumbersome equipment, wearing netted helmets with a scarecrow effect of camouflaging leaves. Their faces were dark and shiny with a mixture of cottonseed oil and cocoa; their eyes were young and strained under their weird helmets. They stood in rigid ranks beside their aircraft until the General ordered, "Have them stand at ease!"

Then he walked among them, talking, making little jokes; and the tension went out of the young eyes, as the boys broke ranks and followed him around.

In spite of the green battle dress of the troops, the serried ranks of planes and the wet English wind, Ike felt it was a little like going home to talk with these American boys, many of whom had the familiar speech of the Midwest.

"How many bushels do you get to an acre?" the General asked of a farm boy from Iowa.

"Where did you get that haircut?" of a monkishly shorn youth.

"How does it taste?" he asked another, who was licking the cocoa mixture that ran down his face.

"Damn good!" replied the boy amid a roar of laughter.

From the far side of the field other men began calling to him. "Ike!" "Ike!" "Hey, Ike, come over here!"

Their voices, coming thinly down the wind, brought an unmilitary tightness to the Supreme Commander's throat. They were going on so desperate a venture that their wanting him was infinitely touching.

Ike came to the last field in the northern dusk, which comes so late in England at that season. The men there were already aboard their aircraft and, while he watched, the first C-47 transport lumbered along the airstrip, followed by its glider at the end of a long cable. The wide-winged tow was airborne before the plane had made half its run and soared behind it, tossed by the rough air close to the ground. Other planes followed the first at seven-second intervals. There seemed to be an endless procession of them, laboring upward, each with its glider streaming behind.

Someone suggested that the General could see better from a roof; and he went on top of the headquarters building.

The planes were circling for formation; and the sky was gaudy with their running lights, red and green and white, moving swiftly through the darkness, climbing toward the broken clouds, becoming increasingly numerous until the whole circle of night was filled with moving, colored stars; and the air was jammed with the beat of the engines.

As the last planes took off, the highest lights began to form a recognizable pattern of vees, slanting upward and away. Ike raised his binoculars and watched them diminish down the sky; and he thought of the round metal tunnels which were the cabins of those frail ships, with the boys packed close on the long side benches. He seemed to see their faces in their grotesque war paint; it was the final irony that they should, like old-time minstrels in blackface, go so gallantly to war.

"God keep them . . ."

The Supreme Commander went back to sleep for a few hours in his trailer at the headquarters encampment in a grove of trees. On D-day morning he spoke by radio for the first time to the subject peoples:

"People of Western Europe! A landing was made this morning on the coast of France by troops of the Allied Expeditionary Force. This landing is part of the concerted United Nations' plan for the liberation of Europe, made in conjunction with our great Russian allies.

"I have this message for all of you. Although the initial assault may not have been made in your own country, the hour of your liberation is approaching. All patriots, men and women, young and old, have a part to play in the achievement of final victory . . . The day will come when I shall need your united strength. Until that day I call on you for discipline and restraint.

"Citizens of France: I am proud to have again under my command the gallant forces of France . . . Follow the instructions of your leaders. A premature uprising of all Frenchmen may prevent your being of maximum help to your country in the critical hour . . .

"As Supreme Commander of the Allied Expeditionary Force, there is imposed on me the duty and responsibility of taking all measures necessary to the prosecution of the war. Prompt and willing obedience to the orders that I shall issue is essential. Effective civil administration of France must be provided by Frenchmen ... Those who have made common cause with the enemy will be removed. As France is liberated from her oppressors, you yourselves will choose your representatives and the government under which you wish to live ...

"This landing is but the opening phase of the campaign in Western Europe. Great battles lie ahead. I call upon all who love freedom to stand with us. Keep your faith stanch! Our arms are resolute. Together we shall achieve victory!"

That message was not only a promise of certain relief to the peoples who had suffered so long, it was also an honest statement of the plain straightforward manner in which Eisenhower intended to cope with the complexities of European politics.

Ike spent D-day morning pacing the wooden floor of his headquarters tent, smoking a lengthening chain of cigarettes and writing memoranda to himself. These were the moments he hated worst of all, when his troops were in swift action and he must wait for word from the front. One of the earliest memos expressed his sense of strain with characteristic understatement, "Now I'd like a few reports."

Once or twice he dropped into the big leather armchair in his tent and thought about John, graduating today from West Point. What a day it would be there, and how John would hate the fuss the reporters would make over him because of this coincidence. His son had elected the infantry. Ike wondered how much sentiment had swayed that choice, because it was his own branch. If he could have had one personal wish, unconnected with his duty or his great object, it would have been to stand on the Plain that day and see Mamie pin the golden bars on her son's shoulders.

When the reports of the landings came, they were, on the whole, good; things were going according to plan—almost. The tremendous motley fleet of minesweepers had done their work well in the darkness; broad avenues had been cleared through the German minefields. The fire-support squadrons of battleships, cruisers and destroyers had begun to lay down a tremendous barrage before dawn, under cover of which the Army and Navy demolition units had slipped ashore and, working sometimes up to their necks in water, had blasted away the obstructions on the beaches. Meanwhile every type of Allied aircraft—eight thousand of them—

were paralyzing the German defense. The Luftwaffe had hardly appeared, and already the Allies held the air above Normandy.

British and American airborne divisions had, for the most part fulfilled their first missions of capturing strategic points behind the enemy lines and messing up communications. They had, however, suffered heavy losses. The fact that this must inevitably be the case made the news no less hard for Ike to bear as he thought about the boys with whom he had talked the evening before.

The Allied Forces were making good progress at both ends of the invasion line. The British Second Army had established a beachhead in the eastern sector at the estuary of the Orne River, and were advancing toward Caen; some of the American First Army, under the personal command of Omar Bradley, was ashore near Isigny and moving on the town. But at Omaha Beach from Vierville eastward to Port en Bessin, the hinge of the line between the American and British, there was trouble. By unlucky chance, the Germans had been holding anti-invasion maneuvers in this area, and as the first assault wave of the American 29th Division and the Rangers dashed through the five-foot breakers, they found themselves up against four German regiments armed and waiting. First, second, third and fourth assault waves were checked at the water's edge. LCIs and LSTs were smashed by the heavy guns in the bombproof casemates on the cliffs at Pointe de Hoe. Tanks crawled up to the high-water mark, got hit, and burned, sending up tall black columns of smoke. The few men who lived to get ashore, scooped shallow trenches in the sand and lay there, fighting back with bazookas, machine guns and rifles, while out beyond the heavy surf hundreds of landing craft milled around, warned off that fatal beach by the patrol boats. The 29th had almost lost its beachhead; and as the reports poured in to Ike, it sounded too much like Dieppe.

In these landing operations it was impossible to hold reserves ready to rush in and plug a weak spot or overwhelm an enemy strong point. A commander had to hurl in everything he had as fast as he could, because there was no depth behind the lines where reserves could muster; and the men waiting in the tossing ships—particularly in the smaller craft—became so seasick as to be useless.

But other types of reserves could be used; orders from SHAEF sent Allied planes swarming over Omaha Beach. One pilot said that the traffic was so thick he had to put his hand out if he wanted to make a turn. Medium bombers pounded at enemy gun emplacements, and dive bombers roared down almost into the throats of the guns, while fighters strafed the enemy infantry. It was the Navy, however, that really saved the day. The fire-support group of Rear Admiral Morton L. Deyo's Western Task Force concentrated on this sector. Rear Admiral Carleton F. Bryant, commanding this squadron, anchored his flagship, *Texas,* and *Nevada* and *Arkansas* off the beach; their big guns wrecked those concrete gun emplacements that could not be damaged by bombs from the air. Inshore of the battleships, American, British and French heavy cruisers poured their fire upon the Germans, while Commander W. J. Marshall took his American and British destroyers within light machine-gun range of the beach. The new rocket assault boats charged right up to the surf. Not even the best German troops could stand in the incandescent hell of that naval barrage.

By afternoon, reports indicated that the beach had been cleared sufficiently for landing operations to be resumed, and in the dusk the Rangers scaled the cliffs at Pointe de Hoe and captured the German heavy guns.

The beachhead was safe.

The Supreme Commander was up early on the morning of June 7, D+1. Characteristically his first activity was to catch up with the mail from home; he had dropped a little behind in his letter writing these last few days. Equally characteristic was his next decision: to go over to the beaches and see for himself.

Ike chose a British heavy cruiser for that first trip to the front. The weather had cleared and the sun was bright on the White Ensign flying from her stern, but the wind was still brisk and the tumbling blue waves were crested with white. Ike stood on her bridge enjoying the strong pressure of the salt wind in his face and the rhythmic heave of the ship. He had that important quali-fication for a commander of amphibious operations: he never got seasick.

They came up to the Norman coast near Isigny. To the farthest range of vision, the Channel was as crowded with ships as the narrow Hudson at Poughkeepsie on race day. The vast armada was given a peculiarly gala appearance by the barrage balloons floating like silver bubbles above it and the thousands of small landing craft scooting in and out in the transport area. The hazy blue sky quivered with the roar of motors as steady streams of planes winged back and forth from England; and the air shook with continual explosions.

Through his binoculars Ike could see the swarming activity on the beaches and the heavy surf boiling around the mine stakes and underwater barriers. Long columns of trucks moved inland up the river valley toward Isigny. As the cruiser steamed eastward along the coast, he scanned the line of green hills that were cleft where the little rivers came down to the sea. There were fishing villages at the mouths of the rivers and pretty white villas on the hills, and over them all the smoke banners of battle streamed along the wind. Farther along men were hastily rigging the first floating harbor and the waves were breaking white against the superstructures of the line of ancient ships which had been sunk to form a breakwater.

"That's Pointe de Hoe," said Butcher, standing beside him.

Ike looked at the cliff up which the Rangers had swarmed with ropes and grapnels. Shellbursts farther inland showed where fighting was still in progress.

Texas and *Nevada* were anchored within four thousand yards of the shore, searching the hills with their main batteries. The long guns spurted streamers of flame and then belched brown smoke, which engulfed the squat silhouettes of the old battleships until the wind shredded it away. Each time the great guns flashed, Ike braced himself against the thud and shock of the broadside. So near shore that they seemed almost in the breakers, Commander Marshall's destroyers were shooting with sharp angry barks and British steam gunboats were even closer in.

Eastward from Port en Bessin was the British sector. Off these beaches lay Admiral Sir Philip Vian's Eastern Task Force: the old *Warspite,* wrapped in the smoke of guns that spoke at Jutland; *Ramillies* and magnificent *Rodney,* who could heave her sixteen-inch shells halfway across the Peninsula. Besides these, there were the last of the monitors, *Lord Roberts,* doing splendid work; and destroyers and cruisers, including Vian's flagship, *Scylla.*

When Eisenhower's cruiser anchored, Admirals Ramsay and Hewitt came aboard in their barges to consult with the Supreme Commander. Then a duck waddled out into the breakers and chugged alongside. General Montgomery in his battle dress of fleece-lined jacket and corduroy trousers, and, of course, the black beret with its shining badges, swarmed up a rope ladder over the side. Monty was in high spirits and full of admiration for the Americans who had clung so desperately to Omaha Beach and finally stormed the cliffs.

"They were absolutely magnificent," he told Ike, "and so were my Northumbrians. Our men are in smashing fettle, full of beans . . ."

Ike thought that the famous little Englishman himself was full of beans. His sharp nose quivered with excitement, and he was smiling gleefully as he scrambled down the ladder to his boat. Ike leaned out from a wing of the cruiser's bridge and jerked his thumb up in the spirited British gesture.

"Good luck to you," he shouted affectionately.

Five days later, on D+6, otherwise June 12, 1944, Eisenhower landed on the soil of France. He was in excellent company, for Generals Marshall and Arnold and Admiral King, who had flown over from America, went with him in USS Thompson. It was the first time Ike had traveled on an American destroyer. He was delighted by the speed she showed as she tore through the dark blue hummocks of water, and he enthusiastically complimented her captain, Lieutenant Commander Al Gibelin, on his taut little ship. Captain Gibelin headed for the coast near Isigny, and took Thompson in close to the now peaceful shore. As she swung into the wind, they hailed a duck. It came alongside and its crew nearly popped their eyes out as the four-starred gentlemen scrambled down the landing stage and piled into the little craft.

The duck slid down the breakers in slashing foam and spray, like a chute-the-chutes at Coney Island, while "Hap" Arnold roared with delight. Then it lumbered sedately up the strand, and Ike jumped out onto the drifting sands of Normandy.

A command car met them at the edge of the beach and they drove inland up a narrow lane along which the debris of war was strewn. Every so often they came to a spot in that gentle country-side over which the tide of battle seemed to have leaped. There stood gnarled apple trees, and the meadows were deep with grass. The air was sweet with the fragrance of summer, until a shift of wind brought in the battle stink of sweat and dirt and blood and rotting flesh.

After General Bradley joined them, they inspected the troops of the 29th Division and the fabulous 1st. A few of Ike's airborne troops were there, having fought through from behind the enemy lines to establish contact.

The generals lunched with a regiment in the field. Arnold was like a small boy on a wonderful picnic; Marshall was smiling, and even Admiral King unbent. Ike felt the elation that he always experienced when he went among his troops. He found an abandoned German 88 and climbed about its carriage until someone shouted, "Look out, there!"

Ike jumped off quickly and grinned sheepishly as he noticed a sign hung on its muzzle which read, "DANGER! Booby Trap."

In the afternoon they drove into the petrified wilderness that had been the pretty town of Isigny. Fragments of walls stood like headstones on the graves of human hopes; the streets were choked with rubble and bulldozers roared and clanked, plowing a path through stones and broken bricks which might have been mortared when Duke William sailed to conquer England.

As the car moved slowly over the cobbles, pathetic groups of men and women and children lined the street to watch it pass. Their clothes were ragged and dirty and their faces were gray with hunger and fatigue. But Ike thought he saw a gleam of hope in tired, fearful eyes. Pale lips were curved in unaccustomed smiles and nearly all held up their hands with two fingers spread in the symbol of victory.

Ike's mood was somber as he stood a little apart in the market place, looking over the leveled town. Hardly a wall was left intact and drifts of broken stone covered the cobbles of the square as deep as snow after a Kansas blizzard. He judged that this place had been about the size of Abilene. Even in ruins he could see how lovely it once had been—once—why, only six days ago! The river wound between banks that still were green and shady down to the estuary's sudden vivid blue. Some fishing boats lay at their moorings among the crowding shapes of war, and one small, un- damaged house, sheltered by the hills, poked its steep gabled roof above the trees.

Men had loved Isigny as he loved Abilene—more perhaps, for it had been more beautiful and their roots in the town extended back nearly a thousand years. Men loved it still, for they were poking about in the ruins, setting up little camps with pots and pans and household goods in the lee of some broken wall. It was just the chance of geographical location that he was not as they, searching amid the wreckage of his home.

Fierce anger and renewed determination swept him; this should never happen again. By all the power that was his, and in him, he meant to shatter the enemies of his country and of mankind.

As Ike looked southwestward, he could see black clouds of smoke rising beyond the hills. He could hear the thud of guns as the First Army stormed into Carentan. Eastward ran a straight white road, marked with a broken road sign that read, "To Paris." Eastward toward Paris he would go—and how Patton's tanks *would* go, once they were turned loose—then northward to Berlin. That road was long and bitter, no one knew how long. But Ike did know that he would travel it, whatever the cost.

Sometimes he had let his mind dwell on the end of that journey —the happy end, after the fuss and cheering, when he could go home. It was a rest to think about it; to dream of Abilene, and poker games at Joner's, and of a permanent home for Mamie, who had put up with so much. Not that he intended to rusticate. He was going to travel, to take Mamie with him to all the places he had been, and others he had always wanted to visit. He was going to write a book too, and try to tell other men the things he had learned the hard way.

Those were his dreams. The reality was this shattered town of Isigny, and all those cities and towns and pleasant villages that would be wrecked along the straight white road. Real, too, were Rommel's Panzers, gathering for a counterattack that must be met and stopped before it shook the Allied Force from its narrow foothold; and the lines of Nazi fortifications, bristling with cannon, between him and his goal—the famed West Wall that must be stormed. The saddest of all realities was that death would come to so many of his men along that road.

But Ike felt that he had within him the strength to face all those things. He was secure in his beliefs and confident of the victory of those splendid troops, American and British, who slogged cheerfully onward against all adversities, not riding gallantly into the jaws of death, but driving forward doggedly through storm or cold or heat, through fire and the awful blast of high explosives. They put their trust in him.

The Supreme Commander looked eastward along the road to Paris. The dirty battle smoke stained the evening sky above the shuddering fields where his troops fought desperately against mounting odds. But his faith in them and in himself was sure. He could not fail such men as these.

CHAPTER TWENTY-TWO

"WE WILL WITH GOD'S HELP..."

It was, perhaps, just as well that General Eisenhower could not see all that lay over the hills on the white road leading from Isigny to Berlin. What he imagined was terrible enough, but the reality, viewed all at once, might have shattered even his great spirit.

At first most operations went well. The beachheads were safely established. Field Marshal Karl Rudolph Gerd von Rundstedt and Field Marshal Erwin Rommel, fearing attack from another quarter, stayed their hands until it was too late to throw the Allies from their original precarious toe hold on the sands of Normandy. When the Germans finally committed their reserves and sent Rommel's armor in, Allied power had been built up so well that his thrust was parried and broken.

Secret floating harbors were partly responsible for the German commanders' miscalculations. It seemed impossible that such enormous quantities of men and matériel could be landed in so short a time without the use of at least one great port. And so it would have been, had not American ingenuity put down two ports where none existed. Even the unprecedented gale that swept the Channel in the second week of June and destroyed the more exposed of these floating harbors failed to upset the timetable. The landings had been made so fast and the staff work that routed men and supplies had been so brilliant that the floating dock had already served its purpose.

Without the heroism and élan of the Allied troops, however, even such staff work and such equipment would have been insufficient. This great imponderable was the major force that overthrew the enemies' calculations. It is no wonder the Germans were surprised; even the man who loved those soldiers the best

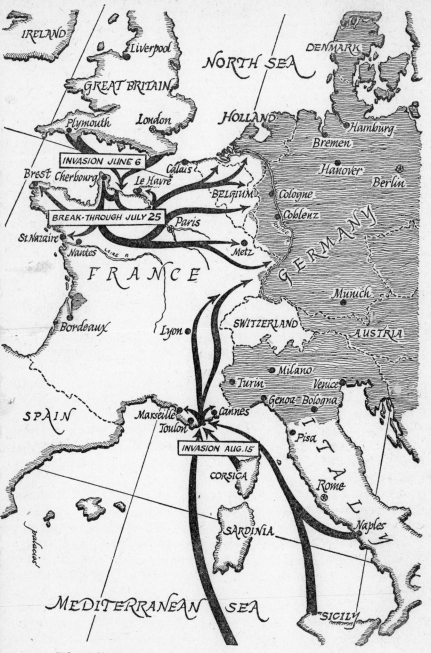

The Liberation Campaign; June 6–October, 1944

and expected the most of them was amazed. On D+7, General Ike sent this message to his armies: "Your accomplishments in the last seven days of this campaign have exceeded my highest hopes."

At the same time, always preoccupied with Allied unity, Eisenhower reported to General Marshall: "Our operations are . . . only part of the far larger pattern of combined assaults against Fortress Germany by Russian armies from the East and our forces in the Mediterranean. The Nazis will be forced to fight throughout the perimeter of their fortress."

Even Stalin paid a sincere compliment: "Forcing the Channel and mass landings of troops in Northern France have fully succeeded. History will write this down as an achievement of the highest order."

The political front began to clear up, too. There had been difficulties between the Allies and De Gaulle's French Committee: Washington and London had refused to recognize the Committee as the provisional government of France until they were sure that the French themselves would accept it. As a result, De Gaulle had not allowed the French officers assigned to liaison work with the Allies to accompany the Allied armies to France. The situation had become very tense at a time when we most needed French co-operation. Eisenhower had been obliged to employ all his talent for diplomacy. On June 3 and 4, before the invasion, he had conferred with General Joseph-Pierre Koenig, De Gaulle's representative in England, but could reach no agreement. Then De Gaulle himself had arrived in England from Algiers.

The French leader was probably the most difficult man with whom Ike had ever dealt. The very qualities that had enabled him to represent France when all seemed lost—indomitable will and unshakable faith—made him temperamentally unable to compromise on even a minor issue. He had the impassioned single-mindedness of a Hebrew prophet or a medieval saint. Negotiating with him was like trying to do business with Savonarola. And so much depended on reaching an agreement with the French! If our armies were not to be hamstrung by confusion and civil war in their rear, there would have to be a civil authority to take over the government of the liberated areas; moreover, the wholehearted assistance of Frenchmen in the prosecution of the war might well mean the difference between victory and defeat.

Eisenhower met with De Gaulle on D+1. That day, the Supreme Commander had made a trip down the Channel on a British cruiser to see the Allied armies storming the hills behind the beaches. A thousand vital decisions awaited his attention. Strain, excitement, and fatigue conspired to jangle Ike's nerves as he came to this momentous interview, but he was able to banish them all from his mind. He handled the touchy Frenchman with exquisite tact, yielding gracefully on nonessentials, but standing firm where he deemed it necessary. By his broad reasonableness and evident good will, he made a common meeting ground, and that evening was able to announce that he and De Gaulle had reached an agreement "on military levels."

Nothing was settled, however, about the vexing question of civil authority; and pursuant to the policy of his government, Eisenhower was careful to add, "When victory is won the French people will be free to choose the government under which they want to live."

Two days later he announced that "members of the French Military Mission attached to SHAEF will aid French patriots during the liberation campaign."

A few days later De Gaulle crossed the Channel to his own country. During the few hours he spent in the small strip of France that was free, the question of his standing with the French people was settled. In the tiny towns and villages crowds greeted him with almost religious fervor. He was at once their savior and the symbol of France reborn.

Immediately upon his return to England, De Gaulle strode into Eisenhower's tent headquarters and announced that he had established a provisional government in the liberated districts!

It was a coup d'état. By every agreement and convention, Eisenhower was responsible for the maintenance of order in military areas; and certainly the term applied to that small section of Normandy, shaking under the bursting shells of German 88s, and held, precariously still, against the concentrated might of the Wehrmacht. De Gaulle's action was not only unilateral; it amounted almost to a defiance of the Supreme Commander's authority.

A lesser man would have rejected it with every justification. But Eisenhower had the reports from France; he knew about those cheering villagers, the people kneeling in the flower-strewn streets. There was no longer a doubt in his mind that the French wanted De Gaulle. And what was this war about, if it were not to enable people to live under the government they chose? Furthermore, this man could give him what he needed most: a stable government behind his lines and the enthusiastic co-operation of the French, which would save uncounted American lives and bring victory immeasurably nearer. Beside those factors, what weight had personal pride or even the cautious attitude of distant statesmen?

The Supreme Commander grinned amiably up at the controlled, expressionless face of the defiant Frenchman.

"That's fine," he said cordially.

With those two words the future of France was settled and all the fatal errors inherent in the situation were avoided. It took weeks for London and Washington to accept the situation officially. But in that moment the thing was done. And well done.

With the French off his mind and the troops pouring ashore, Ike had time to take a deep breath. While he was savoring the first flavor of victory, his soldier son arrived in England. General Marshall, with his usual thoughtfulness, had ordered young Eisenhower to spend part of his thirty-day graduation leave at Supreme Headquarters on an "inspection trip." Six hours after he had graduated from the Military Academy, John had sailed for England.

Father and son greeted each other with the casualness that they invariably assumed to conceal the embarrassing depth of their feelings. Ike thought that the boy had matured greatly in the eighteen months since their last meeting under the bluffs at West Point. In his new uniform, John was more handsome than ever. He was, Ike thought, the very archetype of those magnificent young men whom it was his privilege to command.

As always, the shyness of meeting soon wore off, and the two men spent hours in excited professional discussion. The early morning talks which had meant so much to both of them were resumed. But they were not together all the time. John was immensely eager to profit by his unique opportunity to get a first-hand view of the greatest military operation in American history. He did not waste a moment of the time allotted to him.

The days were much too few, and the time came for John to return home. Once more emotion had to be masked as those two said good-bye. This time the separation might be longer still, for the probabilities were that John would be sent to the Pacific Theater. Remembering the steaming jungles and steep mountains of Luzon, Ike wondered, as he knew so many other parents were wondering, how his son would fare.

Meanwhile, the strong initial impetus of the campaign bogged down. The Normandy countryside was cut up into small fields surrounded by high, impenetrable hedges. It was ideal for enemy defense—each field became a fort surrounded by a high stockade; but, for our invasion forces, it was like fighting through a gigantic house, room by room.

The timetable fell behind. Caen, which was scheduled to be taken the first week, defied the British Second Army, and Cherbourg held out while the Germans wrecked its port facilities. The weather was unbelievably bad; fog, wind, and rain grounded our planes and turned the roads to mire. Despite these delays, however, Allied power built up a tremendous potential, and the troops slogged slowly onward through the mud.

Ike spent all the time he could spare at the front. Still intent on welding the American and British armies into unity, he divided his trip almost equally between them.

The first fighter planes to be based in France were a Royal Air Force Squadron under the command of Group Captain Russell Bullimore. They were a crack outfit of war-tempered young veterans of the Battle of Britain, who asked no favors and took no nonsense. Their present unique position led to considerable interest on the part of the Allied Command. Generals kept coming on inspection tours, which irked them considerably—they wanted to get on with the war.

Once it was Montgomery, but Monty had won the right to inspect whom he pleased. The RAF was glad to see him. When word filtered into the ready room that General Eisenhower was coming, the atmosphere became, as they put it, "a bit thick." These men had had no previous contact with the Supreme Commander, and there was more than a touch of resentment that an American should be Supreme Commander.

On the designated morning a battered, topless jeep turned up the narrow lane and wallowed through the mud and driving rain to the temporary building on the edge of the improvised air strip. A bulky figure jumped out and dashed through the door.

The British officers in the barnlike room rose politely and stood at attention as General Eisenhower took off his dripping helmet and shook himself like a terrier after a bath. Then he smiled at them and said gaily, "Hello, fellows!"

Even the Battle of Britain boys weren't proof against the genuine warmth of that greeting. They stopped being polite and crowded up. Ike stayed with them perhaps half an hour, noticing by the ribbons what action each had seen, talking in his intimate, friendly way. When he left, that Royal Air Force Squadron had definitely become part of his Army.

As June turned to July things began to go a little better, though the timetable was still dropping behind. Some genius had conceived the idea of fastening a bulldozer blade to the front of a tank. Thus equipped, the General Sherman tanks tore great gaps in the stubborn hedges, through which the infantry could pour. Cherbourg fell and the engineers began clearing the port with miraculous speed.

Ike celebrated the Fourth of July by going on a fighter sweep over the enemy lines. He rode in a *P-51* (Mustang) piloted by Major General Elwood Quesada, Chief of the 9th Air Force Fighter Command. It was one of the rare fine days that occurred in Normandy that summer. The sun flashed in and out through scurrying white clouds, and on the gentle wind the salt smell of the sea was mingled with the sweetness of the meadows. Ike, bareheaded, climbed into the rear seat of the fighter plane and "Pete" Quesada lightly swung his stalwart form into the pilot's cockpit. They buckled on their helmets and earphones and took off in an almost vertical climb. Other fighters climbed beside them, and still more circled above, waiting.

The squadrons reached the designated altitude and swung into close formation. All around him Ike could see the slender, deadly Mustangs, with their long fuselages and gun-studded wings, rising and falling on the currents of the air. It took but a few moments to cross the busy rear areas to the front. The battle was marked by an apparent absence of life. Below Ike's plane the small, neat fields sharply edged by dark bands of hedgerows looked empty. Occasionally he could see a small herd of tanks crawling forward, and behind a slope a line of Long Toms firing in succession. But there was a startling absence of soldiers; it seemed incredible that some hundreds of thousands of men could make themselves invisible.

That day, Bradley's First Army was closing in on La Haye du Puits. From the plane Ike could see the small circle of the beleaguered town, and beyond it the blue plain of the Channel. From the air the battle assumed a coherence and a design which could be only imagined by a commander on the ground. American troops were storming into the villages of La Broquiere, St. Remy des Landes and Baudreville to the west of La Haye, and Neufmesnil and La Poterie to the east. Eisenhower could see moving guns and armor, the flash and billowing smoke of shell-bursts, a haze of machine-gun and rifle fire, and the black-smoke columns that rose from burning houses and equipment.

The Mustang squadrons wheeled, wings flashing in the sun as they banked. They followed the front line east, then north. Ike saw Saint-Lô, the anchor city of the German center; and presently they were over Caen, the northern bastion of the Nazi line, on which the British Second Army was pressing close. As they passed over the enemy lines there were sharp cracks and the woolly balls of flak floated in the air. Quesada gave an order over the radio and the planes wheeled away. . . .

Patton's new secret Third Army started across the Channel. Men and guns were ferried over the water and massed in the narrow strip of France behind the lines. The potential of power built up was enormous and Omar Bradley, Commander of the American Ground Forces, picked the spot—Saint-Lô—where it was to be released. "Give me three hours of good flying weather any morning," he said, "and we'll break the German line."

The clear day came on July 25, and at ten o'clock the first of three thousand planes started going over, smothering the German lines under an incandescent blanket of bursting bombs. But not all those bombs fell in enemy territory. The smoke line indicating our forward positions drifted back on the light wind, and at 21,000 feet, the Fortresses could not see what was wrong. Some of their bombs rained down on the waiting Allied troops. There were casualties in the forward echelons, and Ike's old friend, General McNair, was killed. Quick communications changed the bombers' aim, but too late to prevent the heartbreaking, irreparable accident.

Massed American artillery added to the inferno of the Nazi positions, and, as the barrage lifted, the 4th Division went in, followed by Patton's armor. They ripped right through the shaken German line, crumbling the enemy's entire left wing.

It was a clean break-through. The next day Patton took Coutances, and within forty-eight hours he had Avranches at the base of the Brittany peninsula. The tanks were loose at last; nothing to stop them now. The level fields and fine white roads of France beckoned them onward.

George Patton was riding high. He handled his swift armored columns as Jeb Stuart once handled his cavalry. They *were* the armored cavalry. Across the base of Brittany they stormed, and up the coast and through its center. Only the main ports, garrisoned by suicidal Nazi expendables, held out. The original plan called for taking these ports before moving on Paris, but Eisenhower saw that the Germans were on the run, and he decided to keep them running. It was another of his considered gambles, and it succeeded brilliantly.

Delightedly following his new orders, Patton swung his army eastward. Right across the heart of France they streamed. The long columns of trucks, tanks, mechanized infantry, tank destroyers, motorized artillery, ambulances, sound trucks, repair trucks, motorcycles, and jeeps hurtled forward between the rows of poplars. Now and then there would be a check as the jeeps, scouting ahead, reported an isolated German detachment, and the boom of the 88s confirmed their words. The trucks and soft-shells would be flagged down; the tanks and self-propelled guns would go through to smash the German resistance. Twenty, thirty minutes might pass, while the men lay in the shade of their vehicles. Then word would come back along the column that the way was clear, and off they would go again.

One armored force came over the hills to Chartres finding the beautiful city and the great cathedral completely untouched. It came down the slope at such speed that engines ran red hot and trailers leaped crazily from side to side, threatening to twist their trucks off the road. That column took Chartres so fast that the Germans had no time to damage a single house. Prisoners dazedly admitted that they did not know that there was an American within eighty miles.

From Chartres the same armored force went racing on. It passed south of Paris, turned sharply northward through Fontainebleau, and eventually reached Metz, where German resistance stiffened and the gasoline began to give out.

Other columns fanned out across France. The Germans were pulling out their troops as fast as they could, but hundreds of thousands were cut off. Only along the Channel coast in the Pas de Calais area did they fight stubbornly, retreating yard by yard. General Model, who had succeeded von Rundstedt in command, lost half an army in the pocket between Argentan and Falaise. Rommel, on whom so much depended, had been killed in either an accident or a bombing raid.

It looked almost like the end. On August 14, Eisenhower, who had moved his headquarters to Normandy by air, issued an order of the day asking his troops for special effort, inasmuch as "the victory we can now achieve is infinitely greater than any it has so far been possible to accomplish in the West." Hopeful though he was, he told reporters that he foresaw no early German collapse.

On August 15, Lieutenant General Alexander M. Patch landed with the Seventh Army on the Mediterranean coast of France, and marched northward with the ultimate intention of joining Eisenhower's army and cutting France in two.

So far the American armies had avoided Paris. It was Ike's tactful intention to let the French take the city themselves, and Major General Jacques Philippe Le Clerc's First French Army, equipped with American matériel, was sent in to do the job. German resistance was stiffer than anticipated; though the Nazis risked annihilation, they could not bear to surrender without a fight the greatest prize of all their conquests. Accordingly, Patton's 5th Corps was sent to lend the French a hand. On August 25, in the oddest battle of the war, Paris was finally freed, with French Forces of the Interior, Le Clerc's Army, and the American armor fighting block by block through the streets, while joyful Parisians danced around the tanks, dodging bullets, throwing flowers, and kissing every American who raised his head. At seven o'clock in the evening General de Gaulle made his triumphal entry.

Three days later, on August 28, General Eisenhower came to Paris. The big official car, flying the flags of all the Allies, circled the Arc de Triomphe and started slowly down the wide Champs Elysées. The sidewalks and even the roadways were jammed with celebrating people who cheered wildly as they recognized the Supreme Commander. It was all too much for Ike. He climbed out of the back seat. Laughing, waving, and shouting to the people, he rode down the stately avenue, standing like a Kansas farm boy on the running board of his great car.

That evening, Eisenhower, Tedder, and Bradley met with Generals Koenig and Le Clerc in French Headquarters in the Hôtel des Invalides and formally turned over the city of Paris to the French Provisional Government, represented by Koenig.

On August 29, the American 5th Corps marched through Paris on their way to further action. Armored cars and tanks moved slowly down the Champs Elysées four abreast, with their engines roaring and their crews riding on top. The infantry marched in battle dress to the beat of drums. As they wheeled past the obelisk in the Palace de la Concorde a group of generals took the salute. There was De Gaulle, with his face like a mask but his eyes shining with exaltation. Beside him stood Montgomery, jaunty in his beret, and Bradley, beaming through his spectacles. Le Clerc was there, too, and Koenig.

But the Supreme Commander was not present. Fearful that his presence would dim De Gaulle's hour of glory, Ike had quietly left the city, "to get on with the war."

On August 31, Eisenhower announced that General Bradley had been given direct command of all American ground forces under himself, while General Montgomery, who had been Commander of all Allied ground troops, was placed in charge of the 21st Army Group consisting of the British Second Army and the First Canadians.

The reason for Montgomery's changed status was that the battle line had become so far-flung that he could not oversee its entire length, and still give the British Armies in France the careful direction needed for the difficult and exacting tasks which they would soon be called upon to perform. While this change had been decided upon before D-Day, there was some rumbling in British quarters at Monty's apparent demotion; to prove it was nothing of the sort, the British government made him a field marshal. Thus, he theoretically outranked the Supreme Commander.

All the complaints came from outsiders. Montgomery and Eisenhower understood each other very well. The British general's loyalty to his chief never wavered. Nor did Eisenhower lack confidence in his brilliant subordinate, as he was to prove dramatically when the hour of crisis came.

Meanwhile, old names rang like familiar bells in the news. The Marne, Chateau-Thierry, Soissons, Reims, Verdun fell to the onrushing Americans. The Pas de Calais was cleared at last, and the British and Americans swept on to liberate Belgium.

But as the Allied armies neared the German frontier, the great offensive ground slowly to a halt. The Nazis were fanatically determined to defend the soil of the Fatherland at whatever cost, and when the remnants of their armies found shelter behind the powerful fortifications of the West Wall, they put up a terrific fight. The Allies might yet have broken through before the enemy had time to re-form had it not been for the insoluble problem of supply. A miracle had already been accomplished in keeping Patton's racing columns from running out of gasoline, ammunition, and food. Only once had they been delayed by lack of ammunition. On that occasion Patton had telegraphed to Eisenhower, "I'll shoot the next man who arrives with a truckload of food. Send us ammunition. We can eat our belts!"

Thousands of tons of supplies had been carried by the trucks of the famous "Red Ball Express" over the long French roads from Normandy to the border. But with the French railway system disrupted and the most of their Atlantic ports still held by Nazi suicide garrisons, it was impossible to mount a full-scale offensive immediately.

In these circumstances, Eisenhower decided to try an end run through the Netherlands around the northern flank of the Siegfried Line. On September 11, a spearhead of Lieutenant General Courtney Hodges' First Army made the first break into German territory northwest of Trier. This was a sort of raid in force. The main attack came on September 17, when Allied air-borne divisions were dropped behind the German lines in the Netherlands and the ground forces attacked. The 1st British Air-borne Division took the city of Arnheim and the Nijmegen Bridge. For a few breathless days, the British air-borne troops stood off the whole available might of the Wehrmacht while the British Second Army bucked forward to effect a juncture. It was a near thing, but German power was still too great. On September 27, the remnants of the 1st British Air-borne Division filtered back through the German lines. They had fought with incredible valor. Out of a total strength of 8,000 men, 6,000 were killed, wounded, or reported missing. Only 2,000 got back. The British Second Army failed to reach them by only five miles; that was the narrow margin by which victory was missed.

The loss of the Nijmegen Bridge ended the chance of a quick break-through to victory. There was a breathing spell while the Allies gathered their forces for a frontal attack and the Germans re-formed their shattered armies. Not that all action ceased. The British fought a bitter battle to clear the Scheldt estuary so that ships could reach the great port of Antwerp, which had been captured intact. The First Army slugged its way yard by yard beyond the Belgian border into Germany and took Aachen after a desperate fight, during which 300,000 large-caliber shells were fired into the little city. General Patton completed the siege of Metz and moved into a thin edge of the Ruhr while the American Seventh Army and the First French Army—now consisting of nine divisions in GI uniforms armed with American weapons—fought their way through the Vosges Mountains to the Rhine.

It was nevertheless a comparative lull during which a man could take stock. General Ike thought that his team had not done too badly. The citadel of German power had been stormed from across the sea and the Nazis' boasted Atlantic Wall breached—something that many men had called impossible. In less than four months France and Belgium had been liberated, and the Germans had lost more than a million men, of whom nearly 800,000 were prisoners. Our own losses were, perhaps, a fifth of that figure. One reason for the disparity in casualty figures was the extravagant use of American supplies. In war there is a mathematical ratio between the expenditure of matériel and the loss of life. Ike and his generals were profligate of the former and miserly with the precious human component.

Our losses, comparatively light though they were, weighed heavily upon the Supreme Commander's spirit. They might have been less had he been able to get more supplies to the front. So many of those splendid young men might have been able to pursue their lives in happiness and to contribute their talents to the greatness of America. . . .

Up to now the shortages had been unavoidable, owing to lack of transportation and to the German strategy of holding the French ports at all costs. With the opening of the great port of Antwerp and the partial restoration of the French railroads, that problem could be licked, but the stock piles in England were diminishing too fast. On November 23, Eisenhower wrote an eloquent appeal to his countrymen for more production: "Unless everybody all the way through the nation—those at the front and those at home—keeps on the job everlastingly and with mounting pressure, we are only postponing the day of victory."

Meanwhile, Supreme Headquarters had moved to Paris with Advanced Headquarters near Verdun. Ike had a fine house near Paris and his official family were with him: Butcher and Ernie Lee and, of course, Mickey, who was more than ever in love with Pearlie Hargrave—they were now officially engaged. Most of Ike's time, when he was not actually with the front echelons, was spent at Advanced Headquarters. He seemed rather embarrassed on the rare occasions when visiting dignitaries caught him at Paris Headquarters.

Ike continued his practice of making personal reconnoissance flights. On one such occasion his plane made a forced landing on a strip of beach. It squashed down on heavy sand and stopped with a jerk, kicking its tail in the air. There was no damage, and when the pilot had made the necessary repairs to the faulty motor, he said, "Now if we could get her down to the hard sand we could take off."

"Let's try it," Ike suggested.

The two men put their shoulders against the wing struts of the light plane, but as Ike heaved with all his strength the loose sand gave beneath his feet and a sharp pain shot through the old football knee.

Eventually some GIs arrived and pushed the plane to a take-off position. The flight was resumed, but Ike's knee stiffened badly. He did not allow it to slow up his work or to interfere with his visits to the front, but it did keep him from getting his daily exercise for nearly six weeks.

In November, Ike started on a 3,000-mile inspection tour of all his armies. Fog, rain, and snow made flying too uncertain, and so he went by automobile. His route took him through many of the towns he had visited with Mamie when he was assigned to the Battle Monuments Commission. As his car raced through the winter landscape, he met memories at every turn. The contour of a hill was suddenly familiar, and he knew that beyond the next curve he would find the little inn where, on a sunny August day, they had had such a good lunch of *pigeonneau en casserole* and *vin rosé*. The yellow peeling façade of a provincial hotel facing a cobbled square reminded him that there he and Mamie had experienced their first feather bed, and had been waked in a golden dawn by deep singing bells that pealed matins.

There was a dreamlike feeling about seeing all those places still the same when so much else was changed; it was like fourth-dimension traveling backward in time. When Ike had last come this way he had been intellectually preoccupied with the possibility of another war; but this present reality was beyond all imagining. It was an infinite turmoil of machines and men—boys far from home calling "Ike!" as he passed; generals waiting for his decisions; maps and enormous plans that dealt with nations and continents; wounded patients in long, white rows of cots. And the four silver stars pressed down upon him with the awful weight of Supreme Command. It was all so fantastically improbable that for the moment only memory seemed real.

His nostalgia was deepened by the dripping rain and the sad autumnal smell of wet earth and fallen leaves. Usually he was too busy to think of personal things, but now the chill of loneliness seeped through him like the pervasive fog, and he knew how much he missed Mamie. He wrote to her one night: "We went over so many of the same roads and it seemed as though you were riding in the back seat with me. . . ."

When he was actually with the troops his mood was different. The devotion they showed him was heart warming—more than that, it filled him with selfless exaltation. His arrival produced a riot that no discipline could quell; and always they shouted "Ike! Ike!"

At each unit Ike set aside ten minutes for a special purpose. After the salutes and the cheering he walked up to some GI standing in the ranks and said, "How about taking a walk with me?"

They would go off alone over frozen fields or through dripping woods, the General limping slightly as he swung his stiff knee, the GI wondering and nervous until the friendly ways and homely phrases of his commander made him feel that Ike was an old friend.

Then the General would ask, "What's bothering you, son?"

And the boy beside him usually talked freely about personal troubles, fancied injustice, fear of battle, or, perhaps, some deficiency in Army procedure. That was how Ike kept in contact with his men. It was a sort of personal Gallup poll of GI opinion prompted by sincere affection and the determination that if any remedy for the trouble was within human power it would be applied.

On December 15, 1944, General Eisenhower was at Supreme Headquarters. Omar Bradley was staying with him for consultations with the staff on the situation at the front. That was the day the fifth star was added to the constellation on Ike's cap. The advancement neither troubled nor elated him too much, for all the stars in the firmament could not add one gram to his responsibilities. But behind the smoky fog that rested like an earth-bound cloud upon Western Europe, Field Marshal von Rundstedt, again in command of the Nazi armies, was preparing an ironic salute to this new honor.

Though Ike's visit to Headquarters was occasioned by military necessity, there was a matter to which he desired to give personal attention. The next morning there was to be a social event which, contrary to habit, he was anxious to attend.

When the morning came it was as dark and dreary as the preceding days. The square in front of the great palace of the kings of France was almost deserted. Fog veiled the long façade so that its extremities seemed dissolved in vapor.

Those same mists swirled through the Schnee Eiffel Forest beyond the Belgian border, covering a vast uneasiness as machines by the thousands and men by the hundred thousands moved silently through that muffled world.

Before the great wrought-iron gates of the French palace there was a squad of military police, very smart and alert despite the sullen dripping moisture. Presently a jeep drove up. Some American officers got out and went inside. Another followed and then a couple of olive-drab Army cars. The few French civilians about took notice that something was going on, and a small crowd collected. They were rewarded when an official car with a staff of multicolored flags hanging damply turned into the square. As it stopped, General Eisenhower jumped out and strode through the gates. Just inside he turned to wave and grin in response to the scattered cheering.

Close behind came another limousine. Some of the onlookers recognized Lieutenant Colonel Ernest Lee, aide-de-camp to General Eisenhower. Then the crowd laughed and cheered, for beside him was a girl in a tulle veil and gleaming white satin. Colonel Lee gallantly assisted the bride from the car and offered his arm. The crowd caught a glimpse of blonde hair and laughing blue eyes as she turned to wave to them, and then she, too, disappeared into the palace.

Thus did Pearlie Hargrave of Pillager, Wisconsin—promoted by Ike to the rank of Sergeant before the wedding—go to her wedding to Sergeant Mickey McKeough of Corona, Long Island, in the Royal Chapel of the Kings of France. General Ike, the master planner, had found relaxation from his cares in planning the wedding of these two young people of whom he had become very fond. The staff work was excellent. Mickey's best man was his brother, Staff Sergeant Frank McKeough, who was in France with another unit. The groom's mother, Mrs. Joseph McKeough, had purchased the rings in New York and sent them to Mrs. Eisenhower, who had entrusted them to an officer leaving by air for

SHAEF. Pearlie's wedding gown was made by a great Paris couturier and she carried a bouquet of white camellias.

The party made a small group, but for all that, the beautiful classic chapel seemed warm and friendly. Father Keegan, a chaplain attached to SHAEF, performed the ceremony. Afterward Ike gave a reception at his own house, though he stayed only long enough to receive guests and accept a slice of wedding cake from the bride. He was careful to appear very gay. It was a long time before he could smile again. . . .

On that same morning of December 16, 1944, the last great striking force of the German Wehrmacht, which lay like a gigantic Wagnerian dragon in the fogbound forests along the borders of Belgium and Luxemburg, began to slither and clank forward in a desperate effort to burst through the ring of men and steel that was slowly closing in. During the next two weeks, the very existence of the Allied armies in Belgium and the Netherlands—perhaps even the ultimate outcome of the war—hung in so delicate a balance that more than once the gallant behavior of a single battalion turned those fateful scales. Owing to the rapidity and vast complexity of the movements of men and machines, only an outline of the main action can give any clear picture of what happened.

To understand the battle at all, it is important to know the disposition of the Allied forces. On the extreme right of their line, touching the Swiss border and advancing along the west bank of the Rhine, was the First French Army. Next came General Patch's Seventh Army, which had recently taken Strasbourg. On its left, Patton's great Third Army had seized Metz and was battering into the Ruhr. Next to Patton, General Hodges' First Army was spread out thin on a long front through the Ardennes in Belgium and Luxemburg, its main strength centered at Aachen, which represented the only serious Allied penetration of German territory. Just north of Aachen the fresh Ninth Army was concentrated for an attack. The northern end of the line was held by the British 21st Army Group. Field Marshal Montgomery was building up supplies for a tremendous attack.

This disposition of the Allied forces was necessarily a compromise. Eisenhower and his generals simply did not have enough men to hold the lime from the Swiss border to the North Sea at full strength all the way. To win the war they had to attack,

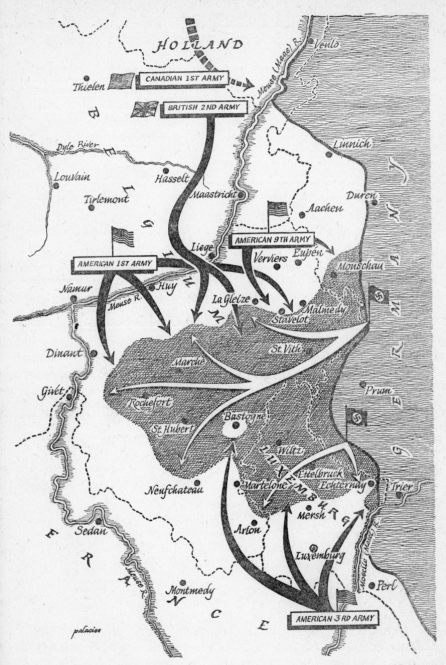

The Battle of the Bulge, December 16, 1944–January 31, 1945

hence their dispositions were offensive; they took the calculated risk of leaving the unpromising Ardennes section of the line lightly held, in order to concentrate sufficient forces for the offensives in the Ruhr, at Aachen, and the Netherlands. But this does not mean that they disregarded the possibility of a German thrust through the Ardennes. They expected it, and made plans to meet it. Thus it is not true that the Germans achieved strategic surprise in their skillfully planned offensive.

Von Rundstedt did effect tactical surprise, however. The Allied Command knew that German troops were being concentrated in the forest area beyond the First Army line, but they did not know what tremendous power von Rundstedt had managed to build out of the forces released by the shortening of Nazi lines on the shrinking perimeter of Fortress Germany. Weeks of fog and rain had prevented aerial reconnaissance; deep forests made concealment easy; and the Germans had been skillful in moving great masses of men and vehicles at night. And when that enormous force was loosed against the soft spot in the Allied lines, there was real danger that it might sever them, and overwhelm the British and American armies piecemeal.

All through the morning of December 16, reports of German activity in the Ardennes sector came to General Eisenhower. These indicated heavy artillery fire and attacks up to battalion strength. Eisenhower watched the situation closely, but it was too early to commit his reserves. By afternoon it was evident that the 106th Division, which was spread out on a twenty-five-mile front, was the subject of a heavy attack. The unlucky 106th had arrived at the front only five days before and had been sent to this "quiet" sector to get its baptism of fire.

Eisenhower and Bradley agreed that this might be the counteroffensive they had anticipated. Countermeasures previously agreed upon were put into effect. Bradley threw his belongings into a suitcase and started for the front. On Sunday, December 17, the full fury of the German attack tore loose. Headed by the 1st SS Adolf Hitler Armored Division and the 12th SS Hitler Youth Armored Division, two prongs of the Nazi offense swept through the game but hapless 106th. Two of its regiments went down fighting. The third was pulled back to Saint-Vith, where it became part of the heroic defense. Before it was relieved, the 106th's casualties numbered 8,663, nearly all its combat strength.

The front was chaotic and every weapon the Germans owned was used to increase the confusion. Robot bombs came over in flocks; *V-2* rockets fell in awful silence from the opaque sky. Nazi paratroopers in American uniforms dropped behind the lines to tangle up communications.

In some places the limit of vision was ten feet. The troops fired by ear at unseen foes, and German infantrymen materialized out of the fog like ectoplasm. American boys were fighting King Tiger tanks with artillery at fifty feet. They were fighting them with bazookas and cans of gasoline, with machine guns and rifles; and when the ammunition gave out they died with knives in their bare hands.

Bradley threw in his reserves to plug the hole. Brigadier General Bruce Clarke's 7th Armored Division drove at full speed all through that Sunday night to beat the Germans to the important road junction at Saint-Vith. They won the race, and the German tide, split by that rock of resistance, flowed on around it. The 7th was surrounded, but fought on furiously to deny the Germans those vital roads. Meanwhile, the weather gave the air force half a day—half a day in which to smash at the long columns of German vehicles and to estimate von Rundstedt's power.

Now, at last, Ike knew what he was up against; twenty crack German divisions—200,000 men—were pouring through his broken lines. He was at field headquarters and he summoned his generals there. The council lasted but fifteen minutes. In that time Ike appraised the situation and made his decision.

It was evident that von Rundstedt was striking for Liége, Antwerp, and the Channel. If he succeeded, he would cut off all the Allied armies in the north. Without supplies they would be helpless; surrender would be inevitable. Then the Germans could turn back and sweep through France.

He decided not to try to meet that German flood head on, but rather to throw up strong walls on either side—to canalize it away from the precious bases. Let it run its course through the barren, unprofitable Ardennes country. Already those walls were being formed along the sides of the German bulge. A single battalion of the 2nd held the northern hinge near Monschau long enough for its regiment to form; cooks, engineers, and truck drivers fought along with them to gain vital minutes. When the regiment was formed, it sold its lives to gain time for the whole division to wheel into line. The German host passed on, seeking to swing north beyond the Americans. Allied reserves must be brought up to strengthen the extending line—it was like improvising a levee before the crest of a flooding river.

The 1st Division, enjoying its first rest since D-Day, was yanked out of camp and ordered to form the next section of the dike. Racing toward the front near Butgenbach, it collided head on with the Hitler Youth Armored Division; and it was Hitler's boys who gave way.

Then the 82nd Air-borne Division came in to link up with the 1st at Stavelot; another section of the levee was in place. The 30th Division was pulled out of the Ninth Army to extend the line still farther. They cut through the forest behind an advancing Nazi column and blew up a bridge, leaving sixty German tanks helplessly out of gasoline. The 99th followed the 30th.

Meanwhile, von Rundstedt, seeing his way blocked, turned southward toward that twice-fatal city of Sedan. The same race to build a levee began along the southern shoulder of the bulge. It was the 4th Infantry Division which held the hinge at Echternach in Luxemburg. Just as the 7th Armored had been sent to Saint-Vith, the 101st Air-borne Division, with parts of Patton's 9th and 10th Armored Divisions, was rushed by truck into the vital communications center of Bastogne. Brigadier General A. C. McAuliff barely had time to form a two-mile circle of men and guns around the little city before the German tide surged up and hit with four times the defenders' strength. The bastion held and the Nazi mass swirled on. Bradley radioed anxiously to the 101st, "What is your position?" Replied McAuliff, "We're the hole in the doughnut."

On Tuesday, December 19, the situation was bad and getting worse. The shoulders of the bulge were barely holding. Saint-Vith and Bastogne were surrounded, and the Nazis were streaming ahead at full speed. They cut direct communication between Bradley's headquarters and both his Ninth Army and the greater part of his First Army. In this situation Eisenhower made a typical decision, which was possible only because of the unity he had fostered in the Allied forces. He placed Field Marshal Montgomery in command of all the armies north of the bulge.

It was a brilliant move, for not only did he thus make use of the extraordinary talents of the battlewise veteran, but he made sure that the full resources of the British and Canadian arms would be brought into the battle.

Monty was always at his best when things looked worst. He

acted surely and decisively. As he himself described it later to the correspondents, "The first thing you must do in a battle is to shape it to your desire. The battle area was untidy, so I busied myself with getting it tidy and getting things in balance. . . ."

While Montgomery was "tidying up" the north side of the battle, the southern side was getting worse. On December 20, Ike called on Georgie Patton. It was well that he had saved his ace of armor when the crowd was shouting for Patton's head because of the slapping incident. Now, in the hour of crisis, the right man was at hand to lead the counterstroke. Patton was ordered to attack the south side of the bulge.

"At what hour do we move?" asked a Third Army staff officer, when the orders came through. Ordinarily it takes at least ten hours to start an army moving.

"That's a damned fool question," roared Patton. "We start now!"

December 22, 1944, and the point of the German attack was still moving forward, though the levees were holding at the sides. German tanks were nearing the Meuse River and the 7th Armored had given up Saint-Vith. "We must get those fine fellows back from there," Montgomery had said.

Bastogne was besieged by eight German divisions, and the weather prevented the Allies from delivering supplies to the outnumbered garrison by air. Nevertheless, to the Nazi demand for surrender McAuliff replied in the classic American manner:

"To the German Commander
NUTS
The American Commander."

Air power, the Allies' strongest arm, was paralyzed by fog and rain and sleet, and the grounded airmen cursed.

The correspondents in Paris were panicky. To keep the Germans from learning about our countermeasures before they took full effect, Eisenhower had imposed a forty-eight-hour delay in releasing news of the battle position, but there was no censorship of criticism of himself or his staff. The correspondents could comment as they chose, and they did. According to them, the Allied Command had failed lamentably. Intelligence was terrible, they said, and what reports there were had been grossly misread. Some claimed that Eisenhower was too kindly for the ruthless business of war; others, that he was too optimistic—forgetting that only an optimist would have dared invade Fortress Europe from across the sea. There was a contingent which held that Eisenhower had been given too much to do, and had therefore been delegated too much authority. It was suggested that the command be divided between Eisenhower and Montgomery. Meanwhile, Monty, unknown to them, was already tidying up beautifully for his superior.

Nearly all the dispatches implied that the Supreme Commander was to blame for what was called, in hysterical exaggeration, the worst disaster ever to befall American arms. Apparently no one paused to consider that it was no disaster, but a battle only half fought.

In America the reaction was naturally even worse, for, added to the cabled dispatches, was a bumper crop of rumors hinting at catastrophe.

But there was no panic any nearer the front than Paris. In the mists and confusion of the shifting battle lines, men did their jobs with competence and courage unsurpassed; and in the very center of the vortex, at Advanced Headquarters, a quiet man issued orders and made dispositions with swift, unhesitating decision.

On that dark December 22, a calm voice spoke above the confusion of battle and the clamor of frightened voices in the rear. General Ike addressed his armies in an Order of the Day:

"The enemy is making his supreme effort. . . . He is fighting savagely to take back all that you have won and is using every treacherous trick to deceive and kill. He is gambling everything, but already in this battle your gallantry has done much to foil his plans. In the face of your proven bravery and fortitude, he will completely fail.

"But we cannot be content with his mere repulse.

"By rushing out from his fixed defenses the enemy may give us the chance to turn his greatest gamble into his worst defeat.

"So I call upon every man of all the Allies to rise to new heights of courage, of resolution, and of effort. Let every one hold before him a single thought to destroy the enemy on the ground, in the air, everywhere—destroy him.

"United in this determination and with unshakable faith in the cause for which we fight, we will, with God's help, go forward to our greatest victory!

Dwight D. Eisenhower."

That was actually the way the Supreme Commander saw it, for he was incapable of sham optimism, least of all in addressing those brave men who had put their faith in him. To General Ike, at the crisis of the battle, the moment was not one of disaster, but of opportunity!

Clouds still hung heavy over Europe, denying the Allies all the potential power of their air forces. Georgie Patton scanned the dripping skies, and the old blasphemer did a thing that seemed most curious, unless one remembers the poet and mystic beneath his armored shell. He wrote a prayer for his army:

"Almighty and most merciful God, we humbly beseech Thee of Thy great goodness to restrain these immoderate rains with which we have had to contend. Grant us fair weather for battle. Graciously listen to us as soldiers who call upon Thee that, armed with Thy power, we may advance from victory to victory, crush the oppression and wickedness of our enemies and establish Thy justice among men and nations. Amen."

To the confounded Nazi meteorologists, who had predicted unending storms, and our own bemused weathermen, who agreed with them, it must have seemed as though the God of Battles lent an ear to the old soldier. For at the dawn of December 23, the skies turned gloriously red and gold, and then to flawless blue.

That was the turning point. From half a thousand airfields the impatient planes took off. Over the German lines they went in swarms that rivaled our legendary flocks of passenger pigeons: quite literally the skies grew dark with their wings. Fortresses, Liberators, Lightnings, Marauders, Spitfires, Hurricanes, Typhoons, Mustangs and Thunderbolts bombed and strafed, and fired rockets, machine guns and cannons into the Nazi host, while Piper Cub pilots flew up as artillery observers. The last hoarded reserve of the Luftwaffe came up to meet them and 178 Nazi planes went down in flames.

In Bastogne, the valiant defenders, short of food and ammunition, of gasoline and medical supplies—short of everything but courage—looked upward and saw a great aerial cargo fleet climbing up the sky. The thunder of their motors was a celestial diapason, and as they swept overhead the sky became gay with thousands of brightly-colored parachutes, beneath which swung the boxes of succor. Laughing and shouting, regardless of danger, the troops ran to catch them like children at a birthday party. More planes came over with tows streaming behind them. The laden gliders loosed their hawsers and, spiraling slowly down, settled down, settled heavily on the snow. . . .

Good weather held. The planes were out again the next day, seven-thousand strong, and at 4:20 P.M. on Christmas Eve, a column of General Sherman tanks, led by the "Cobra King" (Lieutenant Charles P. Boggess, Jr.) of the 37th Tank Battalion, 4th Armored Division of General Patton's Third Army, tore through the German lines into Bastogne.

The battle wasn't over by many a long shot. The Nazis were still advancing at the tip of the bulge; German tanks rolled to within three miles of the Meuse at Dinant. But Ike's chosen team —Tedder, Montgomery, Bradley, Patton and Beedle Smith—was functioning with superb synchronization, and his army—British, American, French—was fighting magnificently.

On the north Montgomery had formed a new offensive army corps of mixed British and American divisions under the command of Major General Lawton J. Collins. Monty skillfully brought this new corps across the communication lines of the Ninth and First Armies and flung it at the tip of the great German offensive. That intrusive spearhead was "stopped and then lopped."

From the south Bradley and Patton bored into the sides of the bulge, and Montgomery's armies to the north put on the pressure, too. Between them they squeezed the waist of the bulge until von Rundstedt saw that he must fly or be cut off.

Meanwhile, a blizzard had succeeded the clear weather. Slowly, lashing out viciously with the sting in its tail, the armored Nazi serpent crawled back through the shrunken salient. Over the frozen fields the American tanks charged, throwing off great plumes of snowlike rotary plows. The white fields turned crimson in the light of burning Nazi tanks and vehicles; they were littered with the black bodies of Nazi dead. . . .

By the time the Germans had been pushed back they had lost approximately 200,000 men and a vast number of tanks, artillery and other matériel. Four Panzer divisions were smashed, and four more Panzer or Panzer Grenadier divisions were badly battered.

One parachute division was completely destroyed, and eight Volks-grenadier divisions lost half their total strength.

The only advantage the Germans gained by their desperate sacrifice was a little—very little—time. And the order of the Allied plan was reversed. For the Russians, not the Americans and British, opened the attack on the German homeland. But Nazi losses in Belgium left them with nothing for a counterblow in the East, while Eisenhower was able to rebuild his reserves at once for a mighty lunge from the west.

But if the Germans had been able to achieve a real break-through whole Allied armies might have been cut off. There were moments when that catastrophe was averted by a hair's breadth. If the 9th Infantry Regiment had not held near Monschau or the 101st Air-borne Division had folded at Bastogne; if Patton had not moved so fast or Montgomery had hesitated to throw in the British, the ensuing course of the war would have been different.

Thus the battle was not won by mathematical superiority; the odds in that area were against us. It was won by great imponder-ables; by quick thinking and sound generalship; by valor and by faith; and above all, by loyalty, which is another word for team-work. The commander who can inspire these qualities is a great general.

The tremendous joint effort of American and British armies that broke the Wehrmacht was complete fulfillment of General Eisenhower's patient building of Allied unity. An Englishman best put it into words:

"It was a remarkable thing," Field Marshal Montgomery said, "how in time of danger the Allied team rallied together. Team-work wins battles and battle victories win wars. On our team the captain is General Ike. I am devoted to him. . . ."

By January 31, 1945, the last thin curve of Von Rundstedt's Bulge had been flattened out. Another lucky break in the weather had given the Allied Air Force their chance at the crucial moment, and the Nazi retreat became a ride through inferno. The Allies stood once more along the line of Germany's inner citadel. The Russian armies coming down from the east breached the fortress walls and rolled to the outer defenses of Berlin.

At Yalta, Roosevelt, Churchill, and Stalin made certain there would be no weakening of the Allied bonds. The Nazis were to be forced to fight along the perimeter of their fortress, and that perimeter was shrinking fast.

The Allied armies in the west stood poised for attack all the way from Switzerland to the Channel. General Ike in his jeep rolled over the snowy roads to visit his troops once more. They were awaiting his word to launch the last assault.

None knew better than they how desperate it would be, how much toil and suffering lay ahead, how many would fall. But they also knew that this was the last campaign. And as the little five-starred jeep with the big friendly man in the back seat drove through the combat commands, they pledged their confidence, their lives, and their love shouting:

"Ike! Ike!"

INDEX

There was a deeper vibration in the air, a humming that was not the wind. It grew in volume to a brazen diapason that drowned out the small sounds of wind and waves and trees. Now he could see the black shapes against the pallor above, flying in vees like the wild geese crossing Kansas. The